CONFESSIONS

OF A

RECOVERING ENGINEER

CHARLES L. MAROHN, JR.

CONFESSIONS

OF A

RECOVERING ENGINEER

TRANSPORTATION

FOR A

STRONG TOWN

WILEY

For general information on our other products and services or for technical support, please
contact our Customer Care Department within the United States at (800) 762-2974, outside
the United States at (317) 572-3993 or fax (317) 572-4002.

Wiley publishes in a variety of print and electronic formats and by print-on-demand. Some
material included with standard print versions of this book may not be included in e-books or in
print-on-demand. If this book refers to media such as a CD or DVD that is not included in the
version you purchased, you may download this material at http://booksupport.wiley.com. For
more information about Wiley products, visit www.wiley.com.

Library of Congress Cataloging-in-Publication Data

Names: Marohn, Charles L., Jr., author.
Title: Confessions of a Recovering Engineer : Transportation For a
   Strong Town / Charles Marohn.
Description: First edition. | Hoboken, New Jersey : Wiley, [2021] |
   Includes index.
Identifiers: LCCN 2021015785 (print) | LCCN 2021015786 (ebook) | ISBN
   9781119699293 (hardback) | ISBN 9781119701194 (ePDF) | ISBN
   9781119699255 (ePub)
Subjects: LCSH: Urban transportation—United States. | Cities and
   towns—United States—Growth. | Engineering—United States.
Classification: LCC HE308 .M37 2021 (print) | LCC HE308 (ebook) | DDC
   388.40973—dc23
LC record available at https://lccn.loc.gov/2021015785
LC ebook record available at https://lccn.loc.gov/2021015786

COVER DESIGN: PAUL MCCARTHY
COVER ART: © GETTY IMAGES | JUNXIAN ZHU
SKY10028638_072921

This book is dedicated to the memory of Destiny Gonzalez and all whose lives have been cut short by America's transportation system, and to Sagrario Gonzalez, her husband, Luis, and all who have suffered great loss on our nation's roads and streets, and to Sandra Zemtsova, along with everyone who must live knowing that others did not.

May this book reduce your pain.

Contents

Introduction: Conversation with an Engineer

"Hello, I'm the project engineer. I heard you have a concern about the street improvement we have planned for your neighborhood."

I was feeling nervous about going out to speak with her, though I had no reason to believe that this would go poorly. I extended a hand as she stepped out her door and into the front yard. We had a firm but friendly handshake, and she gave me a smile.

I was the project engineer, and this was my job. I needed to be able to speak with the public, smoothing over concerns, if I was going to advance in my chosen profession. I had been on many such visits with other, more senior engineers, watching and learning from how they handled sensitive interactions like this. Now it was my turn. I waited for her to speak next.

"Yes, I heard that you are planning to improve my street. What will this mean for my neighborhood?"

Perfect. I had anticipated this question, of course, and I knew exactly how to answer it. This is the reason why I was here. My confidence growing, I responded.

"We plan to correct deficiencies in the grade as well as deficiencies in the curvature of the existing alignment. We also plan to enhance the clear zone in order to bring the street up to an acceptable and safe standard."

She gave me an odd look, like I was speaking a foreign language.

"So, you are going to make the street safer?"
"Yes, of course."
"How are you going to make the street safer?"

Civil engineering is a four-year program, although most of my peers took five to earn their degree. The four-year pace is rigorous, while the coursework is deeply technical. Upon graduation, an engineer wishing to be licensed will take a grueling, eight-hour test called the *Fundamentals of Engineering Exam (FEE)*, after which they become an *Engineer in Training (EIT)*.

The path to licensure then requires the EIT to work for four years in an apprentice capacity under the direct supervision of a licensed engineer. This is a time to go beyond theory and become knowledgeable in the standards and practices of the profession. After four years of gaining wisdom through working, and only with the support of another licensed engineer, an EIT becomes eligible to take the licensing exam and become a *Professional Engineer (PE)*.

I attained my degree in four years. I passed the FEE on my first try. I had done my four years working as an EIT for some distinguished engineers, and I passed my licensing exam on my first attempt.

I stood in this yard, adjacent to a street I had been asked to design, as a licensed PE — the proud steward of wisdom that, in some respects, dated all the way back to the ancient Romans, Greeks, and beyond. This might be my first solo project, but I was confident because I knew what I was talking about.

"Well, first we are going to correct deficiencies in the grade and in the alignment."
"What does that mean?"

Safety is the primary responsibility of any licensed engineer. There really isn't a close second. It's written into our codes of ethics.

It's embedded into our design processes. Safety is the reason why the state requires a license to practice engineering. It's why the city hired my firm for this job. It's why I was standing there.

If there was one single thing motivating me on this project, it was the desire to make this street safer.

> *"It means the grade and alignment of the street do not meet the standard, and so we are going to fix that."*
> *"What is the standard?"*

My understanding of safety in this situation comes from accepted industry practice. Engineers have books of codes and standards that outline all aspects of safe design, from how wide to make a street to where to put the signs. I not only had access to these texts, I had been trained in how to interpret them properly.

I recognized that my role in this interaction was to simplify all of the complicated factors that go into designing a street — all of the institutional knowledge of my profession — into something that a layperson could understand.

> *"Basically, the street must be relatively flat and straight."*
> *"So, you are going to make the street flat and straight?"*
> *"Yes."*
> *"How does that improve safety?"*

My ability to stay friendly and professional here was important. The woman to whom I was speaking hadn't sat through the traffic engineering courses that I had taken — the ones that taught me the history of roadway design. She didn't know the horrible death rates of the early automobile era — the time before engineers established modern best practices.

She didn't have the training and the background that I had, including access to all of the code books and standards that my profession had developed over decades. She hadn't done the continuing education, sat around the table with my fellow engineers hearing the tales about how bad decisions led to bad outcomes and sometimes even death. I forced a half smile and went on.

"It will allow cars to navigate more smoothly, which makes it safer."
"I don't understand."

In traffic engineering, randomness is the enemy of safety. The more variables that we can remove, the more the driver can predict what is going to happen and the safer things become. For the driver, a road that is straight is safer than one with a lot of curves. A road that is flat is safer than one with a lot of hills.

It was difficult for me to explain something so self-evident, so I tried to expand the conversation to an aspect of design that would hopefully be easier to grasp — someplace where we could develop a common understanding and build to more complicated concepts.

"Along with fixing deficiencies with the grade and the alignment, we will be widening the driving lanes."
"What will that do?"
"It will improve safety."
"How does widening the lanes improve safety?"

Okay, this was getting frustrating. It is a little too obvious that wide lanes are safer than narrow lanes. Anyone who has tried to drive down a narrow street, having been forced to slow way down to avoid hitting things, knows that having more space gives the driver a higher safety margin. This was Road Design 101— the most basic of concepts. I was starting to think that this woman, despite her friendliness, just didn't want to get it.

"Along with fixing the deficiencies in the grade and the alignment, it will allow traffic to flow more smoothly."
"What do you mean by allowing the traffic to flow more smoothly? How does that improve safety?"
"Cars will be able to move without worrying about hitting things, so it will be safer. That is why we are also expanding the clear zone."
"What do you mean by expanding the clear zone?"

Having a *clear zone* on each side of the roadway is another one of these basic design concepts universally understood to improve safety. If a car goes careening off the road surface, all that kinetic energy needs to be dissipated. We don't want the car to be brought to an abrupt stop by hitting an obstacle; we want the process of slowing down to happen more gradually.

All traffic engineers have heard the story of a driver losing control, the car going off the road and hitting an obstacle that should never have been there, with tragedy being the predictable result. Establishing an area on each side of the road that is clear of obstacles increases the chance that people will walk away from such an incident. I was taught to insist on it. No compromises with safety.

> *"We will be removing obstacles from the clear zone to improve safety."*
>
> *"What is the clear zone?"*
>
> *"It is the area on each side of the street that we need to keep clear of obstacles in case cars go off the road."*
>
> *"What kind of obstacles?"*
>
> *"Mostly trees."*

I steadied myself because I had been in this situation before and knew what was coming. We were standing in a yard full of trees, many of which were going to be cut down. I knew she wasn't going to like that. It seemed a selfish reaction to me.

Most people seem to want progress. They show up at public meetings and demand all of the conveniences that come with driving. They want it, that is, until it impacts them directly. *Then* progress must be stopped. Then they all turn into environmentalists. I'd seen it many times. She seemed to fit the profile, especially with her next question.

> *"So, you are going to remove the trees from the clear zone to improve safety?"*
>
> *"Yes. Exactly."*
>
> *"How big is the clear zone?"*

I took a deep breath and looked down. "The clear zone is 25 feet on each side of the street."

> *"Twenty-five feet! That is my entire front yard!"*

I wasn't going to compromise on safety. I had a code of ethics demanding that I put the welfare of the general public ahead of concerns like this. I had worked years to get my license, and I wasn't about to risk it by not following the design standard.

Plus, the firm that I worked for had professional liability insurance, which I knew was expensive. We live in a litigious society. There was no way that I was going to be bullied into doing something irresponsible — something that threatened my client or my firm, let alone the people who would drive along this road.

> *"I'm sorry, but the standard requires that for the road to be safe, all obstacles must be removed from the clear zone."*
>
> *"Do you understand that my children play in this clear zone?"*
>
> *"I would not recommend that. It would not be safe."*
>
> *"But it is safe today. I thought you were doing this project to improve safety. How is the street safer if my children can't go outside?"*

I was having a conversation with this woman at the request of the mayor. She was one of his constituents. I knew that my job was to listen to her and answer her questions, but it was also to demonstrate that the city had performed due diligence on the project. If she showed up at a future council meeting complaining about her kids not being able to go outside to play, she was less likely to be taken seriously if everyone knew that I had personally met with her, answered her questions, and seen her property firsthand. I'm the professional and, after being on site and meeting with her, I can confidently say that nothing unique is happening with her property, regardless of what she might suggest at a public hearing.

> *"Building the street to meet the standard will enhance safety by allowing cars to flow more smoothly."*
>
> *"More smoothly. The cars will just drive faster, will they not?"*

By statute in my state, the city is not able to enforce any speed limit lower than 30 miles per hour. There are exceptions, but those require extensive studies and proof that there is some unique circumstance justifying the lower speed limit. We weren't going through that effort here. The city didn't have the budget for such a study and, even if they did, there were no special circumstances that would justify doing so.

Once the street was built, if there was reason to believe that 30 mph was the wrong speed, I could do a speed study and make that determination. Such a study would involve monitoring the speed that traffic was naturally flowing, which my experience suggested was unlikely to be less than 30 mph. She should be careful what she wishes because a speed study is more likely to result in a higher speed limit than a lower one.

> *"We will post a speed limit after we do a speed study and determine the safe speed for the street," I said with some added authority in my voice.*
>
> *She replied with equal authority. "But cars drive slow now. Slow is the safe speed through my neighborhood where my children are playing in my yard. How does it improve safety to have a drag strip out my front door?"*
>
> *"It will increase safety because traffic will flow more smoothly. That is the standard."*

At this point, the two of us had cycled through all of the typical objections that people bring up to oppose such projects. We had started with a friendly line of inquiry and eventually proceeded all the way to unresolvable acrimony. I had done everything that had been asked of me, and I was thinking it was time to move on.

She was not ready to let things go, however, and I started to sense that this conversation would get very emotional before we were done. Her next words reinforced my uneasiness.

> *"I am not aware of anyone being killed in an accident on this street, and I have lived here for thirty years. Are you aware of anyone being killed?"*
>
> *"No, I'm not." I tried not to roll my eyes or sound like the teenager I was just a few years earlier.*

"I am not even aware of any accidents that have occurred on this street. Are you aware of any accidents?"

I repeated, "No, I'm not."

"Then why do you say that the street is not safe today?"

One of the frequent justifications for making roadway improvements is a tragic incident, especially a death. While those cases often seem random, they form a powerful justification for doing an improvement project, especially where you can tap into available federal or state funding. Multiple incidences can even create a sense of urgency. Since there is a seemingly endless list of roads that need improvement, prioritizing by death rate or accident rate can almost seem natural.

That wasn't the case here. We were proactively making the improvements to this street to make it safer — to bring it up to an acceptable standard in a way that would ultimately save lives. We weren't waiting for the accident rate to rise; we were getting out in front of that. It gave me a feeling of satisfaction in my work.

"The street is not safe because it does not meet the standard."

"So, today cars drive slowly and it is safe, but you want to flatten the street, straighten the street, widen the street, and remove all of the trees so that cars can drive fast? Only afterwards will you post a speed limit so that cars will slow down? And you say this is safer?"

It was a clever recitation, but while the woman with whom I was speaking was clearly sharp-witted, she lacked the background knowledge and understanding that allowed her to grasp the situation fully. I would try one last time to enlighten her.

"Yes, it will meet the standard. And please understand that there are high traffic projections for this street."

"What do you mean by a high traffic projection?"

"We project that a lot of cars will use this street in the coming years."

We've all been on roads that lacked capacity, where the traffic was at a standstill. From the perspective of the traffic engineer, this is an absolute failure. We even give it a grade of F.

Traffic engineers use a scale to measure "level of service" that runs from A, for "free flow condition" where all traffic is moving unhindered, to F, where the flow of traffic breaks down and travel times are unpredictable.

Cities spend a great deal of time and resources analyzing and projecting traffic patterns. For this project, our models suggested a large increase in traffic, something that would create congestion and reduce traffic flow to Level of Service D — or potentially worse. All of the improvements underway were a proactive attempt to avoid bottlenecks and keep traffic flowing. We were being proactive with this project and I was proud of that.

> *"Why would a lot of cars drive down this street? It is a small, narrow street where you have to drive slow."*

Now we were getting somewhere. Now she was asking the right questions — the ones that explained exactly why this project was so important. And I could surely sympathize with her not understanding what was coming. She hadn't seen the models my colleagues and I had put together. She wasn't the expert working with this every day. I felt a renewed sense of optimism. We were making progress. I replied excitedly.

> *"That is why we have to improve the street — to meet the standard."*
>
> *She gave me a sideways glance. "Won't that just encourage more people to drive?"*
>
> *"We have anticipated that, and we are adding two more lanes to handle the additional cars."*

That insight was not received in the way that I anticipated. There was an uncomfortable period of silence — the kind where the person expected to speak is too startled to do so. Her eyes widened and she stared at me, not blinking.

> *"You are adding two more lanes?"*
>
> *"Yes." I was nodding knowingly.*
>
> *"For cars?"*
>
> *"Yes. An additional two lanes will allow the street to meet the standard."*

I looked down at my feet. I wasn't sure how to react to this conversation. It was clear that the woman with whom I was speaking was upset, but certainly she didn't want traffic congestion in front of her home. I bet she'd be the first one calling City Hall if she was stuck in traffic every day at Level of Service F.

I just needed to help her understand what was already so clear to me. Yes, she might have to give up some trees and a little bit of her front yard, but didn't she want things to be safe? Didn't she want the road to work for everyone? She spoke next.

> *"Let me see if I understand. You are projecting a high volume of traffic where there is none today and then building a street to handle this traffic. Aren't you just encouraging more people to drive?"*
>
> *"No. We are anticipating a lot of growth and need to make this improvement to handle the growth."*

While I'm an engineer, I'm really in the growth business. All of us who work for the city are in the growth business in one way or another. New growth is how we get the money we need to fix the streets, pay for police officers and fire fighters, keep the library open, and all of the other things that taxpayers say they want. Growth is how people get jobs. It's the unifying focus that we more or less all seem to agree on.

The more growth that we can generate, the better off things are for everyone. Yes, there are some people who are anti-growth. They sometimes come to council meetings with a sentimental attachment to some old building, a concern over an environmental issue, or maybe expressing their concern with economic dislocation. There are generally a few speaking out against each project, but they usually aren't taken very seriously. What are we supposed to do? Stop growing? That would be a disaster.

> *She asked, "Where is all of this growth happening?"*
>
> *"New growth is being created in the tax subsidy zone."*
>
> *"Where is the tax subsidy zone?"*
>
> *"The tax subsidy zone is on the edge of town."*

In a recent planning process with the city, my colleagues and I identified many sites where infrastructure could be extended. These are places primed for growth, where public spending can be a catalyst for quick private investment. All of the major developers and business leaders were at these meetings, and they were enthusiastic for that kind of public support. That makes sense because they know what it takes to create growth.

To their credit, the city leadership followed through. They took on a lot of debt to invest in additional capacity. They applied for economic development grants from the federal and state governments. They waived fees and other development charges, and they streamlined the approval processes. Even more proactively, they established some tax subsidy areas, a move that had paid off with an initial round of development proposals. It was all very exciting.

> *"What kind of new growth is going to occur in the tax subsidy zone?"*
>
> *"On the edge of town, there is a proposal for a grocery store as well as a drive-through restaurant and a gas station."*
>
> *"Okay. But I go to the neighborhood grocery store across the street, I eat at the restaurant up the block, and I don't drive much, so I don't need another gas station."*

I had heard this kind of thing before, but what she referred to as a "grocery store" was just a small neighborhood grocery. You couldn't get much there, nothing like the big box store that my family bought groceries from, not to mention all of the families I knew.

The same thing with the restaurant. I knew the family that owned it from way back. They didn't really invest in their own place and, economically, they were being left behind. It was obvious. The whole neighborhood had been officially listed as blighted. It had seen better days, for sure.

Even so, if we were to get growth going out on the edge and get a good, high-capacity street running through here, there was a chance that someone would buy up these old buildings, tear them down, and build something new. That's about the only hope I saw for this neighborhood. The zoning codes wouldn't allow this old stuff to be rebuilt here again anyway. And for good reason.

> *"Yes, we know. That is why we have planned for a pedestrian overpass on this block."*
>
> *"What is a pedestrian overpass?"*

"It is a bridge that will allow you to get from one side of the street to the other safely."

"But I can walk across the street safely right now. My kids can walk across the street safely right now. Why will I need a pedestrian overpass?"

I felt like the answer was obvious here and that, once again, she was almost deliberately trying not to understand. She had just told me that she wanted to cross the street. With all of the additional cars speeding through here, how did she think that was going to happen?

"With four lanes for traffic, you will not be able to walk across the street without slowing down the cars. Slowing down the cars would not be safe."

"But I am not going to be able to haul my baby stroller up a pedestrian overpass every time I want to cross the street to buy milk. How does this benefit me?"

I was out there working on a project being done for the greater good. All of the safety improvements, all of the new growth that would result, all of the jobs that were going to be created — including mine — were a benefit to the entire region.

Here was one person asking how this benefited them. Did she not see the larger picture? Did she not care? Did she not recognize how selfish she sounded? It was clear to me that I needed to end this conversation.

"You will benefit from the added tax base from the new growth."

"But the new growth is in a tax subsidy district. How much will they contribute to the tax base?"

"Nothing today, but in 10 or 15 years, they will contribute a lot to the tax base."

"Why would we make an investment that will not start to pay back for 10 or 15 years? By then, the grocery store will be turned into a dollar store and there will be a new tax subsidy zone."

There are always people against tax subsidies. Generally, I would be one of them, but I had been in the meetings with investors and developers. I knew that none of this investment was going to happen without the tax subsidies. And if this city didn't have new investment, more places would start to look like this blighted neighborhood.

> *"If we do not provide the subsidies and invest in improving streets, the growth will not happen. Without growth, our city will die."*

> *"But if I can't walk across the street to the grocery store, it will go out of business. If I can't walk up the street to go to the restaurant, it will go out of business. Nobody is going to want to buy my house with a highway outside my front door. Do you care that my neighborhood is dying?"*

It was precisely because her neighborhood was dying that I was out there. This project was the neighborhood's best hope for revival. If I could get more traffic flowing through here, more people from outside of the neighborhood passing by, this neighborhood would have a chance for some investment. Why couldn't she see that I am part of the solution?

> *"Yes. That is why we are investing in new growth. That is why we are improving the street."*

She looked past me, off into the distance, one of those long stares that people do when they are collecting their thoughts. I reminded myself that she had a lot to process here. My patiently exhausting her line of questioning was part of that process. I waited for her to speak.

> *"So how much will this street improvement cost?"*

Now we were back on solid ground. I had prepared the cost estimate and knew this answer.

> *"The total project cost is nine million dollars."*
> *"Nine million dollars! Our city is broke. We can't afford to keep the streetlights on overnight. We have laid off our fire fighters and half our police force. Where are we getting nine million dollars?"*

I understood the sticker shock. This was a large project, especially for this community, but now I had a chance to impress her. All of this new investment, all of these improvements, all of the new growth that would result, and all of the jobs and economic development was going to happen and most of it was being paid by others. As a taxpayer in this city, she was getting a tremendous gift.

> *"Seven million dollars is stimulus money coming from the state and federal governments. The other two million dollars will be assessed to the property owners that benefit from the project."*
>
> *"What does that mean, 'assessed to the property owners that benefit from the project?'"*

Cities are limited in the taxes and fees that they can charge property owners. Some of this limitation comes directly from equal treatment provisions in the U.S. Constitution itself. One exception to treating everyone equally is the assessment process. When assessing, a local government can charge a property owner whatever amount they want to so long as the property value they own increases by that amount.

If the project increases a property's value by, say, $10,000, the city could charge the property owner up to $10,000 for doing that project. The engineering firm where I was employed did this kind of work all the time. In fact, this neighborhood had been so neglected, the public infrastructure in such a state of disrepair, that just having new pavement was likely to improve this woman's property value.

Nonetheless, I dialed back my enthusiasm, reverting to the classic-speak I had heard other engineers use in public hearings on assessments.

> *"It means that the property owners who benefit will pay a share of the cost."*
>
> *"Who is it that benefits from the project?"*
>
> *"Everyone who is on the street."*

The vacant stare evaporated. She looked me straight in the eyes, a combination of frustration and confusion apparent on her face.

> *"Wait, are you saying that I benefit from this project and will pay an assessment?"*

I again looked down at my shoes. I tapped the ground with my foot, a reflexive behavior.

"Yes. You are one of the benefiting property owners who will be assessed for the project."

"You must be kidding me. I have a nice quiet neighborhood street today. My kids play in the yard and it is safe. I can walk across the street to the grocery store, or up the street to the restaurant, and it is safe. To make it safer, you are going to flatten, widen, and straighten the street and add two more lanes of fast-moving cars. This is done because of traffic projections — because we want new growth in the tax subsidy area on the edge of town. And while my neighborhood crumbles and my home drops in value, you are going to assess me, too."

I felt bad for her. She truly didn't get it.

"I'm sorry. But the traffic projections require a four-lane street for safety reasons. We must follow the standard."

This conversation is a composite of many conversations I participated in during my years of working as a civil engineer and urban planner for cities across Minnesota. The thoughts and words I attribute to myself in this dialogue are all ones I've believed or expressed at one point or another during my career. In 2010, I shared these impressions in a YouTube video I titled, "Conversation with an Engineer." The eight-minute exchange between two computer animations is now used in university courses and other training sessions. It has been watched over 340,000 times and can now be viewed at www.confessions.engineer.

For many years, I believed that my education, training, and license gave me superior insight into how cities work. I believed that I was uniquely positioned to know what was best for society — at least when it came to transportation.

I believed that the optimal approach to city-building was reflected in the codes and standards that had been developed by others in my profession and that adhering to them was the only responsible approach an ethical person could take.

I believed that the straighter, flatter, and wider we could make a street, the safer it would become, and that requiring clear zones free of obstacles on each side was a critical component of public safety.

I believed that the speed people drove reflected their own level of responsibility or recklessness, that my designs had no influence on traffic speed, and that the only real way to address speeding was through police enforcement and public awareness campaigns.

I believed that automobile crashes, and the frequent incapacitations and deaths that accompanied them, were random events mostly caused by driver error, that the best thing I could do to reduce human suffering was to strive to continually improve our transportation systems to higher and higher standards.

I believed that I could use models and simulations to predict future traffic flows and that I had an innate sense for how drivers would respond to the designs that I and other engineers put in place.

I believed that Level of Service and other measurements of traffic efficiency were strongly correlated with economic success and that the potential for increased jobs, growth, and economic development were all directly tied to the free flow of automobile traffic.

I believed that government transportation programs, public debt financing of infrastructure projects, and local tax subsidies for development were all responsible actions taken in response to the private marketplace and that government leadership was reinforcing the natural outcomes being expressed in a market-based economic system.

Most of all, I believed that my efforts to plan, design, and engineer transportation systems were a service to society, that I was part of creating a prosperous America that could be shared by everyone, and that the only real impediments to success were a lack of funding and the political courage needed to stand up to naysayers.

In all these beliefs and more, I was wrong. Utterly and shamefully wrong.

What follows here is my confession, along with my insights and recommendations for making things better by using a Strong Towns approach to transportation.

1

Embedded Values

Sagrario Gonzalez was at the Central Library on State Street in Springfield, Massachusetts, near closing time on December 3, 2014. As many loving adults are prone to do, she brought her niece and daughter to enjoy the library's children's section. Springfield was the home of Theodor Geisel, better known as Dr. Seuss. It has a great children's section.

It was lightly raining when they left the library, the December kind of rain that stings when the wind whips it against your neck. Their vehicle was in the library's parking lot, directly across the street from the front door. As Gonzalez walked down the front steps, two small children in tow, she made a fateful decision.

At the bottom of the library steps was a sidewalk. To get to her vehicle, Gonzalez could walk the 275 feet south to the traffic signal, push the button and wait for the light to turn in her favor, cross the four lanes of State Street, and then proceed back up the street another 275 feet to the parking lot.

She could do that, or she could do what most people seem to do when they leave the library. She could follow a well-worn path through the grass, step over a small decorative fence erected along the side of the street, wait for a gap in the traffic, and then quickly walk, maybe run, across State Street to the parking lot.

The quickest path between two points is a straight line. With the rain coming down, darkness well established, and the bedtime hour fast approaching on a school night, Gonzalez chose the quicker route. It was the wrong decision.

The group was struck by a vehicle while crossing State Street. Sagrario Gonzalez's daughter and niece were taken to the hospital with serious injuries. Gonzalez survived, as did her niece. Tragically, Destiny Gonzalez, the seven-year-old daughter of Sagrario Gonzalez and her husband, Luis, was killed.

I will never forget that night. I was in Springfield, having just given a public lecture on behalf of the nonprofit Strong Towns. I was homesick for my family, especially my two daughters, who were roughly the same ages as the pair of young girls who had been struck. It was 10 days before Christmas. My heart ached, and it still does, for Sagrario Gonzalez.

It was not her fault.

The Crossing

What happened that night on State Street seems obvious. In a karmic world where we all, to one degree or another, must live with the consequences of our decisions, it's easy to see how Gonzalez made a series of bad choices.

She could have walked to the traffic signal, but she didn't. Traveling four feet per second with two kids in tow, it would have taken her roughly one minute and ten seconds to get there. Depending on her luck, she might not have had to wait at all to cross if the light happened to be green in her direction. If it was red, she might have been there another minute, perhaps longer. It would have taken an additional minute and ten seconds to walk back along the opposite sidewalk. To walk to the signal instead of crossing directly meant it would take an additional two to four minutes to get to her car.

Two to four minutes. That is what was saved by crossing directly in the middle of the block instead of walking to the signal — one dead, one seriously injured, and lives forever damaged. It seems like an extraordinarily high price to pay for what could casually be described as impatience.

That's not to suggest that crossing the street mid-block was effortless. To cross in front of the library, Gonzalez had to walk around a row of shrubs. To reach the street, she also needed to step over a small fence, nothing more than a couple of decorative chains hanging between posts. These obstacles were put there to discourage people from crossing in this location, a fact that is self-evident to anyone who chooses that route.

We can think of these obstacles as a warning: DO NOT CROSS HERE. Gonzalez did not heed this clear warning.

From curb to curb, State Street is 40 feet wide in this location. At a normal walking speed, the three of them would be exposed to traffic for at least 12 seconds, assuming that they could proceed in one smooth crossing.

That is 12 seconds in an area where Gonzalez knew that a traffic signal would not be stopping oncoming traffic. She also had to have known that at least some of these drivers might not anticipate people crossing mid-block, especially at that hour. Those drivers would not be alert for the possibility that she and the girls would be there.

Of the four lanes on State Street, two convey traffic to the north and two to the south. Crossing safely here requires one to time a gap within the multidirectional traffic flow, a task made more difficult at night. What often happens in these situations is that the person crossing can anticipate the gap only in the two nearest lanes. They venture out and often find themselves trapped in a traffic lane, fully exposed, waiting for the furthest two lanes to provide the gap that they need to finish the crossing.

Sagrario Gonzalez had done this crossing many times. She knew all of this. Everyone in Springfield knows this, and most of us, if we visited the site and looked at it, would intuitively understand it as well.

What Gonzalez did was very dangerous. She did it despite the clear warnings. She did it to save a couple minutes of time. She did it despite having two small children in her care, young people who would face the risk with her and pay a heavy price.

This was Gonzalez's choice. It is easy to say this was Gonzalez's fault.

Too easy. It wasn't her fault.

Hidden Values

That night Sagrario Gonzalez made fateful decisions about how to navigate an environment where her existence was, at best, an afterthought, and at worst, a nuisance. The options she had available to her were the result of the underlying values applied to the design of State Street — values reflected in similar environments across North America and wherever around the world American design practices are being emulated.

The professionals who design streets follow a practice codified in the decades since the Great Depression. Engineers who do this work learn it as a practice, as a body of technical knowledge that has been amassed over generations. While one book or another of engineering standards is often referred to as "the bible" by those who use them, that reference is due more to their centrality to the practice of engineering than to the type of wisdom imparted.

While the religious debate passages of the Bible, contrasting different teachings in a search for deeper truth, the codes of an engineering manual are more like a cookbook. If you wish to make a certain type of chocolate cookie, a cookbook will provide the common ingredients found in cookies and the specific way to arrange them for a particular recipe. Likewise, if you wish to build a certain type of street, an engineering manual will explain the way to assemble all of the components so that you get the desired outcome.

What is expected in a religious text, but not in a cookbook, is deeper meaning. Few people question the underlying values contained in a fruit salad recipe. None search for hidden truth in the list of ingredients for a souffle. The recipes in a standard cookbook do not have an underlying ideology or belief system attached to them. A cookbook is viewed as value free. It is merely instructions for assembling ingredients into finished foods.

Transportation professionals consider their texts, and by extension their entire profession, as being similarly value free. This is wrong.

At the foundation of traffic engineering is a collection of deeply infused values. These values are so deep, and so core to the profession, that practitioners do not consider them values. They bristle at the suggestion. For practitioners, these values are merely self-evident truths — something like gravity that it is not necessary to believe in because it just is.

These values are expressed in the range of options that engineers consider, the way that they discuss different approaches, and the transportation systems that they build. This would not be a problem, and we could allow this entire profession to retain their sacred texts and practices unchallenged by heretical viewpoints, if they could find a way to address the damage traffic engineering is doing to our communities.

They cannot do this for a simple reason: The damage being done is the culmination of those values. The injuries and deaths, the destruction of wealth and stagnating of neighborhoods, the unfathomable backlog of maintenance costs with which most American cities struggle, are all a byproduct of the values at the heart of traffic engineering. Addressing the damage requires addressing the values, but you cannot address something that you deny even exists.

The underlying values of the transportation system are not the American public's values. They are not even human values. They are values unique to a profession that has been empowered with reshaping an entire continent around a new, experimental idea of how to build human habitat.

Let us identify those values.

The Design Process

When an engineer sits down to design a street, they begin the process with the design speed. I have been in countless meetings where engineers presented technical design sheets and even in-depth studies for a street project. Never, and I mean never, was any elected official or any member of the public asked to weigh in on the design speed.

Never once did I hear one of my fellow professional engineers say, "So, what are you trying to accomplish with this street in terms of speed?"

No. The design speed is solely the purview of the engineering professional, with a preference for accommodating higher speeds over lower.

Why?

Choosing a design speed is, by its nature, an application of core values. When we pick a speed, we are selecting among different, competing priorities. Is it more important that peak traffic move quickly, or is it more important to maximize the development potential of the street? Do we compromise the safety of people crossing on foot in order to obtain a higher automobile speed, or do we reduce automobile speed in order to improve safety for people outside of a vehicle?

These are policy decisions, and like all policy decisions, they should be decided by some duly elected or appointed collection of public officials. In a democratic system of representative government, representatives of the people should be provided the full range of options and be allowed to weigh them against each other. That rarely happens, and I have never heard of an instance where it has happened for a local street.

Many of my engineering colleagues will reply that they do not control the speed at which people drive — that travel speed is ultimately an enforcement issue. Such an assertion should be professional malpractice. It selectively denies both what engineers know and how they act on that knowledge.

For example, professional engineers understand how to design for high speeds. When building a high-speed roadway, the engineer will design wider lanes, more sweeping curves, wider recovery areas, and broader clear zones than they will on lower-speed roadways. There is a clear design objective — high speed — and a professional understanding of how to achieve it safely.

There is rarely any acknowledgment of the opposite capability, however: that slow traffic speeds can be obtained by narrowing lanes, creating tighter curves, and reducing or eliminating clear zones. High speeds are a design issue, but low speeds are an enforcement issue. That is incoherent, but it is consistent with an underlying set of values that prefer higher speeds.

Once the engineer has chosen a design speed, they then determine the volume of traffic they will accommodate. How many motor vehicles will this street be designed to handle? This is the second step of the design process, and the second instance where the design professional independently makes a decision that is, at its heart, a value decision.

Standard practice is to design the street to handle all of the traffic that routinely uses it at present, plus any increase in traffic that is anticipated in the future. There is no consideration given as to whether that is too much traffic for the street, and rarely is there a conversation of whether other alternatives should be considered. If traffic is present, it is the traffic engineer's calling to accommodate it. No nonprofessional is given an opportunity to suggest otherwise.

Now that they have identified the design speed and traffic volume, the traffic engineer consults one of the books of standards to determine how to assemble a safe street. Given a certain speed and volume, how does the design cookbook indicate the street's ingredients be assembled? Within the design process, the answer to that question is, by definition, safe. Any other design would generally be considered a compromise of safety.

The final step of the design process then is to take the "safe" design and determine how much it will cost. This dollar amount is the price for a responsible street design. Any questioning of this minimum effort would be considered a reckless endangerment of human life.

Now we have the traffic engineering profession's values as expressed in the design process. In order of importance, those values are traffic speed, traffic volume, safety, and cost.

I have presented the profession's values in this way to dozens of audiences, comprising thousands of people, across North America. I then ask them to identify their values. These are mixed audiences of professionals and nonprofessionals, people involved in local government decisions and those who are not. There is always a broad consensus (Table 1.1).

I ask them to think about a street where they live, or one where they shop or like to go out to eat. I then ask them to shout out, in unison, which value they consider most important as applied to that street. The answer, overwhelmingly, is safety.

And of course, it is. Most humans, including most traffic engineers when they stop to consider what is being asked, would sacrifice much of the street's performance in terms of speed or volume in order to make it safer. Safety is the top value nearly all people apply to street design.

As we continue, I ask for them to shout out their second most important value. Again, there is no real ambiguity. Nearly everyone chooses "cost."

Again, most Americans today would sacrifice the ability of someone to drive at speed, and the capacity of a street to accommodate a specific volume of traffic, to have a more cost-effective design. I acknowledge that this collective response may differ from the preferences of the individual driving the street,[1] but there are always competing interests between an individual and society. In public policy, we routinely ponder such tradeoffs.

While safety and cost are the top values for nearly everyone, the third value expressed by the groups with whom I have interacted is perhaps the most telling. I ask, "In a tradeoff between speed and

Table 1.1   Values Applied to the Design of Streets*

Current Practice	Most Humans
Design Speed	Safety
Traffic Volume	Cost
Safety	Traffic Volume
Cost	Design Speed

* In order of priority, highest priority first.

volume, would you prefer a design that moves fewer vehicles at a higher speed, or one that moves more vehicles but at reduced speed? Would you emphasize speed or volume?" The answer, overwhelmingly, is "volume."

And that makes sense. To the extent that the street is used to convey traffic,[2] sacrificing the number of cars that can pass through in a given time frame just so those drivers can go faster is counterproductive by any meaningful measure. If we can slow down traffic speeds, and it means that more vehicles can pass through and people arrive at their destinations sooner, why would we not do that? Most people would.

The values of the design process — the values applied to street design —are not values that most people would identify with. I would assert that this includes most traffic engineers, which suggests that design professionals are not morally deficient people but simply that they have accepted these underlying values without debate, internal or otherwise.

State Street was designed using a process that values speed and volume above safety. Sagrario Gonzalez was expected to overcome this design. A different set of values, a more human set of values, would not have put that burden on her.

Biased Language

As an engineer, I have worked on any number of improvement projects. I've improved roads. I've improved streets. I've improved parking lots, frontage roads, and alleys. Like King Midas, everything I and my fellow engineers work on, we seem to improve.

At least that is how we describe what we do. As I write this, my city is seeking bids for what they say in the official notice is a "street improvement project." It does not seem like an improvement to me, nor to many people who unsuccessfully fought against it, yet formally it is called an *improvement*.

The project involves the widening of a residential street. The many young families who live there believe that the changes will dramatically increase automobile speeds, which already seem too fast. To widen the street, quite a few mature trees will be removed, and the city has acquired part of the front yards of many of these neighbors, often against their will. To add insult to injury, to help fund the project, these aggrieved property owners are being forced to pay the city a special assessment fee of thousands of dollars. This is the kind of experience that makes my "Conversation with an Engineer" video seem universal.[3]

What makes this project an improvement? In my eyes, it is a diminishment. Yet, from beginning to end, it has been presented by the city engineer as an improvement project. The subtle bias of this language provides another glimpse at the values embedded within the engineering profession.

From the perspective of the design professional, the current street is "substandard" because, given the design speed the professional has chosen and the number of vehicles they want to accommodate, it does not meet the recipe in the design cookbook. The way to "fix" the "substandard" street is to "improve" it to be consistent with the recipe.

This is merely a reinforcement of the underlying values already discussed, but in a way that manipulates the conversation in favor of the engineer's perspective. Who would want something to be substandard? Who could possibly be against improving things? Yet, obviously, whether a project makes things better depends entirely on a person's perspective.

Instead of a "street improvement project," why not just call it a "street project." Or, if we need an adjective, how about a "street modification project." If the profession is free of values, as its practitioners claim, such a change in language should not be the least bit threatening.

The same goes for the word "enhancement." For example, when we "enhance the clear zone," what we really mean is that we are removing all of the trees within a certain distance of the roadway edge. This may indeed be an enhancement to the person wanting to drive quickly through that area, but it may also be a huge diminishment for the person who uses those trees as a sound and visual buffer between their home and the traffic. Why don't we just say, "remove the trees"?

I think the reason is abundantly clear. For the design professional with speed of travel as the highest value, removing the trees from alongside the road is an enhancement. It allows traffic to move at higher speeds. In the eyes of the traffic engineer, "remove the trees" focuses on a negative, and "enhance the clear zone" focuses on a positive, all while being an equally valid yet still value-free, description.

Even deeply technical terms like "Level of Service" are projections of the underlying value system. When evaluating the performance of a street using Level of Service, the traffic engineer will consider how well things are operating from the perspective of the driver. The street is then given a grade, like an academic course, with A being the best and F signifying failure. Level of Service A means that traffic flows freely with no hindrance, while Level of Service F merely means that travel time for the driver is not predictable.

Never mind that Level of Service A is often horrific for people trying to cross a street on foot. And never mind that a high level of service generally means a lower level of financial productivity for the community (higher costs, lower financial return), especially on local streets.[4] For the engineer who values traffic speed above all else, there is no conflict in using this grading system to prioritize "improvements."

When engineers do not recognize their own values and how they are being projected in the words they use, we must do that for them by correcting their language to remove the bias.

Understanding the Bias

One of my colleagues who has repeatedly done that is Ian Lockwood. Ian is a transportation engineer with Toole Design, one of the country's leading engineering firms working outside of the current transportation paradigm. His work on changing the language within the profession has inspired and informed me and many others. In a 2017 essay for the *ITE Journal*, he wrote:

> The field of transportation engineering and planning has its own biased language. Much of the technical vocabulary regarding transportation and traffic engineering was developed between 1910 and 1965. The foreword of the Highway Capacity Manual, first published in 1965, states, "Knowledgeable professionals, acting in concert, have provided the value judgements needed to. . .and have established the common vocabulary. . ."

Notice the acknowledgment of making "value judgments" and the purposeful development of a "common vocabulary." The period prior to 1965 was the golden age of the automobile in the United States. Automobiles were equated to freedom, mobility, and success. Accommodating automobiles at high speeds became a major priority in society and, thus, a major priority for the transportation engineering profession. It is no coincidence that these values were built into the transportation vocabulary.[5]

While civil engineering itself is one of the oldest professions, with techniques and insights dating back thousands of years, the subspecialty of traffic engineering is very young. Some of its earliest practitioners are still alive today. This was an entirely new pursuit, developed on the fly, in a period of tumultuous change.

Coming out of the Great Depression and World War II, the United States desperately needed a program that would keep the economy going. While the war had created jobs and economic output, demobilization threatened to shift the economy right back into depression. The redirection of American industry and capital from war-making into suburbanization created a kinetic growth machine that fueled a postwar boom.

We built a new version of America, one centered around the automobile, transforming an entire continent in a generation. Traffic engineers were tasked with making transportation in this newly imagined approach work. To do that, they needed to standardize nearly every component of this system so that it could be recreated, at scale and with urgency, across a vast continent. It is difficult to overstate how monumental an undertaking this was, nor how astounding their success was in accomplishing it.

In those early days, significant gain in travel speed could be achieved merely by improving driving surfaces and roadway conditions. With new highways connecting distant places, an increase in speed also meant an increase in overall mobility; people could reach more places with the same amount of time investment. Distances previously unheard of were now being routinely traveled by millions of Americans. Under these conditions, focusing on increasing speed was an easy proxy for increasing mobility.

In the decades immediately after World War II, increased mobility was driving economic growth. Whether it was families living in new housing in the suburbs, the ability of employees to switch jobs more easily, or the capacity for farmers, loggers, and miners to get their materials to distant markets, the fact that Americans could reach more places in less time provided accelerating levels of prosperity.

This notion became a self-evident truth embedded within the traffic engineering profession. Out of it sprung many beliefs that are now orthodoxy. These include the following:

- Faster speeds are better than slower speeds.
- Access to distant locations by automobile is more important than access to local destinations by walking or biking.
- Accommodating a full range of movement for large vehicles is more important than minimizing construction costs and increasing safety for people walking.
- At intersections, minimizing delay for automobile traffic is more important than minimizing delay for people walking or biking.
- Economic growth is a greater priority than community wealth preservation or financial productivity.

Today, the American transportation system is fully mature. We finished building the interstate system over four decades ago. The easy mobility gains have long been tapped. We are now left almost exclusively with expensive modifications that provide comparably modest changes in travel time, a theoretical benefit that is quickly denuded by shifting traffic patterns. To the extent that it once was, designing for speed is no longer a proxy for increasing mobility.

Yet these core insights of the early profession persist. State Street was designed for speeds far in excess of what is even legal there. The entire street is built to favor commuters driving into Springfield from distant locations in the morning and departing in the opposite direction at the end of the workday, prejudicing the person who lives close to the downtown and commutes on foot in the process. This is not only dangerous, but it has also had a disastrous impact on property values within the core of the city.

The lane widths, recovery areas, and turning radii at the intersections are designed for the ease of large vehicles, even though they are infrequent, and even though this design makes State Street more dangerous for drivers at nonpeak times, and more dangerous at all times for people walking and biking. Each intersection where assistance to cross the street is provided, the burden of delay is shifted away from the driver on State Street and to the person walking, even at the hour when Sagrario Gonzalez was making her decision on where to cross.

We cannot in good conscience blame Sagrario Gonzalez for the tragedy that occurred on State Street. She was navigating a space that was, at best, indifferent to her and her children's safety. At worst, it was outright hostile. It remains that way to this day, as do most local streets in the United States.

We can be generous in our interpretation of history and thereby more understanding of how the traffic engineering profession came by its core set of values. Even so, these values must be acknowledged if only so that they can be consciously set aside in favor of a more modern and universal set of human values.

The Strong Towns Approach

Traffic engineers are a critical part of designing transportation systems, but the values of the public need to dominate decision-making. Value decisions need to be stripped out of the design process and given over to nonprofessionals, preferably elected officials and the people living within the community— those directly affected by the design.

Table 1.2 gives an example of who should make what kind of decision during a street design process.

Elected officials must be given the ability to set the values for the project. It is their responsibility, on behalf of the people they serve, to establish the automobile design speed, the number of vehicles that should be accommodated, the size of vehicle that should be considered in the design, and the degree of deference that should be shown to people walking or biking at a given intersection. These are not design decisions; they are value decisions.

We must also insist that engineers use value-free descriptions for the work they are doing. If they are proposing to widen the street, it should be called a "street widening" and not a "street improvement." If they are cutting down all of the trees adjacent to the street, it should be

Table 1.2 Who Makes the Decision?

Nonprofessionals	Technical Professionals
Design Speed	Pavement Thickness
Design Volume	Pavement Cross Slope
Design Vehicle Size	Lane Width
Intersection Priority	Bituminous Mixture

called "tree removal" and not brought forth as an "enhancement." The goal for everyone is to communicate as clearly, factually, and value-free as possible. Elected officials must insist on this.

The burden and responsibility of making value decisions should not rest with technical professionals. Traffic engineers are incapable of representing the complexity of human experience that needs to be considered in a street design. That is especially true when industry orthodoxy is adhered to. This is not so much a statement on the engineering profession as it is an acknowledgment that city streets are the frameworks of human habitat, a complex-adaptive environment that must harmonize many competing interests.

As I will demonstrate in upcoming chapters, if we align the design approach with the values of the community, we can reduce death, create places of greater prosperity, spend less money on transportation, and get a better functioning system. We can do all of this, but only if we address the underlying values of the design process. To build a strong and prosperous community, local leaders must assert their community's values and see them reflected in the transportation system.

State Street in Springfield is designed with the wrong values. Its purpose is to move a high volume of automobiles at speeds much higher than what is safe for that area. Instead, it should be redesigned to prioritize safety. The value decisions for State Street were made without presenting the value options to elected officials, let alone the community at large. Both almost certainly have different priorities.

More information on State Street in Springfield, including maps, photos, and supporting documentation, is available at www.confessions.engineer.

Notes

1. This will be discussed in greater detail in Chapter 7, "Intersections and Traffic Flow."
2. There is way more to a street than moving traffic. We'll discuss this more in Chapter 5, "Great Streets."
3. See the Introduction for more on this video.
4. More on this in Chapter 5.
5. *ITE Journal*, January 2017. https://tooledesign.com/wp-content/uploads/2019/02/ite_language_reform-by-ian-lockwood-pdf.pdf

2

The Difference Between a Road
and a Street

The following words and phrases, when used in this Manual, shall have the following meanings: 225. Street — See Highway
— Manual on Uniform Traffic Control Devices[1]

Destiny Gonzalez was killed on State Street. There are many reasons we call it a "street" instead of something else. Likely, that is the name given to it in the original plat: the initial layout and design of the city of Springfield. That would make the designation of "street" a tradition more than anything else.

Some communities use "street" for places that are more residential — or less residential. It is often used in parts of the community that are designed with a network of grids, although not always. When used in places that also use terms like *lane, access, boulevard,* or *drive,* it might just be a random choice. For State Street, it could also be a preference for alliteration.

What is not often seen is calling something in the center of town a "road." I am not saying that it never happens, but when one thinks of a road, it is often in the context of the "open road," the conjecture of a more expansive kind of space.

Before I became a civil engineer, this is how I understood things: Streets were in the city and roads were outside them. I grew up on a farm, so we lived on Mapleton Road. My grandmother lived in town on I Street NE. It seemed clear to me that roads were rural and streets were urban.

Clear, until I began designing transportation systems.

Hierarchical Networks

Traffic engineers and transportation planners classify streets and roads according to their status in a hierarchy. Classification is determined based on how much traffic the street or road handles, or how much it is expected to handle.

The smallest of these with the least amount of traffic are called "locals." They provide access to "collectors," which collect traffic and funnel it to "arterials." Sometimes a community will have "major arterials," which is another step up the ladder of intensity. Theoretically, these different streets form a cascading system with many small streets emptying into fewer large streets.

- Locals
- Collectors
- Arterials
- Major Arterials

There is an obvious tradeoff in this hierarchy between what engineers call "mobility" and what they refer to as "access." Consider a cul-de-sac, the ultimate local street. A cul-de-sac provides plenty of access to the properties along it, but it does not provide much in the way of mobility. It is a dead-end street that is not expected to handle many vehicles. In contrast, an interstate is the ultimate major arterial, providing lots of capacity for vehicles to move at high speeds but with limited access to adjacent property.

With these two as the extreme endpoints, a standard classification analysis gently blends the tradeoff between mobility and access as we move from cul-de-sac to interstate. We can impair the mobility of the interstate to provide a bit of access, and we can give up some local access on the cul-de-sac to improve our mobility. This is a simple and comfortable relationship best represented in Figure 2.1.

The relationship in Figure 2.1 is firmly grounded in the profession's priority values of speed and volume. Note the apparent happy compromise in the middle where we can have our transportation cake and eat it, too. Those are the collectors, where there is a lot of access but still plenty of mobility. At least, that is the way a transportation planner might explain it.

Another way is to note that collectors combine high travel speed with complexity. Collectors facilitate the flow of traffic at speeds above what is safe for a local street with a lot of access, yet they provide just enough access to ensure that there will be random starts and stops, turning movements, and people walking around outside of a vehicle. High speeds combined with complexity create environments that are extremely dangerous.

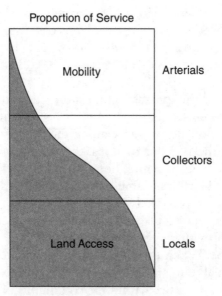

Figure 2.1   Relationship of functionally classified systems in serving traffic mobility and land access.

It would be dangerous enough if State Street were designated a Collector. State Street, which runs through the heart of Springfield, is actually a Principal Arterial, a designation often used for highways.

Roads and Streets

The embedded values of the engineering profession prioritize speed and volume in order to maximize mobility, with the belief that increasing mobility is the ultimate good provided by a transportation system. Discarding these antiquated values also allows one to move beyond the hierarchical classification system to one that creates greater value for a local community.

The starting point is the pre-automobile understanding of the difference between a road and a street.

Road: A high-speed connection between two places
Street: A platform for building community wealth

Think of a modern road as a replacement of the railroad, which, as its name suggests, is a road on rails. A railroad does not have frontage railroads or drive-through railroads. That would obviously be silly. For a railroad, a passenger gets on at one place and off at another, with the road providing a high-speed connection between those two places.

A road creates the greatest value by providing the fastest connection between two places that people want to be. This is done by limiting things that slow down traffic along the road. For a railroad, that means reducing the number of stops, the amount of merging traffic, and congestion along the route. For automobile roads, the concept is the same. The higher the sustained speed, the lower the travel time and the greater the value provided by the road.

While roads connect places, streets are the framework for building a place. Streets provide the greatest value when they create places that people want to be. When people choose to buy land, build something on it, and then maintain and improve what is built over time, they are building measurable wealth within the community. The most accurate measurement for the value of a street is the financial productivity of the land adjacent to it — how much value is created per acre of land that abuts the street?

The tension between achieving mobility and providing access in the current model is rightly replaced with the tension of either building a productive place or connecting productive places. This is a financial constraint more than anything else because the wealth created on the community's framework of streets is what must be tapped to pay for building and maintaining both the streets and the roads.

A railroad, again, is the easiest way to think of this system. During westward expansion, major railroad companies established cities along their train routes. They would do minimal development work to establish the community, mostly laying out the network of streets and establishing lots along them. The railroad company would then sell the lots to pioneers, builders, and speculators, who would pay a premium because of the presence of the railroad and the exclusiveness of being located near one of the stops. The profit from improving the land is what the railroad company used to cover the cost of the rail line.

Without a road, a network of streets will have no value. They will not build any real wealth. A city needs connections to other places for the streets to sustain anything beyond a village level of development intensity. The better these connections, the more value they will provide to these places and the more investment the community will attract and retain.

Similarly, a road that fails to connect places to each other is worthless. A circular train that connects back to itself but does not stop anywhere is merely an exercise in frivolity. Connecting one place to another is the minimum threshold a road must meet to be truly viable. That viability, however, will ultimately manifest, and be measured by, the wealth created in the places that it connects.

Roads and streets are yin and yang for city building. They are at cross purposes and antithetical to each other, but both are necessary for ultimate success. We must have great roads that provide high-speed connections between productive places, places that build wealth and prosperity. We must also have great streets that produce enough wealth not only to sustain themselves, but also to fund a proportionate share of the roads that connect them to other productive places.

Degrading roads to make them more street-like, or degrading streets to make them more road-like, reduces the overall value provided by the transportation system.

Thinking of roads and streets in terms of the value they provide, the functional classification chart in Figure 2.1 should be replaced

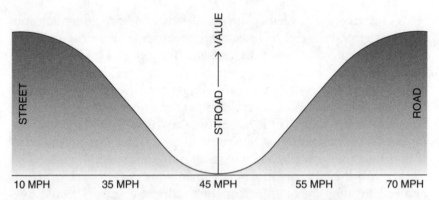

Figure 2.2   Which transportation investment provides the
most value?

with the chart shown in Figure 2.2. The chart provided in Figure 2.2
places speed along the horizontal axis and value along the vertical,
answering the question: Where do transportation investments provide
the most value?

The greatest value is provided where speeds are very low (street)
and where they are very high (road). We get the most value from our
transportation investments when they are used as the framework for
building a productive place, or when they are used to move quickly
between productive places. The further an investment strays from
these objectives, the less value it provides.

There is a large amount of space in the middle of this chart where
increasing speeds reduces value. Once speeds exceed 15 or 20 miles
per hour, traffic is moving too quickly for a place to really thrive. Value
does not start to be created again until speeds get up above 55 miles
per hour; the point where the transportation investment is providing a
meaningful level of mobility.

State Street exists in that middle space, as does nearly all of what
has been built on the North American continent over the past century.
In the classification system of the engineering profession, these are generally called collectors or arterials. I have taken to calling them stroads.

The Stroad

A *stroad* is a street/road hybrid. It is the futon of the transportation
system. A futon is an uncomfortable couch that converts into an

uncomfortable bed, something that performs two functions but does neither well. A stroad tries to be both street and road, providing both mobility and access, yet fails miserably at both.

If you are traveling in an automobile faster than 20 miles per hour, but slower than 55 miles per hour, you are most likely traveling on a stroad. Stroads have the wide driving lanes, turning lanes, recovery areas, and other features used to facilitate high speeds on roads. Despite this large investment in asphalt, concrete, steel, and land, nobody is legally allowed to move fast along a stroad. They are typically designated for speeds between 30 and 45 miles per hour, with frequent traffic signals that inflate travel times by stopping traffic entirely.

A stroad also tries to function like a street and provide a platform for building wealth. By providing access to homes and businesses, a stroad creates an environment where individuals and the community make investments in property with the expectation of a return. Yet, because of the speeds, development on a stroad tends to be spread out, which increases the cost of infrastructure and other public services and decreases overall financial productivity. I will discuss the dynamics of financial productivity for a street in more detail in Chapter 6, "Traffic Congestion."

Stroads squander community wealth. They are significantly more expensive to build than a street. For the level of investment, they have a comparably poor financial return and fail to provide a meaningful level of mobility. Yet, the financial impact is far from the only price paid for building stroads.

Stroads are the most dangerous environment we routinely build in our cities. If we applied a fraction of the level of scrutiny to their design that we have to the design of such items as baby carriers, lawn mowers, or beach toys, we would have made radical reforms decades ago. Thousands of people die each year on stroads, with countless more maimed and permanently injured. This happens for reasons that are not difficult to discern.

Stroads facilitate traffic speeds that ensure a high frequency of violent collisions. A collision with a change in speed of 30 miles per hour can result in a severe traumatic brain injury for the driver or passengers, an AIS-4 on the Abbreviated Injury Scale.[2]

For people outside a vehicle, the average risk of severe bodily injury (AIS-4) jumps from 50 percent at just 31 miles per hour to 75 percent at 39 miles per hour. The average risk of death for a person outside a vehicle jumps from 10 percent at an impact speed of 23 miles per hour, to 25 percent at 32 miles per hour and 50 percent at 42 miles per hour.[3] Obviously, age and health impact an individual's chances of survival, but horrible injury and death are common at speeds that are routine for stroad environments.

On roads the speeds are much greater, but they are achieved in a simplified environment that generously corrects for routine human errors (see Chapter 3, "Whose Mistakes Do We Forgive?"). In contrast, stroad environments have all of the complexity of streets. There are vehicles randomly stopping. There is cross traffic. There are vehicles that make 90-degree turning movements. There are vehicles randomly entering the flow of traffic and there are others that are randomly exiting it.

In auto-based transportation systems, randomness is the enemy of safety, especially as speeds increase. With hundreds of millions of people driving through stroads each day, some of the randomness results in high-speed collisions between two or more vehicles, or between a vehicle and a person outside of a vehicle. The complexity of the stroad environment makes this kind of tragedy inevitable.

For people walking, biking, or using a wheelchair within the stroad environment, the risks are even greater. A person on a sidewalk has no defense at all if a vehicle leaves the roadway at stroad speeds. The person crossing the stroad is even more exposed and vulnerable. That is true even when they cross at designated places and at specified times.

Stroads magnify that vulnerability by making it necessary, yet difficult, to cross. When Sagrario Gonzalez left the library on the evening of December 3, 2014, it was necessary for her to cross the stroad in front of her. Her car was parked where it was supposed to be, in the designated library parking lot on the opposite side of State Street.

While State Street is a street, it is not designed like one. It is also not designed to be a road. State Street is a stroad, so it is designed primarily to facilitate traffic flow at high speeds during peak times while also providing a modest framework for places like the library to exist.

This means that there were four wide lanes to cross with no sanctuary anywhere in the middle. It also means that the traffic signals, the only place where Gonzalez could have crossed with some assistance, are spaced out and timed to keep traffic moving. All of this makes a simple thing like walking to the car frustratingly difficult.

The irony is that stroads are frustrating for everyone, including drivers. Someone driving a stroad is continually presented with mixed messages. The wide and forgiving scale of the design is throttled back artificially by speed limits and signalized intersections. The turn lanes and wide curb radii make movement easy, yet getting from one building to another often requires lengthy detours, U-turns, and delays. There is a veneer of safety that comes from having plenty of margin for error built into the design, but the complexity of the environment creates an underlying tension that randomly disrupts the comfort.

While engineers have tried, it is impossible to make a stroad safe. State Street in Springfield has one of the highest crash rates in the state of Massachusetts.[4] The only way to improve safety on a stroad is to convert it into a street or a road.

Stroad Conversion

In the years following the death of Destiny Gonzalez, there have been other collisions and near-collisions in the same location on State Street. In response, neighborhood activists in Springfield requested that the city install a flashing crosswalk system, one that a person walking could activate to alert drivers that someone is crossing. I am not in favor of this approach as anything more than a temporary measure. While it may improve things somewhat, it reinforces the underlying danger created by the stroad.

To fix a stroad, there needs to be a decision on whether it should be a street or a road. Do we want this section to be about moving vehicles quickly from one place to another (road) or are we trying to build wealth and productivity within a place (street)? To get out of the stroad zone, we need to improve safety by either increasing or decreasing speed — by changing the design to function as either a street or a road.

State Street should not be converted to a road, but consider what would need to happen if that were the decision. To go from stroad to road, the first thing to be done is to remove access to State Street. That means closing all of the cross streets, dead-ending them before they reach State Street. That would reduce or even eliminate the need for signals because there would be no cross traffic.

All of the entrances to parking lots and drive-throughs that accessed State Street would also need to be closed. There could be no parking along the road, either, because that would create random start-stop conditions as people back in or pull out of open spaces, a condition that would be extremely dangerous at roadway speeds.

To make State Street a proper road, the sidewalks will need to be removed or, at the very least, a physical barrier would need to be erected between the traveled roadway and any space where people are expected to be present outside of a vehicle. There is no way to build safe space where humans are standing, completely unprotected, just feet away from tons of steel being propelled down the road at lethal speeds. The physics of this are not possible.

To protect the roadway investment, the city of Springfield would need to use their planning and zoning authority to regulate building along the corridor. Any new development should not undermine the roadway investment or degrade its capacity to move vehicles quickly from one place to another. Anything built along State Street would need to be accessible from some other side street, alley, or property.

Converting a stroad to a road is a process of simplification. Removing elements of complexity improves safety, allows higher travel speeds, and improves financial productivity by allowing the road to function as a high-speed connection between places. Every American city has miles of stroads that should be converted into roads.

State Street, especially in the vicinity of the Central Library, is not one of them. This is the core of Springfield. The library is surrounded by blocks of homes, businesses, and civic buildings. This is a *place* — the exact thing a framework of streets is trying to improve to grow the community's wealth.

The stroad that is State Street is undermining that wealth, not least by making the area around the library extremely dangerous. To convert State Street from a stroad to a street, the travel speed of the street needs to be reduced to compensate for the complexity of the environment. That means a human speed — something close to 15 and no more than 20 miles per hour.

The design needs to shift to prioritize people walking, those in wheelchairs, and others who are not within a vehicle. This means traffic passing through becomes a lower priority. That will change the emphasis of intersection design, walkway widths, the placement of trees and vegetation, and any number of other design items necessary to enhance the experience of being in that place.

Since the purpose of the street is to build the community's wealth, the city of Springfield will need to use its community development tools to facilitate investment in the neighborhoods around State Street. The objective is to continually improve the wealth there, a condition closely correlated with the value of the underlying land. As that land value increases, as the place becomes more valuable, a natural redevelopment pressure emerges that attracts investment and generates leaps in financial productivity.

This is an exercise in adding complexity, something I discussed at length in my book *Strong Towns: A Bottom-Up Revolution to Rebuild American Prosperity* (Wiley, 2019). Allowing neighborhoods to respond, incrementally, to stress and opportunity is the path to building broad-based, long-term strength and prosperity. Here's what I wrote in Chapter 8 of *Strong Towns*, "Making Strong Investments":

> To remove as many distortions as possible, to give neighborhoods a chance to evolve, to build wealth in neighborhoods that is not merely transactional but reflected in the net worth of the people living there, cities must allow, by right, the next increment of intensity throughout all neighborhoods, and they must limit by-right development to only the next increment.
>
> The goal is to thicken up neighborhoods, to create feedback loops that allow emergent prosperity to build on itself. No neighborhood can be exempt from change, but no neighborhood should experience radical change all at once. This is the prudent discipline we must impose on ourselves.
>
> Complex systems overwhelmed with resources stop behaving in complex ways. They become merely complicated, losing the feedback mechanisms that drive adaptation. The temptation to work only in bold ways, to embrace instant and comprehensive transformation as a strategy, guarantees eventual atrophy and decline. If our cities are to be truly strong, they must resist the easy path and dedicate themselves to the work.
>
> Cities can and should grow rapidly where that option is available to them, but that growth needs to be one step at a time, not huge leaps in the dark.

The environment around State Street is perfectly situated for such a bottom-up revolution. The buildings are underutilized and atrophied, but quite salvageable. The population trends toward impoverished, but with a high capacity for ingenuity and entrepreneurship. By making State Street a street for the people of Springfield instead of a stroad for commuters, the city can unleash the productive capacity of its citizens and build a prosperous place.

Whether street or road, the city must abandon the stroad approach on State Street and throughout the community. The hierarchical classification system needs to be retired and replaced with an updated understanding of how to make productive transportation investments, as illustrated in Table 2.1.

Table 2.1   Stroad Conversion

Stroad to Street	Stroad to Road
Slow traffic	Limit access
Prioritize people over throughput	Prioritize throughput over access
Build a productive place	Connect productive places
Embrace complexity	Embrace simplicity

Note that the decision on whether a transportation investment is a street or a road is not a technical one. It requires knowledge of the community's goals and objectives, but no technical expertise regarding engineering or design. This is a decision that must be made by an elected body — one directly accountable to the people of the community. It should never be made by technical professionals.

If we leave this decision to traffic engineers and transportation planners, the result will almost certainly reflect the embedded values of their professions. An emphasis on speed and volume creates trade-offs between mobility and access, a tension that technical professionals inherently address by prioritizing speed. It does not take much in terms of added speed to make a street into a dangerous and unproductive stroad.

If State Street were designed to be a street and not a stroad, it is very likely that Destiny Gonzalez would still be alive.

Productive Stroads

I started to develop my understanding of the difference between a street and a road as a teenager visiting Disneyworld. The theme parks and resorts are fantastic places. People pay thousands of dollars to spend time in them. If you stay in one of their resorts, you can walk to everything you want or need, including shops, restaurants, and recreation. The attention to detail in designing those human spaces impressed me as a young man and continues to do so today. These are great places that create enormous wealth for the Walt Disney Corporation.

If you are in Disneyworld in one place and want to visit another place — say a theme park, one of their shopping districts, or another resort — you can quickly drive there on roads that are unencumbered by excessive amounts of traffic, despite the incredible number of people being transported on them. Part of this is because there are almost no stops along the way. All of the complexity has been removed and what is left is high speed and simple to navigate.

Another reason for the productivity of the roads is that most people do not drive but instead take another form of transit. This could be a bus, monorail, boat, or even an aerial gondola. These systems carry huge numbers of people between productive places, quickly and efficiently, where those people then exit the transportation system and immerse themselves in their place of destination. It is not lost on me that the most successful pre-automobile cities were built in this way, with the roads connecting them being waterways and railroad lines.

It was on my first trip to Paris in 2001 that I experienced a different kind of stroad than what I had come to know from living in North America. One of the most iconic streets in the world, the Avenue des Champs-Élysées, was a stroad back then. It combined the function of both street and road, building wealth and moving traffic, but it did both exceptionally well. The Champs-Élysées is one of the wealthiest and most exclusive streets in all the world.

This productive stroad trick was accomplished with what an engineer would call a slip lane. The outside lanes of the Champs-Élysées, those closest to the buildings, were designed to be streets. There were slow speeds, parking, street trees, and an emphasis on people. In fact, people walked back and forth across these lanes all the time, an indication to me that Parisians and the tourists flooding their city felt secure in this space.

The middle lanes of the Champs-Élysées, the road portion of the stroad, were separated from the slip lanes by wide, tree-lined boulevards. There was physical separation between the street portion and the road portion. This allowed the traffic in the middle to operate safely at relatively higher speeds. (The Champs-Élysées was no highway, but it would not surprise me if traffic safely reached speeds of 45 miles per hour on the road portion.)

The ability to cross the Champs-Élysées was the only real impairment, something for which long delays in signal timing could somewhat compensate. When it was time for people to walk across, they were given a fairly long time to make that crossing. When it was time for drivers to operate their vehicles, they were likewise given a long turn at dominating the space. I was deeply impressed.

Years later, I visited the great incremental developer R. John Anderson when he was living in Chico, California. There he introduced me to the Esplanade, a two-mile stroad through a gorgeous neighborhood. It was a more modest version of the Champs-Élysées, with the interior road lanes physically separated from the street slip lanes by a tree-lined boulevard. The neighborhood along the Esplanade is a great place that makes for pleasant walking, a fact reflected in the high property values.

Five blocks east is Mangrove Avenue, a nasty stroad that runs parallel to the Esplanade. Mangrove Avenue has the gas stations, strip malls, and other auto-oriented businesses typical of American strip development, a style not only less productive financially but far more fragile than that found along the Esplanade. In 2018, both stroads accommodated around 22,000 vehicles a day, despite the radically different design and outlook.

The Champs-Élysées and the Esplanade are exceptions to the norm, but I include them here because they are not only good models to understand, they reinforce the notion that the critical tradeoff is not between access and mobility but between street and road, between building a place and traveling between places.

Incidentally, I had the opportunity to visit Paris again in 2019. This time my wife and I were joined by our daughters. In a way that I am sure is doing long-term psychological damage to my children, I was excited to show them the layout and design of Paris, including the slip lanes along the Champs-Élysées. After building them up to my family and eagerly anticipating them myself, I could not find them anywhere. They were gone.

All the street space that was formerly used for parking and slow-speed driving has now been given over to people on foot. Parisians have wisely decided that the area surrounding the Champs-Élysées is far more valuable when a high number of people can access it on foot, as opposed a lesser number of people accessing it by automobile. Successful experiments in limiting or banning automobiles in parts of the core of Paris are extensions of this realization. The Champs-Élysées is no longer a stroad.

The idea of banning automobiles today on State Street in Springfield is an absurdity, as it is for almost all stroads within North American cities. Our neighborhoods are simply not valuable enough as places either to warrant or sustain themselves without some auto-mobile access. Yet achieving that level of wealth and productivity must be the goal.

Building great roads and productive streets is ultimately about making the places we inhabit so prosperous, so productive, so valuable, and so inviting that they transcend the need to accommodate the automobile.

The Walt Disney Corporation would never make Cinderella's castle in the Magic Kingdom accessible by car. Whatever added value there is from being able to drive right up to the castle would be dwarfed by the lost value from individual automobiles diminishing the overall experience of the park itself. The park is such a valuable place, the streets within it have created such wealth, that it only needs roads to connect it to other places to thrive.

Springfield is not a theme park. It is a city where people live, work, and occasionally take their kids to the library. The automobile is going to be a reality along State Street for years, likely decades, to come. A reality, but not the goal.

The goal must be to turn the stroad of State Street into a wealth-producing street. That will require a shift in emphasis from moving traffic to building a productive place — one focused on the needs and experiences of the people who live there.

The Strong Towns Approach

Roads are high-speed connections between productive places. Streets are platforms for building wealth within a place. The greatest value in a transportation system is provided when building roads or streets.

A stroad is a street–road hybrid. It contains the elements of both road and street but fails to provide the benefits of either. Stroads are expensive to build and maintain and have low financial productivity. The complexity of the stroad environment combines with high traffic speeds to create environments that are extremely dangerous.

Cities must discard the hierarchical transportation networks and instead identify their streets and their roads. Where hierarchical classification is required for federal or state funding, it should be con-sidered advisory and subordinate to a transportation map that iden-tifies roads and streets within the community.

The decision on whether a transportation investment is a road or a street is a policy decision requiring no technical expertise. That decision must be made by elected officials, individuals who are accountable to the citizens of a community. It should not be made by technical professionals.

More information on streets, roads, and stroads is available at www.confessions.engineer.

Notes

1. https://www.mutcd.fhwa/dot.gov/htm/2009/part1a.htm
2. Nordhoff, Larry S. (2005). *Motor Vehicle Collision Injuries: Biomechanics, Diagnosis, and Management* (Burlington, MA: Jones & Bartlett Learning), page 53.
3. Tefft, B.C. (2011). *Impact Speed and a Pedestrian's Risk of Severe Injury or Death* (Washington, D.C.: AAA Foundation for Traffic Safety).
4. https://gis.massdot.state.ma.us/topcrashlocations/

3

Whose Mistakes Do We Forgive?

I worked with some fantastic engineers during my time as an Engineer in Training — people who were conscientious as well as competent. More importantly, they tolerated my diversions and constant questioning, as well as what I am sure was youthful arrogance.

One time, we were working on a curve on a road in Crosslake, a small city in central Minnesota made up mostly of vacation homes, restaurants, tourist shops, and party spots. There was a local legend, never confirmed, that the actor Tom Cruise owned a home on one of the many lakes. I liked imagining him driving a sports car at ridiculous speeds on the roads I helped build there.

This curve, however, was giving us some problems. The original white pine of the area had been logged a century ago, with the virgin forest long replaced by what locals consider lesser species. Yet there on that corner was a gorgeous white pine, towering over everything around it, right in the clear zone that was not supposed to have any trees.

I believed in standard engineering orthodoxy at the time and so understood that the tree had to go, but I was hesitating. It just seemed wrong. It wasn't environmentalism that motivated me but more of a subtle humility in the face of something that survived so long, combined with a youthful calculation of the odds. What was the chance, after all, that this one tree would become a problem? What were the odds that someone, on this low-volume back road, was going to lose control, leave the road surface, skid through the ditch, and hit this exact tree?

It seemed like a remote risk, and I was willing to roll the dice in deference to the rare and impressive specimen in front of me. I shared that opinion with my senior colleague, and I remember his response.

"As soon as we leave this tree, some drunk is going to come around this corner, go off the road, and smash into it. Then we're all in trouble."

Driving under the influence of alcohol was not only common in the early days of the automobile era — it was socially acceptable. Citations were misdemeanors, if any were given at all. It was considered an "accident" and not a homicide to be killed by a drunk driver. The organization that has led efforts for stricter limits and penalties for drunk driving — Mothers Against Drunk Driving (MADD) — was not even founded until 1980, well after the interstates were built and America was halfway into the second generation of suburban expansion.

More important to this narrative, broad social stigma about driving while intoxicated came decades after the standards, doctrine, and values of the traffic engineering profession were established.

This is important because the vehicle that killed Destiny Gonzalez was driven by Sandra Zemtsova, who would later plead guilty to being under the influence of alcohol at the time of the incident.

Forgiving Design

The early days of mass adoption of the automobile were a period of chaos, mayhem, and carnage. In 1935, there were 35,500 roadway deaths, which is 15.1 deaths for every 100 million vehicle miles traveled. Eighty years later, in 2015, the same number of deaths were recorded, but with 300 billion more miles driven. The death rate per 100 million vehicle miles traveled is now down to 1.1.[1]

This reduction is one of the great accomplishments of the traffic engineering profession. It is so impressive that it is worth noting: If 1935 death rates were applied to current traffic volumes, half a million people would be killed on roadways in the United States each year.

In the early days of the automobile, there were few high-performance roads on which automobiles could operate. Outside of cities, the roads that existed were merely cart paths used for horse-drawn wagons, with the best ones given an improved driving surface. This is important because, with the speed of a carriage, there was no need to remove obstacles from the path. A driver would simply go around them. Early roads wound around all manner of large rocks, trees, and gullies, if only for ease of construction.

Even if the driver is intoxicated, a horse is not going to run off the road and into a tree. The animal will make that corner, and it will not be a problem. However, take a two-wheel path and grade it out with a gravel or asphalt surface, then switch to a motor vehicle operating at higher speeds, and the result is easy to predict. All of those obstacles that the horses intuitively avoided become deadly at high speeds, while collisions with them become a statistical function of time and opportunity.

The alarming rate of carnage prompted much public debate and, as is the American way, plenty of litigation. Time and again, courts found that automobiles do not kill people; reckless drivers kill people. In 1907, in *Lewis v. Amorous*, the Georgia Court of Appeals ruled that automobiles were not inherently dangerous:

> It is insisted in the argument that automobiles are to be classed with ferocious animals, and that the law relating to the duty of the owners of such animals is to be applied. It is not the ferocity of the automobile that is to be feared, but the ferocity of those who drive them. Until human agency interferes, they are usually harmless.

> While by reason of the rate of pay allotted to the judges of this State, few, if any, have ever owned one of these machines, yet some of them have occasionally ridden in them, thereby acquiring some knowledge of them; and we have therefore, found out that there are times when these machines not only lack ferocity, but assume such an indisposition to go that it taxes the limit of human ingenuity to make them move at all. They are not to be classed with bad dogs, vicious bulls, evil-disposed mules, and the like.[2]

In the wake of World War I, the Progressive Era push for temperance from alcohol resulted in the enactment of Prohibition through the adoption of the 18th amendment to the Constitution. Prohibition was closely tied to women's suffrage, which was ensured in the 19th amendment the following year.

A significant part of these reforms was a response to domestic violence. Prior to Prohibition, husbands who abused their wives could claim that they were "taken by the spirit," and thus not in full control of their faculties. They were just drunk and not responsible for what they did under the influence.

Prohibition, and the broader movement supporting abstention from alcohol, was a progressive approach that changed the environment around abusive spouses. If men culturally could not be held responsible for what alcohol did to them, then make it difficult and expensive for them to get any alcohol. This seemed to have worked, as suggested by David T. Courtwright in his book *The Age of Addiction: How Bad Habits Became Big Business* (Belknap Press, 2019):

> Asked why her husband, a shipyard worker, was drinking less, a New Jersey housewife replied simply that it was due to liquor's poorer quality and higher cost. Across the Hudson River, in Manhattan, the number of patients treated in Bellevue Hospital's alcohol wards dropped from fifteen thousand a year before Prohibition to under six thousand in 1924. Nationally, cirrhosis deaths fell by more than a third between 1916 and 1929. In Detroit, arrests for drunkenness declined 90 percent during Prohibition's first year. Domestic violence complaints fell by half.

It is instructive to note that overall violence was not really reduced. It merely shifted from one form to another. Domestic violence might have fallen, but violence around the black market for alcohol distribution skyrocketed. Human societies are complex systems, and so any sweeping changes imposed on a culture will always have unintended consequences (although, I will note, those unexpected changes are sometimes positive).

Prohibition was repealed at the end of 1933 during the depths of the Great Depression. The following year, auto fatalities per 100 million miles traveled would peak at 15.9 and then begin a decades-long decline that continues today. More people were drinking alcohol and more people were driving, with many now doing both. Yet travel by automobile was becoming safer.

Since human error is inherent to the operation of an automobile, and since humans are not machines that can be fixed but complex organisms that respond to their environment in emergent and novel ways, there is no strategy to remove reckless behavior completely. In a society that accepts drinking and driving as normal, people will drink and drive.

This is the reality that faced the first highway engineers, and it forced them to make a fundamental breakthrough in understanding — one that has saved a countless number of lives. Instead of exclusively trying to fix the behavior of people driving automobiles, engineers needed to reshape the environment being driven so that it forgives the common mistakes that drivers make. People who drive will make mistakes, but we can keep them safe by anticipating those mistakes and compensating for them in our design.

The application of this profound insight is really simple. Consider a two-lane roadway with traffic flowing in opposite directions. Sometimes a driver in such a situation will drift out of their lane. Perhaps they are distracted by something on the side of the road or a child in the back seat, or maybe they are driving impaired. The reason does not matter because drifting into another lane is a common error that drivers make.

The engineer can compensate for this error by making the driving lanes wider. Now the driver has more room, and a little bit of drifting will not be a problem. The risk of head-on collision is dramatically reduced. Even so, there are times when a driver will fully leave their lane, either accidentally or on purpose. Perhaps their car breaks down, an animal comes onto the roadway, or they are driving with a high level of impairment. Going off the road surface can cause a driver to lose control. The vehicle may flip or spin and cause serious injury.

The engineer can compensate for this error by building a shoulder or recovery zone on the outside edges of the driving surface. That way if the driver exits the lane, they have room to recover control of the vehicle and get it back on course.

Even with wide lanes and shoulders, sometimes things transpire where the vehicle leaves the entire roadway. When that occurs, there needs to be a way to dissipate the kinetic energy of the moving vehicle before it smashes into something. Rapid changes in speed are deeply traumatic to the human body.

For these reasons, the engineer will establish a clear zone on the edge of the roadway. This is an area devoid of trees, large rocks, steep slopes, and other obstacles that would prevent a more gradual deceleration from occurring.

Wider lanes, recovery areas, and clear zones, when combined with gradual curves and the flattening of hills and depressions, form the core of the forgiving design approach. On America's roads, these innovations were revolutionary. They are so successful that they have become standard practice all over the world, saving innumerable lives.

That is the story of America's roads. On our streets, the story is much different.

Risk Compensation

Everyone has a level of risk that they are willing to assume. I have no qualms driving through most blizzards, even when I drove a little Honda Fit. My mother-in-law has an all-wheel drive Subaru, but she stays home if there is a threat of snow. I would never take a ride on a motorcycle, let alone drive one myself, yet I know lots of people feel very comfortable with the risk of cycling a curvy country road at 60 mph, the threat of a deer running across their path omnipresent.

Not only do we all have a different threshold for risk, but that threshold may change depending on time, place, conditions, age, and so forth. For example, I may develop a higher threshold for risk when I am running late for an event than when I am on my way home. I may have a willingness to take on slightly more risk in the car alone than when I am shuttling my daughters and their friends to softball practice.

Understand that I am not talking about recklessness. I am generally not a reckless person. Few people are, but choosing to drive somewhere, or ride in a car, is to assume some level of risk. We all assume risks every day as part of life. What risks we are willing to take is an individual decision based on our own risk threshold.

So, what happens to our threshold for risk when engineers take steps to make a road safer? What happens when lanes are widened, hills are flattened, curves are straightened, obstacles are removed, and recovery zones are established? Does our willingness to take risks change? Does my teenager suddenly realize her mortality? Does my mother-in-law suddenly become more reckless? Of course not. Our individual threshold for risk does not change. What changes is the level of risk we perceive.

Pretend that a person drives the posted speed of 55 miles per hour and perceives that, at that speed, the road met their exact threshold for risk. Then the roadway is modified to be safer, with a wider, straighter, and flatter course along with expanded clear zones. Now that same driver perceives that the roadway at 55 miles per hour is less risky. There is now a gap between the risk that the driver is willing to bear and the risk that they perceive. How does that driver respond?

The answer is that they utilize that gap in some other way. Consider an extreme example to help visualize the effect. Say that you are driving across Nebraska on the interstate. You can see for miles in every direction. The lanes are wide. The road is straight. There are wide shoulders, no trees if you go off the road, and no cars anywhere in sight. Do you feel comfortable looking down to change the radio station? How about talking to someone in the passenger's seat? Talking on your smartphone? Texting? Speeding? Reading a newspaper?

Driving the interstate across Nebraska is below most people's risk threshold. A driver has a tolerance for risk that is unlikely to be reached there and so they will feel comfortable doing other things. Some will feel comfortable changing the radio station. Some will speed. Some will text while driving. I am not making a case about whether this is reckless or not, merely how the human being who is driving the vehicles perceives the risk.

Now, ponder a busy parking lot at an elementary school. How many people text while driving in such a place? Talk on a smartphone? Speed? Read a newspaper? Likely very few, and it is clear as to why: The driver is going to perceive greater risk due to the complex and random nature of the parking lot environment. This is true even though speeds are slow. In fact, and this is critical to note, slowing down is the natural response for drivers perceiving an increased level of risk.

Risk compensation is the topic of a fascinating book called *Risk* (Routledge, 1995) by Emeritus Professor John Adams from University College London. Safety advocates often like to believe that adding safety features to roadways will make driving roads safer, but Adams points out that increased roadway safety induces people to drive more. While the death rate per mile has continually decreased, the total number of dead has remained consistently high.

In *Risk*, Adams describes the complex mental calculation that we all perform:

> The reward of, say, getting to the church on time might induce a prospective bridegroom to drive faster and more recklessly than normally. In the terminology of our model this behaviour is accounted for by the driver balancing a higher than normal propensity to take risks with a higher than normal perceived danger. This propensity and perception are states of mind that are not directly measurable and are assumed to be responses to external conditions that have passed through cultural filters. The mental mechanisms by which such balancing acts are performed are but dimly understood, but behaviour is assumed to seek an "optimal" trade-off between the benefits of risk-taking and the costs.

Analyzing that tradeoff is way more difficult to do when the costs of risk-taking are transferred to others.

Unforgiving Streets

How does a typical driver respond when forgiving design principles developed for America's roads are instead applied to America's streets? What happens when we take a street, the framework for complex human habitat, a platform for building wealth, and forgive the common mistakes of drivers?

What happens when we widen drive lanes, flatten hills and depressions, and smooth out turning movements? What happens when we add buffer areas and clear zones to the edges of our streets?

The answer is obvious. We communicate to the driver that their common mistakes will be forgiven. We transfer the risk from driver to those outside of a vehicle within the place. We induce the driver to utilize their risk gap by driving more often and, for many, driving faster than they otherwise would.

From Adams in *Risk*:

> Over many decades, research, policy, legislation, education and highway engineering have all focused strongly on the safety of people in vehicles, to the neglect of the welfare of vulnerable road users, those on foot or bicycle. The safety measures adopted have created vehicles that are safer to have crashes in, and road environments that are more forgiving of heedless driving.

It is a shockingly common experience across North America to have a street designed to accommodate speeds of 60 miles per hour, traffic flow at 45 miles per hour, and have the legal speed limit designated at 30 miles per hour.

Many traffic engineers look at that scenario as providing a safety buffer. They argue that there is margin for error and greater safety because the design speed is more than the posted speed. This not only ignores what is going on, but it is the exact opposite of the great insight the engineering profession made with forgiving design.

Let me reiterate that insight: Instead of exclusively trying to fix the behavior of people driving automobiles, engineers need to reshape the environment being driven so that it forgives the common mistakes drivers make. People who drive will make mistakes, but we can keep them safe by anticipating those mistakes and compensating for them in our design.

What are the common mistakes that drivers make on streets? The primary one is that they drive too fast for the actual conditions. Let us consider State Street and the collision that killed Destiny Gonzalez.

State Street is a complex environment. Anyone standing outside the Central Library for an hour will witness dozens of people crossing mid-block. Yet the wide lanes, multiple lanes, and recovery area signal to drivers that State Street is a simple environment to navigate.

Sandra Zemtsova was intoxicated. Alcohol can make some people feel overly confident, and they will misjudge risk and speed as a result, but that does not seem to be the case here. It is more likely that Zemtsova's buzz made her more risk adverse. It was dark out. It was raining. The surface was icy. Slow driving is a classic sign of an impaired driver.[3]

The legal speed limit on State Street is 30 miles per hour. Police reports suggest that Zemtsova was driving 42 miles per hour when she struck Destiny Gonzalez and her cousin. That sounds like she was speeding, but based on my experiences on State Street, I believe Zemtsova was driving slower than she would have under normal conditions.

Besides local knowledge of the library and the frequency with which people cross mid-block, she had no reason to suspect that anyone would be standing in the middle of the street at that time. At 42 miles per hour, Zemtsova had exited the signalized intersection just 4.5 seconds prior. There she had received a green signal light telling her that the pathway was clear and, more importantly, that it was exclusively hers to occupy.

If the goal is to forgive the mistakes of the driver, this design is doing the opposite. It tricks drivers like Zemtsova into making more mistakes — more costly mistakes — than they otherwise would. It is not accurately communicating anything near the level of risk that is present.

Am I arguing that it is okay to drive drunk? Absolutely not. Nonetheless, let's not pretend that people aren't driving drunk routinely on State Street. Impaired driving is a crime, and it should be a crime. Zemtsova spent years in jail and will be on probation for many more. She should pay a high price for her recklessness. Yet we are fooling ourselves if we fail to recognize that only the smallest fraction of impaired trips ever ends in tragedy, let alone some type of sanction.

Almost every person who has driven State Street impaired, whether from alcohol, illegal drugs, legal prescriptions, lack of sleep, caffeine, or multiple other things that limit a driver's capacity to engage fully while operating a vehicle, arrives at their destination with no problem. It is extremely rare that the kind of bad decision Zemtsova made results in someone's death. Extremely rare.

While it may be a rare event for any given Springfield resident, run the scenario every day with tens of thousands of vehicles traveling along State Street conflicting with dozens of people crossing on foot at the Central Library, and the statistically inevitable outcome is a tragedy like the one that killed Destiny Gonzalez.

Without change, there will be more people killed on State Street. The design makes it inevitable.

Random, but inevitable.

Forgiving Streets

On our roads, we compensate for the mistakes that drunk drivers make. We spend billions every year building and maintaining elaborate systems to ensure that even intoxicated drivers make it home safely. So how would we compensate for the mistakes Sandra Zemtsova made? How would we make State Street forgiving?

To be safe, the street must communicate the real level of risk to the driver. In other words, the driver must feel discomfort driving in a manner that is unsafe. In *Risk*, John Adams describes one way this communication could occur:

> If all motor vehicles were to be fitted with long sharp spikes emerging from the centres of their steering wheels (or, if you prefer, high explosives set to detonate on impact), the disparities in vulnerability and lethality between cyclists and lorry drivers would be greatly reduced. There would probably be a redistribution of casualties, but also a reduction in the total number of casualties. Motorists driving with a heightened awareness of their own vulnerability would drive in a way that also benefited cyclists and pedestrians.

If this seems grotesque to you, know that it did to me as well the first time I heard it. In a conversation with the late Ben Hamilton-Baillie, the renowned urban designer and shared-space expert, he walked me through a similar scenario, including seats belts that automatically unhooked and airbags that shut off once the motor vehicle entered an urban space. This is the exact opposite of how I was trained to think of design, and I had a hard time getting the moral of the story.

Let me point out something about State Street — something commonly found in cities across North America — that will perhaps make clear the transfer of risk that has already occurred on our streets.

Had Sagrario Gonzalez chosen to walk to the signalized intersection at Chestnut Street instead of attempting to cross State Street in front of the library, she would have been able to see up close the breakaway base at the bottom of the traffic signal. Just feet beneath where she would have pressed the button requesting permission to cross, the signal pole is attached to the ground with a series of sheer pins.

These pins are designed to sheer off and allow the pole to collapse if struck by a motor vehicle traveling at sufficient speeds. In the spirit of forgiving design, if a driver loses control of the vehicle, exits the travel lane, mounts the curb, and comes crashing across the sidewalk, the goal of the design is to have them continue through the signal pole, albeit with some of that force dissipated. This is preferred to having the vehicle come to an abrupt stop, which would magnify potential injuries to the driver and any passengers.

This is preferred even though it will mean horrible damage to anyone standing at the corner waiting to cross. And it is not like someone crossing there is rare. Hundreds of people cross there every day. Crossing there is what Sagrario Gonzalez was expected to do, after all. There is a bench placed right next to this pole, inviting people to sit in a place where the chance of a driver losing control and going off the roadway *at high speeds* is so great that the city installed breakaway poles.

That is grotesque, but that is what has been built.

Designing a forgiving street is the opposite approach to designing a forgiving road. Instead of widening lanes, we narrow them. Instead of smoothing curves, we tighten them. Instead of providing clear zones, we create edge friction. Instead of a design speed, we establish a target maximum travel speed.

On our streets, we want the price paid for mistakes to be paid in fender benders and shattered headlights instead of in human lives and suffering. Sandra Zemtsova should have hit a curb or a bollard long before she ran into Destiny Gonzalez.

Updating Design Wisdom

So much of our approach to traffic safety is stuck in the limited wisdom gained in those two decades after World War II. This is true in government, but it is also true in the private sector.

In 2014, the year Destiny Gonzalez was killed, the insurance company Allstate issued a report suggesting that Springfield drivers were the fourth worst in the entire United States, while Massachusetts drivers overall were the worst in the country.[4] According to Allstate's data, Springfield drivers were 86 percent more likely to have a crash than an average American. A Springfield driver has a crash once every 5.4 years.

> "I wish I could tell you why," said Allstate spokeswoman Julia Reusch. "More congested cities tend to be more dangerous. We really just want to decrease car crashes. We want these communities to be safe places for people to live and drive."[5]

The Insurance Institute for Highway Safety compiles an annual list of the most dangerous states for motor vehicle crashes. Unlike Allstate, they are not looking at total crashes but fatalities. In that ranking, Massachusetts is the best among the 50 states at 4.8 auto-related deaths per 100,000 people, followed by New York, Rhode Island, New Jersey, and Washington. Wyoming was worst at 27.5 behind Mississippi, Arkansas, Montana, and Alabama.[6]

Massachusetts is a New England state, one of the original thirteen American colonies. Its cities are among the oldest in the country. Despite what has happened to State Street, the state's historic neighborhoods have been difficult to retrofit according to forgiving design. The same goes for New York, Rhode Island, and New Jersey, where streets with tight lanes, sharp curves, and edge friction are common.

In contrast, most of the development in Wyoming, Mississippi, Arkansas, Montana, and Alabama came after World War II. These areas were all designed, from the start, with forgiving design as the basis for their local streets. Their residents are killed disproportionately as a result.

Even with these trends, I still agree with something else John Adams suggested in *Risk*:

> Accident rates cannot serve, even retrospectively, as measures of risk; if they are low, it does not necessarily indicate that the risk was low. It could be that a high risk was perceived and avoided.

Nowhere is this more apparent than in the rising level of what is officially called "pedestrian fatalities," the killing of a human being outside of a vehicle by collision with a vehicle. The Governors Highway Safety Association reports that such fatalities are increasing dramatically, with the latest year on record (2018) having the highest number ever recorded.[7]

There are attempts to blame this increase on cell phones and distracted driving, but that should show up in other crash statistics and it does not. I think it is more likely that, as auto-oriented suburbs age and decline (something examined at length in my book *Strong Towns: A Bottom-Up Revolution to Rebuild American Prosperity*), they are becoming home to an increasing number of poor families, including many who do not own automobiles.

It is one thing to walk in downtown Springfield, a city originally designed for people to walk but then retrofitted for stroads. At least in Springfield there is still connected walking infrastructure, even if it is feet away from excessively fast traffic. In America's suburbs, even that base level of accommodation is absent in most places.

The Strong Towns Approach

Road design has demonstrated that traffic engineers can anticipate the common mistakes drivers make and create environments to compensate for those errors. Local officials must be clear on which mistakes designers should be working to forgive. For roads, the current approach to forgiving design is the safest and should continue to be used. On streets, objectives need to expand to include forgiving the mistakes of people outside of an automobile.

This requires street designers not only to abandon the forgiving design approach, but in many ways to do the exact opposite. Instead of providing drivers with an illusion of safety, designers should ensure that drivers on a street feel uncomfortable when traveling at speeds that are unsafe.

On streets, the design speed should be thought of as the maximum speed at which traffic will routinely flow without the need for continual traffic enforcement (which should be reserved for deviant behavior).

Using forgiving design principles on State Street has made it a dangerous stroad. It is designed to forgive the mistakes of drivers, but in doing so transfers unacceptable levels of risk to people not in a vehicle. Without changes that slow traffic speeds, it is inevitable that people will continue to be injured and killed there.

More information on forgiving design is available at www.confessions.engineer.

Notes

1. https://en.wikipedia.org/wiki/Motor_vehicle_fatality_rate_in_U.S._by_year
2. *Lewis v. Amorous*, 3 Ga. App. 50, 54 (59 SE 338) (1907).
3. https://lifesafer.ca/blog/classic-signs-of-a-drunk-driver-slow/
4. Allstate America's Best Drivers Report, 2014 edition.
5. https://www.masslive.com/business-news/2014/08/allstate_springfield_drivers_fourth-wors.html
6. https://www.iihs.org/topics/fatality-statistics/detail/state-by-state
7. https://www.ghsa.org/resources/Pedestrians19

4

Understanding Roads

In response to ongoing safety concerns, some elected officials in Springfield have pushed for changes to State Street. In 2019, council members Jesse Lederman, Marcus Williams, and Andy Gomez used a formal letter to request that a signalized crosswalk be installed in front of the Central Library. They asked for a type of device that could be activated by people when they were ready to cross, something that would flash and alert drivers.

The council members' letter was addressed to the mayor and the director of the public works department, a licensed engineer named Christopher Cignoli. The latter wrote a lengthy response explaining why the request was, to use an engineering expression, not feasible.

Some council members were not pleased with this assertion. Many community members that had been pushing for changes were also upset by what they considered intransigence by the public works department. In this instance, I think these critics are wrong, or at least they are advocating for the wrong thing.

For decades, transportation investments within Springfield have been implemented based on the values embedded within the engineering profession. State Street was once a street, but it has now been

45

converted into a stroad. Much of the complexity of the street has been stripped out, replaced with a forgiving design approach that moves a high volume of vehicles at speed.

At the current speed of traffic on State Street, adding complexity back in is dangerous. A flashing light for a crossing might make things safer for the person on foot, but it will create random and unexpected speed differentials in the traffic stream, a condition likely to make overall safety worse. There is really no way to make State Street truly safer without reducing the speed of traffic.

Many residents and council members want State Street to be a street, the framework for building the place they call a neighborhood. Cignoli considers it a road, a corridor for moving traffic. In his response letter, Cignoli even refers to State Street as a "road" or a "roadway" 13 times. He is not using a Strong Towns framework; he just is not aware of a difference between a road and a street. For him, the words and the design approach are interchangeable.

Council members and residents are willing to reduce traffic speed and volume to improve safety. For Cignoli, the speed and volume of traffic have already been established and are the starting condition for any design. The goals and perspective of the council members and residents are misaligned with Cignoli, so they speak past each other, each frustrated with the other's apparent inability to grasp what is simple and obvious.

The suggested compromise of a crossing signal in front of the library fails because it does not acknowledge how Cignoli views State Street, and subsequently how State Street has been designed and constructed. To understand Cignoli, the advocates for changing within Springfield first need to understand how roads are meant to function.

Warrants

The cookbooks that transportation engineers use to tell them what to do contain an internal contradiction. On the one hand, they are very prescriptive. They describe, with a sometimes bizarre level of precision, exactly what should be done in any given situation. As a young engineer, I recall being more than a little frustrated that a large portion of the practice that I had entered was essentially technician work. Set a design speed, identify the projected traffic volume, then query the table to find out what the lane width should be. It was like studying to be a classical painter and then, upon graduation, learning that your job was putting copier paint in a machine that ran prints of old masters. Some engineers take to this part of the job, but others need to be broken like a wild horse.

The internal contradiction to such a rote approach comes with a statement contained in every engineering cookbook: a call for the engineer to use their own judgment. It is very strange because the cookbook establishes exactly what is supposed to happen in nearly every instance, but then it tells the professional to go ahead and use their own judgment.

Here is how the concept of engineering judgment is presented in the Manual for Uniform Traffic Control Devices (MUTCD):

> The decision to use a particular device at a particular location should be made on the basis of either an engineering study or the application of engineering judgment. Thus, while this Manual provides Standards, Guidance, and Options for design and applications of traffic control devices, this Manual should not be considered a substitute for engineering judgment. Engineering judgment should be exercised in the selection and application of traffic control devices, as well as in the location and design of roads and streets that the devices complement.

It is the matter of warrants where this contradiction is most dissonant. In traffic engineering, a *warrant* is a threshold condition that must be met before taking a specific action, such as putting in a traffic signal or a mid-block crossing. Cignoli references warrants throughout his letter, always as a way to indicate that thresholds have not been met and that the requested crossing should not be installed.

Here are three references to warrants in his letter:

- Mid-block crosswalks across 4 lanes of traffic are not desired unless certain warrants are met.
- As previously stated, part of the warrant study for a mid-block crossing is to determine if any adjacent traffic signals will have an impact on the proposed location.
- Very similar to the installation of a traffic signal, if certain standards for warrants are not met, the device should not be installed.

Warrants are easiest to understand when applied to signalized intersections, where they provide relatively clear and straightforward guidance. Consider a two-lane road through the countryside that intersects with another, slightly less traveled two-lane road. When should that intersection have a traffic signal instead of a four-way stop or some other type of traffic control device?

The MUTCD provides nine warrants to consider. If any of these warrants are met, then the threshold has been crossed and a signal should be installed. Here are the warrants, with a nontechnical explanation of each one:

Warrant 1, Eight-Hour Vehicular Volume: If the amount of traffic in an eight-hour period is sustained at levels where there aren't enough frequent gaps in the traffic stream to allow a driver to turn in or out of traffic, the warrant is met. To make this determination, there are tables that provide a ratio of traffic on the major roadway compared to traffic on the intersecting minor roadway.

Warrant 2, Four-Hour Vehicular Volume: This is the same as Warrant 1, except it is measured over a four-hour period with the tables of ratios accounting for a higher intensity during that shorter time window.

Warrant 3, Peak Hour: Like Warrant 1 and Warrant 2, except looking only at the ratios for the peak hour of traffic. This warrant generally only applies to places where there is a surge in traffic at a specific time, such as a factory shift ending at the same time each day.

Warrant 4, Pedestrian Volume: A signal can be justified if there are a lot of people trying to cross the road on foot. There must be a high volume of auto traffic and a healthy number of people trying to cross on foot for this warrant to be met. A lot of pedestrian advocates get upset with this warrant because it does not account for discouraged pedestrians, that is, those who would like to walk but don't because it's not safe. I will note that discouraged drivers are also not counted. Designing through warrants is a rote approach, not a dynamic one.

Warrant 5, School Crossing: If there is a school where at least 20 children are trying to cross a road in any hour, there are not enough gaps in the traffic stream, other remedial measures like flashers or crossing guards have been considered but rejected, and there isn't another crossing nearby, then a signal is justified.

Warrant 6, Coordinated Signal System: Maybe there is an intersection where a signal is not warranted, but a signal there would be part of an overall system that keeps traffic adequately grouped and the groups properly spaced. If that is the case, then a signal can be installed.

Warrant 7, Crash Experience: Sometimes called the "death warrant," if there have been five or more serious crashes during a 12-month period at an intersection, a signal can be installed regardless of the traffic volumes. The perversion of this warrant is that sometimes more people must die to justify a signal.

Warrant 8, Roadway Network: A signal can be installed if it is part of a preplanned roadway network. Generally, these are areas early in a development process where anticipated traffic volumes will justify a signal.

Warrant 9, Intersection Near a Grade Crossing: With some railroad crossings, when there is a high enough volume of traffic, a signal is justified.

In terms of warrants, engineers tend to look at roads as a parent looks at a child. The child starts in infancy, becomes a toddler, grows through adolescence, becomes a teenager, and ultimately matures into an adult. A road or an intersection may likewise start out small but then, as warrants are justified, graduate into a higher and more sophisticated state of existence.

A two-lane road grows to become a four-lane. Eventually, it will mature into a four-lane divided roadway. Continue to grow, and it could become a highway or possibly an interstate.

The same thinking applies to intersections. An open intersection may become a two-way stop, then a four-way stop, then mature into a signalized intersection, and ultimately blossom into a grade-separated interchange.

Much like an awkward voice change signals a phase shift in maturity for a young boy, passing a warrant threshold signals a new level of maturity for a road or an intersection. I remember an instance where I had to inform public officials who wanted a signal at a specific intersection that it did not meet any warrants, but that we could try again next year. Maybe in a year, traffic will have grown, and this adolescent intersection can become a full adult signalized crossing.

Of course, no council members or Springfield residents are looking for State Street to mature as a road. Adding more lanes or increasing the intensity of intersections is not a desired outcome. Nobody I have ever met is eagerly awaiting the next level of maturity for State Street.

Even if they were, the warrant approach does not apply to streets. It puts the emphasis on traffic flow and volume instead of on building wealth and prosperity in a complex, adaptive human habitat. When

Cignoli cites warrants for State Street, he is misapplying to a complex street a standard that was designed to be applied to simple roadways.

Even as applied to the city's roadways, I doubt that most Springfield council members are eagerly awaiting their opportunity to spend taxpayer dollars on expanding roadways and intersections, all because a random warrant has now been met. While warrants work fine for roadways, I have only seen them used through the engineering mindset, the one that nurtures adolescent transportation investments to full maturity.

Cities that want to be proactive about their budgets and their financial return-on-investment should use their warrants for proactive planning. Given a volume of traffic on a major roadway, it is simple to determine the volume of traffic on an intersecting roadway that would justify a traffic signal. If the community does not want to spend money on a signal — and strictly from a traffic standpoint, we should want as few signals as possible on our roads — then the zoning and development approach for the land along the intersecting roadway should not induce traffic above that threshold.

With the left hand, the city's economic development and zoning approaches encourage more building out on the periphery. With the right hand, the city's public works department must now spend money on low-priority, negative-returning infrastructure because warrants have been met. Cities can change that.

The same goes for adding additional lanes, turn lanes, interchanges, or anything where meeting a warrant prompts action. For road design, no city is hostage to this system, forced to spend money simply because all transportation investments mature and grow up. That is backward.

A city can decide that they are not going to spend their money on a new signal, an additional lane, an intersection expansion, or any other change and then use their land use controls to direct that outcome. Any city with zoning authority has that power; they just need their planning and their engineering people to share goals, objectives, and understandings.

Level of Service

Even more than warrants, *Level of Service (LOS)* is a tool developed for highways that should never be applied to local streets. LOS is a measuring system used to indicate how well a road is working from the perspective of the driver. No other perspective is considered, let alone measured or harmonized.

There are six levels of service. Like a student report card, LOS A represents the best outcome and LOS F indicates the worst conditions for a driver. While it is malpractice to apply LOS to streets, it works well for roads in that it comes the closest to approximating travel time. Here is what each grade is meant to indicate:

LOS A: Highest driver comfort; free-flowing traffic
LOS B: High degree of driver comfort; little delay
LOS C: Acceptable level of driver comfort; some delay
LOS D: Some driver frustration; moderate delay
LOS E: High level of driver frustration; high levels of delay
LOS F: Highest level of driver frustration; excessive delays[1]

According to Cignoli, the pedestrian crossing being requested at the Central Library will have a negative impact on the Level of Service for State Street. He writes:

> Also, based upon the traffic data provided as part of the Casino project and volumes during the peak period, and based upon our experience, introduction of a HAWK system would cause an additional increase in traffic queues by at least 25%, causing the Level of Service (LOS), currently C, D, E, and F, to deteriorate ever further to full failure of the intersection.

Cignoli attached a data table prepared for the city as part of another study. The table shows State Street having an overall LOS of B or C for the cited intersections, with opportunities to improve LOS with what are indicated as "2024 Future Year Build Proposed Geometry." Even if Cignoli's dire assertions are correct and the data is in error, the amount of time each day when drivers are frustrated along State Street is minimal. At the time of night Destiny Gonzalez was killed, there were no LOS concerns.

My own experience on State Street is that there are long expanses of time when drivers experience little delay, largely based on whether they are inconvenienced by a red light at a traffic signal. During the peak period of commuting time on weekdays — I hate to call it "rush hour," because it does not last anywhere near 60 minutes — the geometry of the space conspires to frustrate drivers with some delay, maybe even high levels of delay at times. In a real city, that kind of thing happens.

Imagine a city where the dream of the LOS-focused engineer is fully realized with ubiquitous Level of Service A. In such a place, at any and all times, the driver experiences the highest level of comfort, with free-flowing traffic and no delays. What would that actually mean?

It would necessarily mean no stopping and starting traffic. No pulling in and out of parking spaces. No slowing to turn or merging into traffic. It would mean no people ever trying to cross the street on foot and nobody on a bike trying to navigate in the traffic stream at speeds lower than 30 miles per hour. Such conditions are only possible where there is no city.

This is the paradox of Level of Service when misapplied to streets. LOS A is ostensibly the best, yet it describes an anti-place — the opposite of the platform for wealth that a city is trying to build with its streets. On the other end of the spectrum, LOS F describes a street the way that Yogi Berra might. It's so busy that nobody wants to go there anymore. We should aspire to this much love for all our streets.

When a licensed engineer references Level of Service for a local street, especially one at the very core of their community, it is a tell. It is an indication of a broad misunderstanding of the difference between a road and street, of deep confusion over what it means to build a place and how that is at odds with a driver's level of comfort. We would expect such professionals, if they are intellectually consistent, to live in a home built almost exclusively of hallways.

They don't, and neither should our cities. Keep LOS for roads where it is very helpful, but never allow it to be applied to streets.

85th Percentile Speed

In July 2017, two and a half years after Destiny Gonzalez was killed on State Street, the Springfield city council voted to reduce the default speed limit on city's streets from 30 miles per hour to just 25 miles per hour. This meant that any street within the city that was not designated with a speed limit now had a default maximum speed of 25 miles per hour. People who drive faster than that were subject to enforcement action.

At the time, Springfield Council President Orlando Ramos was quoted as saying:

"The hope is to make neighborhoods a little bit safer by reducing the speeding problem. In response to a lot of complaints we're getting from residents about speeding in their neighborhoods, we felt it was the appropriate thing to do."[2]

The city was able to take this action because of a change in Massachusetts law, one aimed at lowering speeds in thickly settled neighborhoods. Almost all of the streets affected by this change are in Springfield's core neighborhoods. According to Cignoli, the law does not affect streets "already having a posted speed limit such as wider streets in open areas with higher speed limits." One of those wider streets with a higher speed limit is State Street, which remains marked at 30 miles per hour.

It is not clear that the city council understood exactly what they did and did not do. Members of the public with whom I spoke had a confused impression. The city council did *not* change the design speed applied to their streets and, subsequently, they did *not* change the way their streets are designed. It is also clear, which I will explain in a moment, that they did *not* impact the speed that most people would drive. What they did do is give law enforcement the ability to enforce a speed limit of 25 miles per hour.

If the city council wants people to drive 25 miles per hour or less on their streets, there has never been anything inhibiting them from designing their streets for slower speeds. The city has always been free, on streets it controls, to implement a design where measured speeds would be as low as 15 mph or even 10 mph. What the city is not allowed to do, without an engineering study, is to *enforce* a speed limit below 30 miles per hour. That enforceable limit is now lowered to 25 miles per hour.

In terms of safety, this is hardly an improvement. There is a good argument that it makes Springfield's streets more dangerous overall. Part of that is the way that the routine traffic stop is used as a law enforcement technique. (This is discussed in Chapter 11, "The Routine Traffic Stop"). The other part comes from an understanding of how people drive, something measured by the 85th percentile speed.

The 85th percentile speed is the speed at or below which 85 percent of drivers will operate with open roads and favorable conditions. The assumption underlying the 85th percentile speed is that most drivers will operate their vehicle at speeds they perceive to be safe. Speed limits set above or below the 85th percentile speed will create unsafe conditions due to speed differential. Some drivers will work to adhere strictly to the law, while others drive the speed at which they feel comfortable. The greater that difference in speed, the more dangerous the road becomes.

Why don't we just strictly enforce the speed limit that we want? Why don't we simply expect people to drive the speed that the law requires and sanction people who refuse? Enforcement seems like a simple response, but it ignores the underlying reason why people speed, something engineers have long understood yet selectively applied.

People generally do not speed because they are deviants. They speed because driving is a passive activity, one that almost never requires the driver actively to concentrate or be mentally engaged to perform.

In his book *Thinking, Fast and Slow* (Farrar, Straus & Giroux, 2013), Daniel Kahneman describes the human mind as using two systems to process information. He calls these System 1 and System 2.

System 1 is automatic and largely unconscious. It is the fast reaction system — the one where we do not have to put effort into thinking. We know the answer to the math problem $2 + 2 = ?$, not because we paused to think about it deeply, but because we have done that problem so many times that the answer is reflexive.

Things that require mental effort to resolve access System 2. This system is slower and more purposeful. Adding three-digit numbers is something that most people cannot do in their heads, so if presented with that challenge, a person will activate their System 2 and focus on the numbers, crowding out most anything else that they are thinking about.

Here is how Kahneman describes the tradeoff between these two systems:

> The often-used phrase "pay attention" is apt: you dispose of a limited budget of attention that you can allocate to activities, and if you try to go beyond your budget, you will fail. It is the mark of difficult activities that they interfere with each other, which is why it is difficult or impossible to conduct several at once.
>
> You could not compute the product of 17 x 24 while making a left turn into dense traffic, and you certainly should not try. You can do several things at once, but only if they are easy and undemanding. You are probably safe carrying on a conversation with a passenger while driving on an empty highway, and many parents have discovered, perhaps with some guilt, that they can read a story to a child while thinking of something else.
>
> Everyone has some awareness of the limited capacity of attention, and our social behavior makes allowances for these limitations. When the driver of a car is overtaking a truck on a narrow road, for example, adult passengers quite sensibly stop talking. They know that distracting the driver is not a good idea, and they also suspect that he is temporarily deaf and will not hear what they say.[3]

As suggested, out of necessity, driving is largely a System 1 activity. It is passive, automatic, and we do it without really having to think about it. That is necessary because, were it a System 2 activity, driving would be too exhausting for humans. How long could you sit and add three-digit numbers in your head? People who can sustain long periods of System 2 activity while driving are called "race car drivers" or "fighter jet pilots," and they make up a small fraction of humanity. For driving to be something in which most humans can engage, it needs to be a System 1 endeavor.

I have been pulled over by police officers for speeding, and every time when the officer asks if I was aware that I was traveling above the speed limit, my honest answer is "no." In System 1, people tend to drive the speed that they feel comfortable driving, regardless of the posted limit. Here is how the Federal Highway Administration explains this in their report "Methods and Practices for Setting Speed Limits":

> To effectively reduce vehicle speeds, setting speed limits should be included only as a part of a broader strategy that includes geometric changes to the road and other educational and enforcement components.
>
> Studies have shown that arbitrarily raising or lowering posted speed limits alone will result in a difference of less than 2 mph in mean and 85th percentile speeds. This small change is not practically meaningful and it appears that "new posted speed limits alone, without some additional engineering, enforcement, or educational measures, [do] not have a major effect on driver behavior or encourage most drivers to comply with the posted speed limit."
>
> There is also no evidence that shows arbitrarily lowering or raising the posted speed limit will have a statistically significant impact on crash reductions.[4]

A blanket lowering of speed limits, as Springfield has done, will not have any "practically meaningful" results. It will not address the neighborhood speeding problem. It will not reduce crashes or make Springfield's neighborhood safer, at least not without other action.

Enforcement and education measures are effective, but only temporarily. The police officer parked on the side of the road will jolt a driver into System 2, prompting them to slow down, but remove that prompt and, over time, the driver will revert to System 1. This is the way that the human brain is constructed. We can ignore that and wish it were not the case, or we can accept it and build that understanding into our designs.

The only way to have meaningful reductions in speed, and a significant impact on the number of crashes, is through "geometric change." The design of the street needs to prompt people to drive slower.

The forgiving design approach creates an environment that forgives the common mistakes that drivers make. Forgiving design reinforces System 1 driving behavior by removing distractions and other complexity that would interfere with the smooth and predictable flow of traffic. That is a good thing, but only on roads where speeds are high and complexity has been removed. The 85th percentile speed approach is helpful for establishing the proper speed limit on roads.

For streets, where we need complexity in order to build a productive place, traffic needs to flow at a neighborhood speed (15 mph or less is optimum) to make a human habitat that is safe and productive. To achieve this on a street, the street design needs to shift drivers from the passive awareness of System 1 to the mental state of heightened engagement found in System 2.

Whereas traffic engineers have done a brilliant job recognizing the limits of human cognition and adjusting speed limits on roads to reflect the 85th percentile speed, they now need to apply the same insights to streets. The only difference is that, instead of using the 85th percentile speed to adjust the speed limit, on streets we need to use the measured speed to adjust the design.

Where drivers are traveling too fast, the geometry of the street needs to change, and keep changing, until a safe 85th percentile speed is achieved.

Incidentally, Cignoli was supportive of the change from 30 mph to 25 mph throughout the city. He was quoted in the newspaper as saying:

> "If we can get vehicles to slow down on many roads, they become safer. This [reduction in the enforced speed limit] allows us kind of in a blanket way through the city to bring down the speed."

In the same article, Cignoli says the city wants to "get the word out" about the change, that they will place signs on the outskirts of the city to warn motorists that "enforcement is coming" in Springfield.

I have seen other engineers support such blanket speed reductions. I do not doubt the sincerity, but it is long on moral platitude and short on any professional sacrifice or self-reflection.

Not only are stroad-like streets such as State Street exempt from these kind of superficial speed reductions, by focusing on enforcement and education as the proper response, the engineer fails to confront the role that design plays in speeding. The council's actions, while also sincere, do nothing to force the needed reckoning.

In Springfield, speeding remains the sole responsibility of the driver, not the street designer. For streets like State Street, this abrogation of responsibility is deadly.

Speed and Travel Time

Warrants, Level of Service, and the 85th percentile speed are helpful when applied to roads because, on a well-functioning road, there is strong correlation between speed and travel time. A road is a high-speed connection between two places. The value of a road is in getting from one place to another in the least amount of time possible.

The design of a good road is so simple that it almost defies explanation. The highest-quality road begins at one place that people want to be and provides a high-speed connection to another place that people want to be. Anything that lowers the speed of travel along this route — such as traffic signals, merging traffic, or traffic congestion — increases travel time and thus degrades the value provided by the road.

For roads, because there is such a strong correlation between travel time and speed, engineers have tended to focus primarily on the latter. All along a route, engineers default to higher speeds. This has led to some poor tradeoffs in travel times as roads transition to streets and then back to roads.

Consider a standard condition across much of the United States, where the six-mile by six-mile grid established in the Land Ordinance of 1785 set the conditions for land development. It is common in such places to see cities spaced six miles apart. The North American approach to transportation focuses on keeping auto speeds high between cities but also as high as possible within the city itself. This denudes the value of place, inducing demand for development on the periphery of the city, a pattern derogatorily called "sprawl" by many of its critics.

The result is that the road between cities turns into a stroad as it approaches and departs the edge of town. The traffic engineer tries to maintain the high speeds of the road as pressure from development creates an opposing force that seeks to lower speed and provide more access. The result is long stretches on the edge of a city where travel speeds are well below what is optimal for a road. Such a situation is represented in Figure 4.1.

In this scenario, driving from the center of one city to another will hypothetically take 7 minutes and 22 seconds.

Consider a Strong Towns approach, eliminating stroads and shifting to only roads and streets. In such a scenario, traffic speeds are kept low within the city in order to build wealth, while speeds are kept high

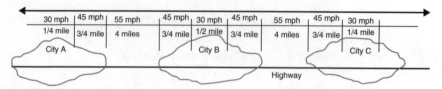

Figure 4.1   American economic development pattern.

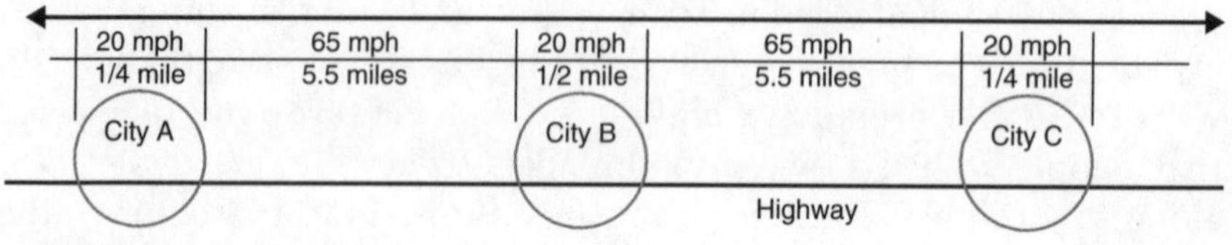

Figure 4.2   City-centric traditional design.

between cities so that the road provides the greatest amount of value possible. This scenario is represented in Figure 4.2.

With the Strong Towns approach, driving from the center of one city to another will hypothetically take only 6 minutes and 35 seconds, nearly a minute quicker than the standard North American approach.

By focusing on sustaining high speeds, especially along streets within the city, the traffic engineer is actually increasing travel time for many trips. This is the exact opposite of the desired outcome.

While a driver can legally speed past the Central Library in Springfield at 30 miles per hour, on the periphery of the city they are forced to travel long distances at between 35 and 50 miles per hour, a time-robbing speed of travel.

From a transportation standpoint, this tradeoff works for nobody. People who live in the city suffer decreased wealth and prosperity while experiencing the danger of fatal automobile speeds on the streets outside their homes, businesses, places of worship, and other destinations. People who are driving into the city suffer unnecessary delays in travel time, plus a large decrease in overall safety despite a level of transportation investment greater than what would be spent for a simple road.

Of course, so many local governments accept this tradeoff because they want the increased tax base that comes along with growth and development on the periphery of the city. I dealt with this topic in depth in *Strong Towns: A Bottom-Up Revolution to Rebuild American Prosperity*, and I will not revisit those insights here beyond pointing out that, long term, this tradeoff is a financial disaster for the community.

What I want to point out here is the asymmetry of costs and benefits for road users and those who own property along the road.

When a road is built between two places, conveying people and goods back and forth creates tremendous value. People living in each place experience part of that benefit, albeit it more abstractly than people who use the road to travel back and forth.

It is commonplace that someone who owns land next to the road would desire to build something — let's say a gas station — to take advantage of their proximity to the stream of traffic. Doing that requires them to tap into the road, to create an intersection of some type of access that slows speeds, creates congestion, and diminishes the overall value of the road. Even if the impact is slight, there is some impact to the quality of the road.

The road was built by general taxpayers. That cost is distributed over many, so the cost to any one individual is minimal. The same applies to the damage of an access. While each person within the community, and each driver along the roadway, will experience some minimal amount of damage from acts that degrade the roadway. Added together, however, the collective damage is significant.

For the landowner, the impacts are the exact opposite. A new access provides them with a very large gain and only insignificant levels of damage from delay. In a public setting, where decision makers hear from affected parties and weigh the costs and benefits of different actions, the landowner has tremendous incentive to show up and make the case that the benefits of the access and the new development are significant. From their perspective, this is true.

In contrast, no individual affected by delay will suffer enough by the action to make it worth their time to fight it. The delay is an annoyance, if anything, but a few seconds lost each day is less time wasted than a two-hour public meeting where one voice is not likely to have much impact on the conversation.

What is happening in these instances is that individual property owners are, in effect, mining the large public investment in the road for their own individual gain. I do not believe that makes them evil, but public officials need to recognize that they represent the collective interest, which is being disproportionately damaged by this transfer of public value to private hands.

Cities undermine their road investments in a death-by-a-thousand-cuts granting of access. No individual action is meaningful, but collectively the damage takes its toll. By understanding roads and the value that a good road provides the community, public officials and their professional advisers can work together to make better decisions on behalf of the public.

The Most Important Roads

While doing engineering and planning work with communities, I have had an opportunity to discuss with public officials, technical professionals, and other interested parties exactly what they consider to be their most important roads. The answer always centers around commuters, people who do not live within the core of the city but nevertheless drive into the city routinely for work or pleasure.

I have struggled to understand this mindset, especially since these planning efforts typically involve people who live within the city and are not commuters. What is it about these magic people who live outside the city that makes people within the city's neighborhoods agree to diminish their own wealth and prosperity so as to accommodate the commuter's expectations for driving comfort?

Springfield's Central Library is amazing. Many people would love to live within a few blocks of such a fantastic place. In Springfield, that would also mean living within close proximity to a world-class symphony hall, an events center that is the home of one professional and one collegiate hockey team, many fantastic local restaurants, and a whole bunch of job opportunities. These are amenities that people generally pay large amounts to live nearby.

In Springfield they don't, primarily because the city has invested its wealth making it really convenient to live outside the city and drive in while simultaneously degrading the quality-of-life and investment opportunities in its core neighborhoods to accommodate that commuting lifestyle. Springfield proclaims itself as the "City of Homes" for its Victorian mansions and unique architecture, but it would be better known as the "City of Stroads" for its emphasis on throughput of traffic over quality of place. If the city set out to develop a more expensive approach that yielded lower financial returns for the community, it is hard to image what it would be.

I do not understand why Springfield's residents tolerate this, nor residents of any community, especially those who are struggling. Even so, I live six blocks from my own core downtown, and I am continually frustrated by how my friends and neighbors will voice support for spending millions on a shortcut to the neighboring city's Walmart yet oppose spending a few thousands making it less dangerous to walk to our struggling downtown.

No property in my neighborhood becomes more valuable because we can now drive to Walmart a minute more quickly, especially if the increased tax burden of sustaining that shortcut is factored in. All of our property values would soar if the walk to the restaurants and shops in our core downtown was safe and pleasant. The value of those restaurants and shops would soar as well. That this isn't abundantly clear is certainly a sign of some syndrome of abuse, a coping mechanism that we have collectively developed.

The most important roads to any community are not those that accommodate commuters. They are not those that allow people to get quick access to the big box store on the periphery. The most important roads are not even in the city limits. They are the roads that connect the city to other places.

For example, Holyoke is a nice little city of 40,000 that is only 12 miles north of Springfield. Like Springfield, it is struggling in many ways, but it also has a lot of assets and some strong sparks of vitality. At a minimum, there should be high-speed buses that go back and forth between these economic hubs, magnifying the energy of each place. There isn't, largely because the roads are instead clogged with commuters, not only wasting the massive transportation investment, but disbursing that economic energy across the region in a way that drives up the region's costs while lowering its overall financial productivity.

Hartford is 26 miles to the south, with Bradley International Airport along the way. All of the interchanges along this highway provide premium access to modest development pursuits. The flood of commuters it induces does more economic damage to Springfield than slowing traffic along State Street ever could.

Albany, and another significant airport, is 90 miles to the northwest. The flooding of this corridor with commuters in single-family vehicles, along with the lack of any high-speed transit alternative that would wring more capacity out of the roadway, is robbing Springfield of investment potential.

Boston is a similar distance to the east. The traffic levels are mind-numbing, despite massive investments in commuter-oriented transportation systems. The more the cities between Springfield and

Boston rely on corridor-focused instead of place-focused growth, the more marginalized Springfield's economy becomes.

If the leadership in Springfield were to get serious about how transportation investments impact the future of their community, they would look far beyond their boundaries to the roads that connect them to other important places. They would fight for those connections and resist plans and approaches that degrade their capacity.

The Strong Towns Approach

Roads are high-speed connections between places. Many of the tools that we have created to guide the construction and maintenance of roads work well for reducing travel time and improving the overall value of roads, but they are misused when applied to streets.

Warrants do not apply to streets. They do apply to roads, where they should inform the community's land use and development approach to minimize unwanted or unanticipated transportation expenditures.

Level of Service (LOS) also does not apply to streets. In fact, the best rating of LOS A is an anti-place, the opposite of what a community is trying to accomplish with a street. Use LOS for roads and be very wary of any professional that references LOS when discussing a street.

The 85th percentile speed measurement is based on deep insights in human cognition. We must set speed limits on roads using the 85th percentile speed measurement. Arbitrarily lowering speed limits on streets will not have any meaningful impact on speed or crash reduction without changing the street design. On streets, use the 85th percentile speed approach to identify when your design has achieved your speed goals.

Success for a road must be measured in travel time, not simply design speed. Having distinct areas of higher-speed roads and lower-speed streets is a tradeoff that increases travel times over the wide adoption of stroad environments.

Local leaders must resist development pressure along roads and not allow the value of their roads to be mined for short-term gain. As stewards of roadways, public officials must recognize the large collective damage done to public investments by ongoing degradation of roadways.

Those in a proactive city need to involve themselves in transportation decisions throughout the region surrounding their community, resisting proposals to degrade critical roadway connections to neighboring communities and even to distant metropolitan areas.

More information on warrants, level of service, the 85th percentile speed, and other aspects of roadways is available at the website www.confessions.engineer.

Notes

1. https://www.trpc.org/DocumentCenter/View/2798/Appendix-O--Level-of-Service-Standard-and-Measurement#:~:text=Level%20of%20service%20(LOS)%20is,and%20LOS%20F%20the%20worst
2. https://www.masslive.com/news/2017/07/slow_down_springfield_adopts_n.html
3. Kahneman, Daniel, *Thinking, Fast and Slow* (Farrar, Straus & Giroux, 2013).
4. https://safety.fhwa.dot.gov/speedmgt/ref_mats/fhwasa12004/

5

Great Streets

One of the remarkable things I learned about Springfield's streets is that they are frequently used for illegal drag racing. This is not the frivolity of teenagers cruising the strip on a Saturday night, but a serious, crash-into-police-cars kind of endeavor.[1] It is so pervasive that the Springfield Police Department has an anti–drag racing detail of officers dispatched specifically to break them up.

As I ponder the great streets that I have seen and experienced in my life, I note that none of them could support drag racing. They are too narrow, too tight, too rough, or have some other characteristic in their design that makes them unfriendly to such contests. This leads to a simple heuristic, albeit an incredibly low bar: If people are drag racing on your streets, those streets are horribly designed. They are destroying community wealth, not building it.

State Street should be a great street, but it is not. Today it is a stroad, an expensive and dangerous piece of transportation infrastructure that neither moves traffic quickly nor builds wealth for the community.

The sole reason why State Street was created was to be a platform for building wealth within Springfield. It fulfilled this role impressively until the street, along with many others, was turned into a stroad sometime in the 20th century. Since that point, Springfield has experienced continual decline. This is more than a correlation.

State Street should be attracting investment. People should want to live on State Street. People should want to open businesses along State Street. Buildings that go into decline should be purchased and fixed up. Parking lots should be converted into some type of higher and better use. If State Street were a street and not a stroad, all of this would be happening. It is not, at least not in any meaningful way.

If it were, not only would Springfield be a stronger and more prosperous place, but it is also almost certain that Destiny Gonzalez would still be alive today. That is because a prerequisite for building wealth is that a street be safe.

Traffic moves too quickly along State Street for it to be safe. It moves too quickly for State Street to be a platform for wealth creation. If State Street is to become the great street it should be, an entirely new approach is required.

The Difference Between Growth and Wealth Creation

Cities are human habitat. Just as a beehive evolved to serve the needs of bees, our cities evolved along with us to serve human needs, both those that we recognize and those about which we are unaware. In *Strong Towns: A Bottom-Up Revolution to Rebuild American Prosperity*, I wrote about the complex nature of pre-Depression American cities and how the trillions of tiny experiments tried by our ancestors over millennia added up to a way of constructing cities that was productive, adaptable, and stable. In a word: strong.

> We are compelled today to acknowledge that the wisdom contained in the cities our ancestors built, in the patterns and approaches they developed over thousands of years, exceeds our capacity to fully understand. There are deeper truths there than we will ever know, spooky wisdom that has co-evolved along with humanity itself, to serve our needs – known and unknown – in ways we have been far too eager to casually dismiss.

As within any organic system, the creation of wealth is a simplified way to express the accumulation of surplus resources. We humans tend to measure wealth in terms of currency, and I find that to be the most applicable proxy to a broader method of accounting, but accumulating surplus resources is really about building the capacity to endure over time.

For example, consider the human body. Some people unfamiliar with our anatomy might think of it as "efficient," yet in an accounting of resources, it is rather inefficient. Humans have two lungs with excess capacity in each. We have two kidneys, yet we only need one. We use a small fraction of our total brain capacity at any one time. Having all of these spare parts and needing to consume the resources to sustain them is grossly inefficient. Yet, obviously, spare parts are necessary for our survival. We know that from studying human evolution because humans without them did not survive while those with them did.

In natural systems, surplus resources are necessary for adaptation to occur. They are also necessary for growth. As human habitat, cities of the past were full of spare resources, the development pattern creating both a base of stability and a mechanism for incremental growth. Cities matured by growing incrementally up, incrementally out, and by redeveloping to become incrementally more intense.

Within this human habitat, streets are the framework for this growth to occur, the platform for building wealth. In simple terms, a collection of structures is a place. The way that those structures are accessed is from a street. Without a street, there is no way to access a structure, and without a structure, there is no need for a street. The two coexist, the street being the platform for the structure.

In community accounting terms, the structure is wealth, and the street is the base cost of attaining that wealth. The structure is an asset, and the street is a liability. Surplus resources are created for a community when the excess wealth from structures exceeds the ongoing liability of the street.

The concept of excess wealth is a difficult one for modern Americans to grasp because we live in a society where success at the community level is measured more by the velocity of money than by the accumulation of wealth. Gross Domestic Product is often referred to as the "size of the economy," but it is merely a measurement of the number of transactions that take place in a country. That is different than net worth, which is an accounting of assets and liabilities.

Cities that grow rapidly often report on their success by measuring the number of transactions that they experience — for example, number of permits issued, miles of street constructed, or amount of sales tax revenue collected. These measurements tell us a lot about the velocity of money within the community, but they do not tell us anything about the community's wealth.

A city may issue a lot of permits for new houses, but if those houses cost the community more to provide services and infrastructure maintenance than they generate in revenue, the community's wealth is declining with each transaction. A city can build miles of streets, but if there is not enough private sector investment on those streets to offset the ongoing maintenance costs, the community is merely growing poorer.

The ledger here is very real. For a community to be stable and prosper over multiple generations, it must have significantly more assets than it has liabilities. It must have a source of stable wealth from which to draw. In *Strong Towns*, I estimate the necessary ratio of private investment to public investment to be 20:1 at a minimum, 40:1 as a more stable target. In those ranges, there is enough wealth within the community to take care of the community's obligations to itself, the baseline of services, and maintenance necessary for the community to endure.

Based on my experience with other communities, I estimate that Springfield's ratio is somewhere between 2:1 and 4:1. Add up all the private wealth within the community, and it will be between two and four times the cost of the public investments that have been made. The latter includes roads and streets, sewer and water systems, parks, public buildings, police and fire equipment, and anything else that would show up in a capital improvement budget.

This means that Springfield needs to become between five times and twenty times more financially productive. Through a combination of building wealth on the current street framework and reducing costs and long-term obligations, likely by contracting on the periphery, Springfield — like nearly every city in North America — is going to be forced to reinvent itself.

Streets can no longer be about moving a high volume of vehicles at speed. They must be primarily about building wealth.

Building Wealth

Having a wealthy city does not mean having a city of wealthy people. In fact, the highest wealth-producing places in the United States today are often where some of the poorest people live. Building a city that values transactions, within a macro economy that prioritizes the velocity of money, at best discounts the poor. At worst, it exploits them, inflicting great harm on vulnerable communities of people.

A core insight of the book *Strong Towns* and the entire Strong Towns movement is that the best financial investments that cities can make are small and, in the present configuration of American cities, almost always in our poorest neighborhoods.

To be clear: My assertion of "best" is not an argument about investments that are the most equitable or somehow judged to be morally superior. The word "investment" is also not meant to indicate some abstract notion of future payoffs, like the suggestion that investing in better healthcare or workforce development will theoretically pay off someday according to some economist's PhD thesis.

From a Strong Towns lens, the best investments are measured in hard currency. Invest a dollar and get back a dollar plus a real return on that investment. This is fundamental economics — the kind that genuinely builds wealth over time.

Not only are small investments in poor neighborhoods the lowest-risk, highest-returning way for a community to build wealth, but they are also the best way to lift a neighborhood out of decline without displacing the people who live there. That is the core of the Strong Towns approach to capital investment, and it is well documented in the book *Strong Towns: A Bottom-Up Revolution to Rebuild American Prosperity*. The following quote from that book references the work of Urban3, a cutting-edge firm doing data visualization, property tax analysis, and return-on-investment modeling:

> The team at Urban3 has modeled hundreds of entire cities around North America. This massive data set has revealed a near-universal set of trends, results that are consistently observed in cities of all sizes, in all geographies, using all taxing systems, across the continent. These include:
>
> - Older neighborhoods financially outperform newer neighborhoods. This is especially true when the older neighborhoods are pre-1930 and newer neighborhoods are post-1950.

- Blight is not an indicator of financial productivity. Some of the most financially productive neighborhoods are also the most blighted.
- While there are exceptions for highly gentrified areas, poorer neighborhoods tend to financially outperform wealthier neighborhoods.
- For cities with a traditional neighborhood core, the closer to the core, the higher the level of financial productivity.
- The more stories a building has, the greater its financial productivity tends to be.
- The more reliant on the automobile a development pattern is, the less financially productive it tends to be.

The traditional development pattern — even when blighted and occupied by the poorest people in our communities — is financially more productive than our post-war neighborhoods, regardless of their condition. Across North America, our poor neighborhoods tend to subsidize our wealthy neighborhoods. The only places this doesn't hold true are communities where the poor have been displaced out to the edge.

From a financial standpoint, four $100,000 homes, each on 25 feet of urban street, is a better return for the community than the one $300,000 home built on a 100-foot lot on the periphery. The more modest homes have the same amount of street frontage as the higher-priced home but cumulatively have 25 percent greater value. That basic analysis does not account for the way that the costs of infrastructure and services tend to increase dramatically the further development is from the core of the community.

This is not an argument for density, a coarse metric that, at best, correlates with productive patterns of development. Some of the worst-performing projects I have ever seen were done in the pursuit of density. Cities will not build themselves to prosperity by tearing down single-family homes in poor neighborhoods and replacing them with apartments or condominium units. Density is never the cause of financial productivity, but it is sometimes the result.

Building stable, long-term wealth requires an ongoing, incremental renewal process driven by positive feedback loops. Neighborhoods need to redevelop naturally over time in order to become more intense and valuable as they mature. That cycle is driven by a feedback loop of rising land values. The mechanism for that is quite simple.

Take any street in the core of Springfield. A strategy to increase land values on that street is essentially a strategy of making that street a better place to live. Make it a better place and more people will want to be there. As more people want to be there, the land values go up. As land values go up, accommodate the people who want to be there, and accumulate greater community wealth, by allowing incremental redevelopment.

Single-family homes add garage apartments or convert into duplexes. Duplexes are redeveloped to become fourplex units. Commercial buildings are subdivided to allow more tenants. Gaps are filled in. Space is used more productively.

The key is to create this feedback loop over a broad area. Freeze neighborhoods in place with zoning and regulation, and rising land values will merely displace existing residents, creating pockets of affluence in a pool of stagnation and decline. Grow neighborhoods in large leaps instead of incrementally and it will crowd out most investments, causing the same mix of dislocation, stagnation, and decline, while landowners and speculators wait for the big payoff from the out-of-town developer.

The aim is not merely to improve a single property or block; that is easy and largely inconsequential. The goal must be to create a virtuous feedback loop that broadly raises land values, drives incremental redevelopment, and ultimately improves the community's entire real estate portfolio, neighborhood by neighborhood, building real wealth neighbor by neighbor.

Improving a Place

The kind of public investments that broadly improve land values begin with low-risk actions that are essentially guaranteed to have a positive financial return. A money manager would do those kinds of investments all day, every day, but cities tend to deemphasize them because they are mostly routine, understated, and boring. They might be, but they are also the foundation of wealth creation.

As I wrote in *Strong Towns: A Bottom-Up Revolution to Rebuild American Prosperity*:

> The low-risk side of our public investment portfolio is as obvious as it is boring: Local governments must prioritize basic, routine maintenance in neighborhoods with high financial productivity (high value per acre).

For example, the downtown of Springfield should never want for basic sidewalk maintenance. The poor neighborhoods next to the downtown should never have streets full of potholes, overgrown ditches, or backed-up pipes.

These core neighborhoods are high in financial productivity and, if not cash-flow positive, then are the closest in the community to being so. This is where Springfield's greatest wealth is; the first thing that needs to be done is to stabilize it.

Just take care of things; for America's cities, it is that simple.

To be clear, I am not suggesting — as the professional staff of many cities are inclined to believe — that maintenance means big, transformative projects. That is what maintenance has come to mean; large projects built all at once to a finished state with efficiency as the value elevated above all others. What results is a short period where everything looks nice followed by a long period of decline that ends in an extended, sometimes permanent, state of dilapidation.

The Strong Towns approach to maintenance in these core neighborhoods is more like the way the Walt Disney Corporation maintains their theme parks: ongoing basic maintenance with an obsessive attention to detail. See a streetlight out: replace it. See a weed: pull it. See a crosswalk faded: repaint it. See a sidewalk broken: fix it. The poor neighborhoods that are already generating such wealth for the community need to be showered with love and attention.

Obsessive dedication to basic maintenance will make Springfield's downtown and core neighborhoods better places to live. Financially for the community, it is self-harm to do anything else.

Layered on top of a dedication to maintenance must be a sustained approach to improve the quality of the place over time. This will not be done at scale. There is no series of large projects, no massive and centralized initiative, that will bring about real wealth creation without also inducing displacement and broader stagnation. Improving the quality of a place, building real enduring wealth, is an ongoing process.

Building wealth begins with the recognition that the best investments — the ones with the highest financial rate of return — address a real and urgent need experienced by people living in the neighborhood. At Strong Towns, we have developed a simple, four-step process for identifying this kind of opportunity and making it happen.

1. Humbly observe where people in the community struggle.
2. Ask the question: What is the next smallest thing we can do right now to address that struggle?
3. Do that thing. Do it right now.
4. Repeat.

The key to the first step is humility. Emptying our minds of as many preconceived notions about the problems and solutions in a place as possible, we humble ourselves to observe as a proxy for sharing that lived experience. As street designers, we try to understand, from the perspective of those who struggle to use the city as it has been built, where those struggles are. A great way to observe is to walk with someone — literally treading the path with them — to understand how they struggle.

Observing is so much more powerful than even asking. When cities do surveys, focus groups, or public hearings, they are using an approach to inquiry that is comforting to decision makers, but not necessarily comfortable to those from whom they are seeking input. Subsequently, public officials are not going to get the insight they really need. If we want to identify the best investments, designers need to get out of their comfort zone.

Where the first step requires humility, the second requires self-discipline. Instead of seeking the comprehensive solution, instead of trying to fix everything once and for all, we take our humble observation (which, if we are truly humble, we must acknowledge is incomplete and may be totally wrong) and just try to make that struggle we have identified a little bit easier. We discipline ourselves to work in the smallest increment possible.

This is not because we are obsessed with the incremental. It is because, as Jane Jacobs suggests, our neighborhoods must be a co-creation. By disciplining ourselves to act incrementally and iteratively, we allow people — our friends and neighbors living in the neighborhood — to react to the change and then demonstrate to us, through their actions, where the next struggle is.

Therefore, in the third step, we do not form a committee. We do not hire a consultant. We do not pause 18 months while our grant application is processed. We have humbly identified a struggle and then identified the next smallest thing that we can do about it, so we just go out and do that thing. We make things better right now with the resources that we have available to us.

And we are comfortable with that action, not because it is a comprehensive solution, and not because it totally eradicates struggles from the neighborhood, but because we are also committed to the fourth step, which is to repeat the process over and over and over. This is the process of co-creating, the way neighborhoods are made by everyone, for everyone.

We can make our cities financially strong while broadly increasing wealth and prosperity. That is the essence of a Strong Towns approach, one that every community has the capacity to put to work right now.

The Street Design Team

Building a great street is more of an art than a science. While some of the techniques can be put in writing, the approach will not be reduced to a book of codes or a set of standard plates. The proper street design cannot be standardized across a city, let alone a state or a continent. Building a wealth-producing street is a nuanced and localized undertaking, one requiring an intimate understanding of a place.

That is because building wealth is not just about lane width, pavement depth, and intersection spacing. Nothing important is ever that simple. A great street is the scaffold for assembling human habitat. Doing it well requires respecting all of the complexities of humans and their habitat.

What is the business owner on the corner looking to do with their building as they transfer ownership to a new generation? What is the young family looking to do now that their kids have all entered school? What is the elderly couple struggling with now that their friend next door has passed? These questions and more are often unknowable — they may not even be known by the people themselves who should be asking them — but they must not be discounted. Wealth will be built by the people who are there. Great street design is an ongoing process that will help them actualize their lives.

What this all suggests is that the street design process is not well suited for the skills of the engineer. The transportation planner is also poorly equipped for this undertaking. There are things that these professionals are trained to do that are helpful in putting together a great street, but they are far from the only skills that are needed. (See Table 5.1.)

In fact, no single individual is likely to be able to pull this off, not consistently and not without ongoing iteration. What is needed is a Street Design Team, a group of people working together to understand the most urgent struggles of a neighborhood and respond to them productively.

The Street Design Team must include the engineer, but it should also include people who understand urban design, housing issues, economic development, transit, parks, recreation, public health, public safety, and maintenance. It should also include nonprofessionals from the community. Depending on the neighborhood, this might be someone with a physical impairment, someone who grasps the needs of local students, or a senior citizen.

Table 5.1 Street Design Skills

Things Transportation Professionals Are Qualified to Do (partial list)	Things Transportation Professionals Are NOT Qualified to Do (partial list)
Make recommendations on the type of pavement to use.	Understand the broad needs of people living within a neighborhood.
Determine the thickness of the pavement.	Determine how a privately owned building will be used.
Estimate stormwater runoff amounts.	Place value on vegetation, benches, lighting, and other parts of a functioning street.
Provide estimates of cost.	Anticipate the future needs of residents.
Observe construction.	Determine how much value individuals will place on different levels of investment.

The goal of the team is to build community wealth by identifying, through observation, the most urgent struggles of people within the neighborhood — the ways that they are struggling to use the city as it has been built — and then directing responses to those struggles using the four-step process already outlined.

Pause and note that this is not designed to be an efficient process. We can build roads efficiently just like we can print a poster efficiently, copying the same print repeatedly. Building a street is less like printing another copy of a poster and more like painting a picture. For it to be done well, it is going to take patience and time so that the subtlety and nuance of the place can have full expression.

For this reason, the Street Design Team should never be run by a transportation professional. I recommend putting the least technical person on the team in charge, someone who is organized and respected but who also has a broad enough vision to ask difficult questions and question orthodoxy.

The worst way to approach a Street Design Team is to allocate money and responsibility to the engineer and then allow everyone else to comment on their work. This not only concentrates power in the wrong place, but it also returns the focus of the design process to code books and standard plates instead of a deep and nuanced understanding of a place and the struggles that happen there.

We will not build great streets, places that produce wealth and improve quality of life, by allowing people to comment on three variations of a bad design.

Iterating to Safety

In the work that Urban3 has done modeling the financial productivity of different places, there is one correlation that stands out above all others. Wherever development patterns are most productive, wherever the highest value per acre is measured, those are the places where people will be found outside of a motor vehicle. Where humans are found in their habitat, those are the places building the greatest amount of community wealth. The more people who are consistently found, the more productive a place is likely to be. To borrow a phrase from ecology: People are the indicator species of success.

Since wealth is created by having humans naturally in their habitat, a prerequisite for building wealth is that a street be safe. The stroad-to-street conversion approach from Chapter 2 is a good place to start: (1) slow traffic, (2) prioritize people over throughput, (3) build a productive place, and (4) embrace complexity. These are not steps to be done in series but four things to work on simultaneously.

As an example, many people — including myself, members of the Springfield city council, and the city's engineering staff — have observed that people routinely struggle to cross State Street. Traffic moves too fast, and the gaps that people must cross while exposed to traffic are too great. The distance to signalized intersections is too great, and the time spent waiting and crossing is a higher threshold than people have shown they are willing to spend. This has been observed and well documented.

This is where we pull out the book *Tactical Urbanism: Short-term Action for Long-term Change* (Island Press, 2015) by Mike Lydon and Anthony Garcia and start trying things. Without collaboration and input from a Street Design Team, I am not completely sure where I would start, but my experience suggests that I would begin with paint and traffic cones at least 500 feet on each side of the entrance to the Springfield Central Library. In those places, I would start temporarily narrowing the lanes, changing the geometry of the street to figure out the best way to communicate to drivers that more caution, and slower speeds, are warranted.

In the previous chapter, I explained the 85th percentile speed and how it relates to the comfort or tension people experience when driving. I wrote the following:

> The only way to have meaningful reductions in speed, and a significant impact on the number of crashes, is through "geometric change." The design of the street needs to prompt people to drive slower.

> For streets, where we need complexity in order to build a productive place, traffic needs to flow at a neighborhood speed (15 mph or less is optimum) to make human habitat that is safe and productive. To achieve this on a street, the street design needs to shift drivers from the passive awareness of System 1 to the mental state of heightened engagement found in System 2.

> Where traffic engineers have done a brilliant job recognizing the limits of human cognition and adjusting speed limits on roads to reflect the 85th percentile speed, they now need to apply the same insights to streets. The only difference is that, instead of using the 85th percentile speed to adjust the speed limit, on streets we need to use the measured speed to adjust the design.

> Where drivers are traveling too fast, the geometry of the street needs to change, and keep changing, until a safe 85th percentile speed is achieved.

I would start with using paint and traffic cones to change the geometry of State Street, but I would keep iterating, trying new things, until I am able to measure the 85th percentile speed consistently at 15 miles per hour or less. At Strong Towns, we put this into a flow chart to draw a contrast between the way to use the 85th percentile speed on a road and a street. (See Figure 5.1.)

The process will produce a design that works, albeit with a temporary installation. The Street Design Team can now get to work on ways to make this temporary design into something more permanent, understanding that the human habitat on State Street is going to

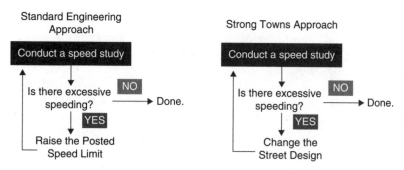

Figure 5.1 How to address chronic speeding.

continue to evolve, revealing more struggles that need to be responded to on a path to greater productivity.

It took Springfield, and cities across America, decades to build such expansive networks of dangerous and costly streets. It is going to take our cities time to unwind this mess. Tragedies such as the death of Destiny Gonzalez must be a catalyst for improving safety.

All cities need to use a Street Design Team to investigate, National Transportation Safety Board–style, every auto-related fatality in the community. Do not allow these incidents to be written off as merely driver error, but probe and document each contributing factor, including design. Respond to any design deficiencies rapidly using a low-cost Tactical Urbanism approach. Study and document driver and nondriver responses to identify changes that improve safety.

Take the lessons learned from investigations and tactical interventions and migrate them to other places within the community that have similar characteristics. Study tactical interventions in these new locations to corroborate or broaden findings. Then use ongoing maintenance as an opportunity to permanently implement the street designs that have been tested in your community and shown to lower speeds and improve safety.

Every city in North America, regardless of size or affluence, has an opportunity to make their streets safer while simultaneously reducing their public cost for infrastructure maintenance, enhancing their tax base to broadly build wealth, and improving the quality of life for people living within their community. That is the essence of a Strong Towns approach to streets. Our cities urgently need to get started.

Complete Streets

The U.S. Department of Transportation (USDOT) has a public health initiative called "Complete Streets" that builds off decades of advocacy work around the concept. From the USDOT website (https://www.transportation.gov/):

> Complete Streets are streets designed and operated to enable safe use and support mobility for all users. Those include people of all ages and abilities, regardless of whether they are travelling as drivers, pedestrians, bicyclists, or public transportation riders.[2]

The idea of a Complete Street is compelling in almost every way, and cities and states across the country have been adopting Complete Streets policies in increasing numbers. The fundamental contribution of Complete Streets to the discourse surrounding the future of our towns and neighborhoods is the recognition that our streets must serve more than just cars. The fact that the Complete Streets model has broken the stranglehold that the auto-only design mentality has had on our streets is something to celebrate.

I first heard of Complete Streets at a conference I attended in the late 1990s. I was working at an engineering firm at the time, doing municipal projects such as road and street design. For me, as well as for the engineers with whom I worked, Complete Streets was a joke. We actually laughed about it, suggesting how ridiculous it was to expect that streets would be used for something other than moving a high volume of vehicles at the quickest reasonable speed. This seemed to be a widely shared reaction.

The overall response of the engineering profession has changed dramatically since then, with Complete Streets now being a standard and accepted design practice. While certainly some engineers have changed their minds about the proper role of streets, I believe that there are two dominant explanations for why the engineering profession has embraced the Complete Street approach.

First, there is more money available to build with a Complete Streets approach. Federal and state governments began by giving out grants to projects to upgrade them to a Complete Street. Many then began to give preferential treatment on funding to projects that incorporated Complete Streets into the approach. Some states and many local governments now require a Complete Streets design in certain areas.

Engineering firms are often paid as a percentage of the overall contract cost. A Complete Street design can sometimes cost less, but generally it is a great excuse to add more features to a project, driving up the cost and driving up the fees paid to engineers. There has been every financial incentive for transportation professionals to warm to the idea of Complete Streets.

Second, and more importantly, is that engineers quickly realized that the Complete Streets concept was perfectly compatible with the profession's underlying value system prioritizing (1) speed, (2) volume, (3) safety, and then (4) cost. To build a Complete Street, a design engineer did not need to compromise at all on the speed of traffic or the volume of vehicles that would be accommodated.

In practice, Complete Streets has taken on an Oprah-like quality where, to the delight of her audience, she starts handing out something for everyone. Automobile drivers get their own lane. Transit gets its own lane. People riding bikes get their own lane. People walking get their own lane. Just open the envelope under your chair and discover that you get a lane, and you get a lane, and you get a lane....

I support Complete Streets as a rational response to a despotic transportation system, but let us be clear about the difference between a Complete Streets approach and a Strong Towns approach. Complete Streets accommodate pedestrians and an auto-dominated realm. Strong Towns accommodate automobiles in an environment dominated by people.

By any meaningful definition, State Street in Springfield is a Complete Street.

The Strong Towns Approach

Cities are human habitat. In natural systems, surplus resources are necessary for adaptation to occur. They are also necessary for growth. Within human habitat, streets are the framework for growth. While roads connect productive places, streets are the platform for building wealth in a place.

There must be enough private wealth to sustain public obligations. Regardless of the taxing mechanism used to tap into community wealth, the necessary ratio of private investment to public investment is estimated to be between 20:1 at a minimum and 40:1 as a stable target.

Having a wealthy city does not mean having a city of wealthy people. Some of the most financially productive places are occupied by a community's poorest residents.

Neighborhoods need to redevelop naturally over time in order to become more intense and valuable as they mature. Building stable, long-term wealth requires an ongoing, incremental renewal process driven by the positive feedback loop of rising land values.

To achieve that feedback loop, local governments must first prioritize basic, routine maintenance in neighborhoods with high financial productivity (high value per acre). Second, they must build wealth using an iterative, incremental approach to making capital investments. The four-step process for capital investments is as follows:

1. Humbly observe where people in the community struggle.
2. Ask the question: What is the next smallest thing we can do right now to address that struggle?
3. Do that thing. Do it right now.
4. Repeat.

Cities should establish a Street Design Team to enact this approach. The team should consist of a broad group of experts, nonexperts, and concerned citizens and be led by someone with a nontechnical background.

A street design process will use the four-step approach to iterate to a safer design. Where drivers are traveling too fast, the geometry of the street needs to change, and keep changing, until a safe 85th percentile speed is achieved.

All cities need to use a Street Design Team to investigate, and learn from, National Transportation Safety Board–style, every auto-related fatality in the community. The findings of these investigations need to inform future design decisions.

More information on building wealth on local streets, along with the Strong Towns four-step process for capital investments, is available at www.confessions.engineer.

Notes

1. https://www.youtube.com/watch?v=2MoWBgqoNnE
2. https://www.transportation.gov/mission/health/complete-streets

6

Traffic Congestion

When the Springfield Director of Public Works expresses concerns to the city council over the Level of Service on State Street, he is using technical language to describe a familiar phenomenon: traffic congestion.

Traffic congestion is the primary technical challenge faced by transportation departments across North America. In Massachusetts, traffic congestion is such an urgent matter that the state's department of transportation, MassDOT, published a 157-page report on it in 2019. In the report, Stephanie Pollack, the Transportation Secretary and CEO of MassDOT, called traffic congestion a "constant and daily reality" while saying that it:

> …chokes growing communities, reduces access and opportunity to jobs, affects people's choices about where to live and work and may undermine the Commonwealth's commitment to reduce greenhouse gases (GHGs), a primary cause of climate change.[1]

The matter of congestion presents the apex of dissonance for traffic engineering and transportation planning professions, politicians and public officials, and the general public. Its causes are so simple to comprehend, yet so seemingly inexplicable. Its appearance is totally predictable, yet impossible to forecast accurately. It is essentially a ubiquitous condition of transportation systems, yet it must be continually fought against as if it were a disease that would overwhelm the body if not fervently resisted.

Traffic congestion is a sign of a public policy failure, yet the absence of congestion is also an indication that things are not working quite as anticipated. For a city, especially in its economic centers, the only thing worse than having traffic congestion is not having traffic congestion.

People often say that they are "stuck in traffic," as if their vehicle is somehow not a literal part of the traffic in which they are stuck. They are not stuck in traffic; they are traffic.

In no other condition of crowding do we entertain this degree of egoism. Nobody goes to Disneyworld and is baffled as to why the lines are so long, begrudging the others who have chosen to visit at the same time. We do not attend a popular movie or board an airplane and experience bewilderment by a desire of other humans to share the same experience simultaneously.

Yet when it comes to traffic congestion, the greater the levels of delay, the more we struggle to comprehend just how it came to be and, more perplexingly, what could possibly be done to rid us of this scourge.

Part of what makes traffic congestion such a wicked problem is that the mechanisms that cause it are so seemingly simple and straightforward. Here is how the MassDOT report describes them:

> Vehicular congestion is a function of traffic volumes and roadway capacity. Once volumes rise enough to slow speeds to a certain point, travel times begin to build. Simply put, as volumes increase, speeds decrease, and people get frustrated. That is congestion.

At this point, it should not surprise the reader that transportation professionals would seek to reduce yet another challenge to a mere simple relationship between the engineering profession's two primary objectives: speed and volume. This simplification suggests a straightforward mechanism for dealing with the problem of traffic congestion: build more capacity. Yet, as aggressive as we may be in combatting congestion, it continues to arise in ways that are mysterious and confounding. From the same MassDOT report:

> What really frustrates people is how that commute can occasionally spike to an hour or more due to accidents, weather, or seemingly for no reason at all.
>
> The congestion measure that best captures this human dimension of congestion is reliability: what matters most to people is not how long it takes to get someplace on a typical day but how long it can take on a bad travel day. Once their commute is unreliable, people have to plan not around the average commute, but around the worst delays.

Sometimes, *seemingly for no reason at all*, traffic congestion emerges as if its properties are not merely a two-variable function of speed and volume. That is because traffic congestion is not as simple as speed and volume, a conclusion that is obvious to anyone not intellectually limited by the toolbox of standard engineering practice.

As is sometimes said about military generals, if you are paid to fight wars, it is difficult to imagine a world without enemies. If you are paid to fight traffic congestion, it is difficult to imagine a world where congestion is no longer the mortal enemy of transportation systems. And it is preposterous to suggest, as I am about to do in this chapter, that congestion is not only not the enemy — it is our greatest ally.

French statesman Georges Clemenceau said, "War is too important to be left to the generals." For our local leaders, traffic congestion is too important to be left to traffic engineers and transportation planners. It is time to move beyond the narrow orthodoxy and embrace a more sophisticated understanding of traffic congestion.

Manufacturing Congestion

If traffic engineers started from scratch with just one goal — to create the maximum amount of traffic congestion possible — they would end up creating the transportation system we now use. Even though congestion is the bane of transportation systems, the hierarchical system of roads and streets deployed in every American city each day manufactures the maximum amount of congestion possible.

As an analogy, consider a river network. Small ditches and creeks empty into brooks and streams. In turn, these empty into tributaries, which ultimately converge to form a large river. This is basic hydrology that every civil engineering student is assumed to know before they even begin a class in drainage systems.

When it rains throughout a watershed, stormwater runoff will flow into the river network. It will run downstream and merge with water flowing in from other parts of the watershed. Again, this is basic hydrology, something taught to every prospective civil engineer.

If this flow is very intense, or if the rainfall persists for an extended period, all that water coming together will create a flood. The cumulative impact of even modest flows, when aggregated over a broad enough area, can sometimes add up to be more than the riverbed can handle. Depending on the size of the flood and the area that is flooded, it can transform ecosystems or cause damage that can run into the billions of dollars.

The mechanics of flooding have been well understood since ancient times. As a civil engineering undergraduate, I was taught how to calculate the amount of stormwater runoff from a rain event, estimate the capacity of the receiving river network, and even compute the volume of floodwater and the area affected. This is anything but a dark art.

When Hydrology 101 ends and, in a classroom across the hallway, Traffic 101 begins, for some reason the civil engineering student is never prompted to recall the very simply properties of hierarchical networks. All that knowledge is segmented off while a completely different set of tools and insights are developed.

When commuters begin their day, they leave their driveways and exit onto a cul-de-sac or other local street. They will then drive to some type of collector street, joining with those in their neighborhood doing the same. All of these collector streets empty into minor arterials, with all of the accumulating traffic continuing to converge on ever larger roadways. Ultimately, minor arterials empty into major arterials, which empty into highways and interstates. This is how hierarchical road networks are designed to function.

And, if there are enough commuters over a broad enough area, or if everyone decides to leave their home at roughly the same time, there will be a flood. It is simple flow dynamics. Just as with a hydrological system, the hierarchical road network manufactures a flood.

It does this every day regardless of the size of the city or the number of automobiles involved. A large city like Boston pulls commuters in from a broad area and experiences a flood of traffic congestion for long stretches each day. As stated in the MassDOT report:

> While the most severe congestion in the state occurs during the morning and afternoon peak travel periods, many roads are congested outside of those time periods, especially but not exclusively in Greater Boston. By 6 a.m., one-quarter of roadway miles inside the I-95/128 belt are already either congested or highly congested and at 10 a.m., 17 percent of those roads are still congested or highly congested. And the afternoon "rush hour" inside Route 128 has begun by 3 p.m., with 62 percent of roadway miles congested or highly congested.

A mid-sized city like Springfield experiences a daily flood as well, but it is smaller in size and has less duration than Boston's. In my hometown, which has fewer than 14,000 people, we also experience a daily flood, where drivers from far-flung parts of the Brainerd region converge their automobiles at a handful of key intersections, everyone attempting to make it to the office or school by 8:00 a.m.

The flood is a shared experience of commuters. If you query people from Boston, Springfield, or Brainerd who find themselves the driver of one automobile in a flood of traffic congestion, they will nearly all attest to the same insights: The amount of traffic is unbearable, there is too much congestion, and something must be done to alleviate this burden. This clarion call of distress is one that traffic engineers are more than ready to answer.

In traffic engineering, we measure the flood of traffic congestion created by our transportation systems and use that data to affirm the need to build more of the same congestion-inducing transportation systems. Instead, we should recognize that the hierarchical networks used in traffic engineering manufacture congestion everywhere they are deployed.

In Greek mythology, Sisyphus is punished for his arrogance by being forced, for all eternity, to roll a boulder up an enormous hill where, near the peak, it always slips free and rolls back to the bottom. If Americans are stuck with traffic congestion as the problem that we urgently need to solve, then traffic engineers have created the ultimate Sisyphean struggle — one we will never solve with the approach we now have.

The Nature of Congestion

Congestion is an emergent phenomenon. It results from the complex interaction of many different people making independent decisions based on their own desires and experiences.

These are self-evident assertions. Consider one's own behavior. If you are anticipating traffic congestion for a trip across town, you may leave early to give yourself more time. You may go exceedingly early and spend extra time doing something else near your destination. You could delay the trip until an uncongested time. Or you could opt to cancel the trip entirely and seek an alternative that avoids the time spent in traffic.

Billions of people around the world independently make decisions just like these every day, adjusting in real time to conditions as they perceive them. They also make larger decisions, like where to work, where to live, and where to enroll their kids in school, partially based on their personal threshold for dealing with traffic congestion.

When I was younger, I was much more tolerant of traffic congestion and, at one point, I even accepted a commute that was an hour of heavy congestion for both daily trips. Today, I refuse to commute by automobile and have instead chosen self-employment and an office location that is within a ten-minute walk of my home. Not everyone has the same range of options, and of course those options change throughout life, but everyone has a set of choices that they make about when, where, and how they move around in their community.

The cumulative effect of all these decisions creates a new set of conditions that are then perceived by people and adjusted to. From the macro perch of the traffic engineer, an equilibrium of traffic may be observed and even measured for periods of time. That apparent stability emerges from the countless number of dynamic adjustments made by people acting independently throughout the system.

The more dynamism that is allowed in a system, and the more options that are provided to people, the more responsive and adaptable a system will be. A bus route with a pickup frequency of once an hour will provide fewer opportunities for people to adjust dynamically to congestion than if the same route picked up every 15 minutes. A gridded street system will provide a driver more options for responding to congestion than a hierarchical network where all drivers are funneled to the same location.

Congestion dynamics transcend the rote variables of speed and volume. Smaller buses with greater frequency provide less-congested, more dynamic service than one large, infrequent bus, even if the volume of passengers is the same. Each street in a gridded network may have less capacity than a major arterial, but the options given to drivers by a grid means that there will be less congestion and fewer delays, even with the same volume of traffic.

The sad reality is that most transportation professionals consider the hierarchical road network to be somehow efficient or optimal, even though, in terms of utilizing the resources mobilized for transportation, it is obviously ridiculously inefficient and wildly suboptimal. At the time of greatest need, during a period of maximum congestion, hierarchical road networks only use a tiny fraction of their overall capacity. The highway or major arterial may be flooded and in desperate need of relief, but simultaneously the miles and miles of local and collector streets are practically empty, providing no relief but, instead, continuing to accentuate the flood.

The emergent and dynamic nature of traffic is frustrating for those who want to view these systems as simple and predictable. When overwhelming capacity is provided — when more lanes are built than are needed or can be used — then traffic flow is predictable. Everyone can consume all of the transportation they want, whenever they want, without restraint, and there are no episodes of congestion. This is the only condition where traffic models work, and it is always fleeting.

This is because, even though traffic flow in that situation is predictable, the underlying human decision-making is still dynamic. Without the restraint of congestion, people will choose to live more remotely, they will take jobs and locate their businesses in distant places, and they will have less incentive to open businesses that cater to local markets as their competitors will be operating at a regional scale. Dynamic humans will adapt to the additional capacity, generally by making decisions that require them to take more auto trips.

As the volume of traffic begins to approach the capacity of the roadway, people begin to adapt to the extent that they are able. For a while, this will keep the roadway from experiencing its maximum level of congestion as people will accelerate or delay their trips, change jobs or shopping habits, or even move to a different location. Even though it has a tremendous effect on traffic dynamics, none of this adaptation is accounted for, or even considered, by traffic modeling that merely looks at speed and volume.

Ultimately, individual adaptation options run out — especially when hierarchical transportation networks are combined with static land use regulations — and congestion becomes, as described by Mass-DOT, a constant reality.

The only time our transportation systems function as planned is when there is overwhelming capacity, a condition where there is no need even to consider a dynamic reaction by drivers or passengers. It should be no surprise then that the standard approach to transportation engineering, which focuses on speed and volume while ignoring the underlying dynamic nature of traffic, addresses traffic congestion by attempting to provide an overwhelming amount of capacity.

This simple reaction has created the niche discipline of traffic forecasting, a practice so lacking in rigor and substance that it should bring shame and embarrassment to anyone who considers themselves an engineer.

Projecting Traffic

To be proactive in heading off congestion, or at least to create the appearance of being proactive, traffic engineers monitor the amount of traffic that currently travels on a road or street and use that data to project how much traffic there will be in the future. They routinely use projections of future traffic to make recommendations and decisions on transportation investments, spending that amounts to hundreds of billions of dollars each year.

Most projection models rely on linear, straight-line projections of past traffic counts. While the engineer doing the work may use a spreadsheet or modeling software that gives the result a veneer of sophistication, it is really no more complicated, and no more precise, than taking a ruler and drawing a best-fit line through past data out into the future. There is no attempt to capture any emergent reaction from a dynamic system.

There are other approaches that attempt to consider dynamic factors when projecting traffic. While millions, perhaps billions, are spent nationwide each year, creating the illusion of sophistication around these various models, they are no better at predicting the future than the straight-line projection with a ruler. In 2015, Congress commissioned a report through the National Academy of Sciences that reached the same conclusion. From the report:

> The committee concluded that existing [Travel Demand Forecasting] models do not offer the national- or regional-level prediction capabilities needed to assess system level impacts from Interstate investments.

That is a long way of saying that the models do not work. Of course they don't. There is no way a model could capture all of the dynamic changes happening with individual decisions, choices that change and adapt in real time based on an infinite number of factors. Later in the same paragraph, the report states:

> Because there are no existing tools with which to analyze these demand responses at the transportation network level for the entire country or regionally, the only alternative was to consult the recent history of travel behavior as indicated by past [Vehicle Miles Traveled] growth rates to develop a reasonable range of future [Vehicle Miles Traveled] growth rates to apply to the. . .models.[2]

"Consult the recent history of travel behavior" is engineering-speak for plotting past traffic data on a chart. "Develop a reasonable range of future VMT growth rates" is a sophisticated way to describe the simple process of projecting the future traffic by applying a ruler to past data. Cities and states spend enormous sums of money doing this work, yet a competent third grader with a straightedge could predict just as well.

Sometimes, the historic data is supplemented with what are called *trip generation models*, an estimation of how much traffic should be anticipated based on what is proposed or expected to be built in a specific location. For example, if someone is building a restaurant, a traffic engineer or transportation planner may examine a chart or table suggesting, based on past observation, how much traffic a restaurant of different sizes can be expected to generate.

Of course, even though it has more effect on traffic than any aggregate study of restaurants, the transportation professionals have no way of taking into account whether the head chef will be amazing or terrible, whether the restaurant will become known for its great breakfasts or exquisite dinners, or whether it will fail in six months or have people lined up around the corner.

Even more importantly, the engineer confidently predicting future traffic flows has no clue as to whether this restaurant will be just the thing the neighborhood needed to become the next hot place, creating a feedback loop that draws all kinds of people in their vehicles to the area, or whether the restaurant will become the kind of obnoxious establishment near which others do not want to locate, depressing traffic throughout the neighborhood. Again, factors far beyond any spreadsheet or chart of expected values will determine the actual amount of traffic.

There is no way for the transportation engineer to know these and other dynamic reactions because they are not knowable. Instead of accepting that fact and developing an approach to traffic management that does not rely on false projections to provide an illusion of certainty, people who do traffic modeling tend to respond to the unknowable by making their models more complicated. This has the effect of creating even more separation between those who would challenge the model's conclusions and those who can understand the methods used to reach them.

The opacity of the models reinforces a power dynamic that is central to the purpose of modeling. It is not the goal of a traffic model to predict the future flow of traffic accurately. That is impossible. Even though the person doing the modeling likely believes their own results, at least enough to bet other people's money on them, the goal is nearly always simply to justify more investment in transportation.

The goal of traffic modeling is not to be right; it is to create a plausible narrative as to why more construction is both needed and helpful.

This sounds deeply cynical, and I hate writing it because there are good, decent, and honest people who do traffic modeling. There are also good, decent, and honest people who consult astrological signs to predict how a marriage will work out. Conviction in one's predictions does not make them any more accurate.

The reality is that it is widely known within the engineering profession that all traffic models are wrong. The conscience is soothed because the profession always seeks better models, and a partially informed guess is perceived to be better than a completely ignorant guess. This known error is accepted because, for the traffic engineer, there is no viable alternative.

That is wrong — there is an alternative — but follow the reasoning because it points to a deeper insight. If the traffic engineer is forced to use a projection of future traffic that they know is wrong, and if congestion is an intolerable condition that is also a ubiquitous foe, then the conservative thing to do when considering a transportation investment is to oversize everything.

It is vastly more expensive to fix congested arterials than it is simply to oversize them to begin with. For an engineer, a conservative approach is not one that reduces the size and budget of the project, opting for a more incremental solution. No, a conservative approach means massively overbuilding everything under the guise of penny-wise, pound-foolish.

For the driver, who pays but a tiny fraction of the cost of any roadway they travel — and even that is paid indirectly — the gain from overengineering is obvious: open roads, free-flowing travel, and a high degree of satisfaction with the transportation system, at least until dynamic responses make claims on that excess capacity.

If the engineer were to err in the opposite way, if they were to under-design even a tiny amount, the hierarchical network would create intolerable levels of congestion. With this asymmetry, most transportation professionals find it better to have double the needed capacity and not use it than to suffer the consequences of being 5 percent short.

This propensity has generated some noted absurdities, including many examples of engineers projecting increasing levels of traffic on roadways where traffic volumes have been decreasing for many years. One of the most egregious is the SR-520 bridge across Lake Washington where the Washington State Department of Transportation three times over 17 years projected massive increases in traffic. Traffic volumes decreased during that entire period. As Clark Williams-Derry wrote for the Sightline Institute:

> It would be funny — if the state weren't planning billions in new highway investments in greater Seattle, based largely on the perceived "need" to accommodate all the new traffic that the models are predicting will show up, any day now.[3]

It causes few sleepless nights among my colleagues that this approach bloats engineering projects and budgets, increasing the size of contracts, fees, and compensation. It also creates few incentives to question the value of traffic modeling deeply or seek alternatives to an approach that relies on projections of traffic known to be false.

Addressing Congestion with Efficiency

Ramp meters are those mini traffic signals that queue vehicles as they enter the highway. Wikipedia explains their rationale succinctly:

> Ramp meters are installed to restrict the total flow entering the freeway, temporarily storing it on the ramps, a process called "access rate reduction." In this way, the traffic flow does not exceed the freeway's capacity. Another rationale for installing ramp meters is the argument that they prevent congestion and break up "platoons" of cars.[4]

There is nearly total consensus among transportation professionals that ramp meters are a positive innovation. Even critics concede that ramp meters allow more efficient use of roadways. With ramp meters, more cars travel through the same lanes in less time. Ramp meters cut overall travel time, improve safety, and make efficient use of highway capacity.

Getting more out of existing transportation investments without needing to build any additional capacity is a level of genius that would make any engineer proud. Sadly, the professional consensus on the benefits of ramp meters is wrong. Understanding why will help us move beyond the fiction of models to an approach not dependent on traffic projections.

In 2000, I was going to graduate school at the University of Minnesota, living in the exurbs of Minneapolis and commuting to the university each day. My commute was about 50 minutes. I never hit a ramp meter on my way because I lived too far out, but there as I drove by were the lines of cars queued up in the on-ramps, kindly allowing me and the rest of the traffic to flow past.

During my first semester, the State of Minnesota did a little experiment regarding ramp meters. Again, Wikipedia accurately describes it:

> In 2000, a $650,000 experiment was mandated by the Minnesota State Legislature in response to citizen complaints and the efforts of State Senator Dick Day. The study involved shutting off all 433 ramp meters in the Minneapolis-St. Paul area for eight weeks to test their effectiveness. The study was conducted by Cambridge Systematics and concluded that when the ramp meters were turned off freeway volume decreased by 9%, travel times increased by 22%, freeway speeds dropped by 7% and crashes increased by 26%.

These results sound terrible and, in fact, the experiment is frequently cited as proving the validity of ramp meters. As an alternative, consider my experience as a participant in this experiment.

Before the experiment began, nearly all of my classmates had apocalyptic fears about their commutes. They were mostly young and lived near the campus in the heart of Minneapolis. In class, they expressed their anticipation that their 20- to 30-minute commutes would take significantly longer without the meters. The opposite happened; without being forced to sit at ramp meters, they all reported much quicker commute times.

My experience was the opposite. The experiment was eight weeks of hell. My 50-minute commute suddenly increased to two and a half hours. I sat in congestion for endless stretches, and it is quite simple to understand why.

Before anyone from a first-ring suburb could enter the city, everyone living in the urban core needed to get to where they were going. Since they were uninhibited by metering, they owned the freeways. Once they reached their destination and parked their cars, the freeways opened enough so that those from the first-ring suburbs could enter the city. The rest of us waited for them to clear out. Then the second ring could enter. Then the third ring. Finally, after everyone closer in had arrived at their destinations, those of us who lived in the exurbs could make our way into the city center.

What shutting off the ramp meters did was effectively meter the highway itself. Instead of the city resident having to wait on a ramp for me to drive by, now I — the exurban dweller — had to wait for them.

With ramp meters, traffic volume is up, speeds are increased, and Level of Service is improved. The values transportation professionals care most about all trend in the right direction, but that leaves out a key part of the story.

What ramp meters also increase is vehicle miles traveled. The engineer's approach of making better use of highway capacity through ramp meters simply allows people to migrate to farther reaches of the system. Once again, the dynamic nature of traffic is not considered.

Whatever cost savings there are in getting more efficient use out of the existing roadway is more than offset by the miles of new lanes demanded in the second ring, third ring, and throughout the exurbs, not to mention the ramps, signals, and other investments that go along with them. Measuring the results of metering at the meter using the metrics that reflect their values, engineers miss the overall impact that their efforts have on the transportation system. While congratulating themselves for saving millions, they are literally inducing billions in new demand in other places.

Building more capacity is a fruitless endeavor. Reconfiguring our systems to make them more efficient in the limited dimensions that engineers find important is doing real damage to our cities, our families, and our economy. The only way to deal with congestion is to allow congestion to drive demand for local alternatives to auto trips.

The only viable alternative to a despotic system of ubiquitous congestion, faulty modeling, and overengineering is to strengthen neighborhoods.

Responding to Congestion Without Fake Projections

A lot of clever minds are working on the problem of traffic congestion, each with their own magic fix. There are those who simply want to build more capacity, relying on the theory that one must acquire a bigger hammer to deal with a problem diagnosed as a bigger nail. This still is probably the dominant philosophy among traffic engineers, even though its adherents have no intellectual credibility outside of their own cohort.

I suspect that most engineers who advocate for adding capacity to fight congestion know that this is a fruitless endeavor, but it is difficult to recommend against something when your job depends on it. My colleagues caught in this intellectual purgatory have my sympathy.

There are others who want to address congestion by overlaying a commuter transit system on top of the dysfunctional hierarchical road network. Advocates for this approach typically argue that switching people from automobiles to transit during peak times will alleviate congestion by reducing the number of cars on the road, a phenomenon never once observed in the real world. When you make it easier to drive, people will drive more. Commuter-based transit does not change that fundamental truth.

That is not to say that shifting people from single-occupancy motor vehicles to carpools or transit has no impact. Quite the opposite: If given priority in the system, such as their own dedicated lane, these systems can make far more efficient use of the road, moving higher volumes of people from one place to another in less time than any auto-based system possibly could. They will move more people, more quickly, and generally at lower cost, but they will not reduce congestion.

Congestion pricing has become the latest fad in the industry. The central idea behind congestion pricing is that a market price can be used to resolve the tragedy of the commons that erupts when everyone tries to use the same free public good at the same time. With this approach, when a road is highly congested, the price for using the road goes up, prompting some people to respond by not using the road. This reduces congestion and allows the price to go down. An equilibrium price is one that allows the maximum amount of use while retaining something near the free flow of traffic.

Congestion pricing can be applied to a single lane, an entire corridor, a bridge, or anywhere that congestion manifests. The MassDOT report recommends that Massachusetts explore different congestion pricing approaches. Many other states and localities are doing likewise.

Congestion pricing is an approach that we should be using both to pay for transportation and to get better use out of existing systems but, much like transit, it is not going to solve the underlying problem of congestion. More precisely, it will solve demand for road capacity in the way that Sotheby's solves demand for fine art and jewelry: by pricing enough people out of the market. It will not get commuters to distant jobs, children to school, and families to goods and services without other significant changes happening in parallel.

It is those other changes that urgently need to happen, and they are elusive to transportation professionals because they lie outside the standard transportation toolkit and the funding systems that support it.

There is only one way to truly address congestion and it goes back to the lessons from Hydrology 101. The only lasting way to prevent flooding is to retain runoff near its source, to prevent stormwater runoff from accumulating to damaging levels. The cumulative impact of tiny amounts of runoff over a broad watershed can be enormous, but that insight also works in reverse. Tiny interventions over a broad area can produce meaningful results that reduce or eliminate flooding.

Small drainage swales, stormwater ponds, and earthen berms are deployed on a site-by-site basis to retain stormwater and allow it to soak into the ground instead of running off the site. Vegetation that is better than sod at infiltrating and absorbing water is often used. Where pavements are required, permeable materials can be utilized to reduce the overall amount of runoff.

For stormwater, none of these individual actions are dramatic. In fact, taken one at a time, they often seem insignificant and even silly. Yet, it is the cumulative effect of all of these small actions that meaningfully reduces or even prevents flooding.

Likewise, the only long-term way address traffic flooding is to go to the source. Auto trips need to be retained near where they originate, or transformed into non-auto trips, to prevent them from accumulating and flowing further downstream. Understanding the dynamic nature of traffic, the way to retain trips is to create local alternatives.

That means building more corner stores and neighborhood businesses. It means creating more local jobs and housing options. It means emphasizing sidewalks and biking infrastructure so that people have more alternative ways to respond to congestion. These things are also good and necessary outcomes if our cities are to become financially strong and resilient.

The key insight is that traffic congestion accelerates these positive outcomes.

The only way to respond to traffic congestion is by creating local alternatives to distant trips. Increases in traffic congestion increase demand for local alternatives. Instead of fighting congestion, we need to embrace it. We need to recognize it for what it is — pent-up demand — and use it to create wealth and prosperity within our cities.

Cities that deny requests to build a new duplex or corner store because of concerns with traffic have things backward. Local leaders should never deny a new apartment building or a new neighborhood restaurant because they may increase traffic congestion. It is traffic congestion that requires us to build more and more local destinations.

Our streets are platforms for building wealth. Traffic congestion is the catalyst for that wealth creation. Congestion is not our enemy; it is our ally.

The Strong Towns Approach

Like river networks generate floods, the hierarchical road network manufactures congestion. It will create the maximum volume and duration of congestion possible wherever it is used. There is no way to productively build enough capacity to eliminate congestion. Stop using hierarchical models and instead designate segments as either roads or streets.

Congestion is an emergent phenomenon. It results from the complex interaction of many different people making independent decisions based on their own desires and experiences. The more dynamism that is allowed in a system, and the more options that are provided to people, the more responsive and adaptable a transportation system will be. Providing more options will not reduce congestion, but it will allow people to adapt and respond in productive ways.

All traffic models are wrong. Approaches that rely on traffic projections trade the insecurity of not knowing the future for the false confidence that comes from modeling. It is better to acknowledge the dynamic nature of traffic and build systems that are adaptable than to make large investments based on models.

It must be acknowledged that the goal of traffic modeling is not to be right; it is to create a plausible narrative as to why more construction is both needed and helpful. A conservative approach to traffic engineering creates far more capacity than is needed. Awareness of this propensity can help everyone involved compensate for it.

The only time hierarchical transportation systems function as planned is when there is overwhelming capacity, a condition where there is no need even to consider a dynamic reaction by drivers or passengers. Humans respond dynamically by using the excess capacity, generally in ways that require more driving. This is a negative feedback loop; building more capacity will only make things worse.

The only long-term way to address traffic congestion is to build alternative destinations locally. Shorter trips, or trips made by walking and biking, retain vehicles near their source and free up arterial capacity for others. In this, congestion is an ally driving investment.

More information on the Strong Towns approach to traffic congestion is available at www.confessions.engineer.

Notes

1. Congestion in the Commonwealth; Report to the Governor 2019, MassDOT.
2. https://www.nap.edu/catalog/25334/renewing-the-national-commitment-to-the-interstate-highway-system-a-foundation-for-the-future
3. https://www.sightline.org/2011/07/13/wsdot-vs-reality/
4. https://en.wikipedia.org/wiki/Ramp_meter

7

Intersections and Traffic Flow

I used to live many miles out of town. The commute to my office required me to drive through the middle of the city of Brainerd, Minnesota. Since I set my own hours, I had the flexibility to time my commute and miss the five minutes of congestion the city experiences during rush hour each day. My route was a four-lane stroad with all of the standard turning lanes and other features that are supposed to speed the flow of a high volume of traffic.

Within the city limits of Brainerd, I passed five traffic signals on my way to the office and then again on my way home. Between signals, I am legally allowed to drive up to 30 miles per hour. If I reach an intersection when the signal light is green, I may slow down a bit out of caution, but I am not required to do so. When the signal light is red, I am forced to stop completely.

With consideration for acceleration and deceleration, I am typically traveling at one of two speeds within the city: 30 miles per hour or zero. I am either moving at the legal speed or I am not moving at all. Most people accept this as a necessary tradeoff, albeit annoying. I find it maddening.

It is approximately 6,500 feet from the first signalized intersection to the last. At 30 miles per hour, if I hit a green light at every signalized intersection, I can travel this entire distance in 2 minutes and 28 seconds. It seems like that happened approximately never.

Depending on the time of day, each red light I encounter will add 20 to 90 seconds to my trip. I will estimate it at 45 seconds as an average. What this means is that my commute time is heavily dependent, not on the design speed of the stroad, and not on the posted legal speed limit, but on the number of red lights I encounter.

Number of Red Lights Encountered	Travel Time
0	2 min, 28 sec
1	3 min, 13 sec
2	3 min, 58 sec
3	4 min, 43 sec
4	5 min, 28 sec
5	6 min, 13 sec

In a scenario where I hit every intersection with a red light for an average length of time, it would take me over six minutes to travel 6,500 feet through the heart of the city. That is an average speed of 11.9 miles per hour, discounting any additional time spent accelerating and decelerating or any delays due to other automobiles.

As a test, for a month I used an application on my phone for tracking bike time and distance metrics. When I hit the edge of the city, I would click "start" and when I reached my destination, I would shut the tracker off. Occasionally, my average speed would be as high as 18 miles per hour, and one time I hit every light perfectly and was over 20 miles per hour, but most trips my average travel speed was less than 10 miles per hour.

I find traffic signals maddening, perhaps the most casual waste of time and resources to come out of the profession of civil engineering. If I could, I would eliminate every traffic signal in every city in North America; just rip them all out and throw them in a landfill.

For most people, a world without traffic signals sounds terrifying. It sounds like anarchy, chaos, and mayhem. People like me who call for the removal of traffic signals in urban areas come across as a Joker level of sadistic. That is because most people, when they think of their neighbors driving through uncontrolled intersections, picture people on stroads traveling at 30 miles per hour, chatting on their smartphones or looking at themselves in the mirror. That would indeed be mayhem.

Instead, picture those drivers traveling at 10 miles per hour, which is slower than most of us travel through a big box store parking lot. Picture the intersection as something that people enter slowly and proceed through in a mostly clockwise direction around a center point, flowing gently with the other traffic. That does not sound so scary.

Traffic signals are only necessary because of the speed of traffic. If traffic moved slower, say a neighborhood-friendly speed of 10 or 15 miles per hour, traffic signals would become largely unnecessary.

Here is the maddening part: If traffic could flow freely at neighborhood speeds with no traffic signals and red lights to impede it, if people could navigate along city streets at 10 to 15 miles per hour — speeds that might result in a fender bender but rarely a fatality or serious injury — most people would arrive at their destination quicker.

If travel speed between the lights in Brainerd were 15 miles per hour instead of 30 miles per hour, but there were no traffic signals, the trip across town would take 4 minutes and 55 seconds, roughly the same time as hitting 3 of the 5 traffic signals red for an average amount of time. A city without traffic signals is a city where most of us arrive at our destinations sooner and all of us travel safer.

Traffic signals provide drivers with the privilege of driving at dangerous speeds when they are afforded a green light and it is their turn to proceed. In exchange, drivers accept longer delays and generally increased travel times due to red lights, not to mention a dramatic increase of serious injury and death, than they would otherwise experience if they were willing to travel at slower speeds.

Ponder this tradeoff the next time you are sitting at a red light. You will likely also find it maddening.

Creating a Gap

The most dangerous traffic movement is the left-hand turn across traffic. Turning across traffic safely requires a driver to do many things. First, they need be aware of the vehicles behind them and clearly relay an intention to slow down and turn. That signaling and braking needs to be done with enough time for those drivers following behind to become aware and adapt. For two-lane roads, that could mean multiple vehicles in the same lane must slow or even come to a complete stop. On four-lane roads or greater, this means altering flow in the left driving lane, which is generally the higher-speed through lane. Failure to do this correctly increases the likelihood of a rear-end collision, or worse.

The driver seeking to turn left must then attain an awareness of oncoming traffic, making judgments as to the distance and speed of cars coming at them. They must also judge their own vehicle's capacity for acceleration and reliability. Taking all of this into account, the goal is to identify a gap large enough to cross, hopefully without depending on the oncoming traffic to alter course.

This is not as easy as those used to driving fully appreciate. As my oldest daughter was learning to drive, she had repeated struggles with this, one time turning directly into the path of an oncoming vehicle whose driver, fortunately, was able to adjust their path and avoid us (especially fortunate for me, as I was in the passenger's seat and would have been the first to be impacted).

Studies have found that the elderly, in particular, have difficulty with this maneuver. The nonprofit TRIP, along with the American Association of State Highway and Transportation Officials (AAS-HTO), released a report titled, "Keeping Baby Boomers Mobile: Preserving the Mobility and Safety of Older Americans," which identified the left turn across traffic as particularly problematic:

> Left hand turns are also more problematic for older drivers, as they must simultaneously make speed, distance, and gap judgments to enter or cross the through roadway. Older drivers generally have problems selecting appropriate gaps in oncoming traffic and estimating the speed of oncoming vehicles with respect to left turns off a mainline highway. According to a 2002 study by University of Kentucky researchers, each advancing year of age after 65 increases by eight percent the odds of getting into a crash that involves turning left.[1]

Stroads are filled with intersections that provide for left turns across traffic, as well as vehicles turning right into and out of the flow of traffic. Each of those turning movements requires a gap, which is another reason why we install traffic signals: to create the gap.

In Chapter 4, "Understanding Roads," I examined traffic signal warrants, the thresholds for traffic flow used to justify the installation of a signal. That section had frequent references to the spacing and group of vehicles and the creation of gaps. One of the goals of a traffic signal is to group vehicles together in a cluster and thus provide gaps in the traffic stream that allow for turning movements.

Let me state that in a different way: One of the goals of you sitting at a red light is to create a cluster of traffic congestion — multiple vehicles that can travel as a group — with the space between groups being used by drivers who need to make turning movements. This is often difficult to perceive when one is driving, but it becomes really obvious when a person views it while on foot. Traffic signals are used to create traffic congestion so that there can be gaps in the traffic flow.

There is a certain absurdity that keeps recurring, especially when engineers and traffic planners speak of this approach as efficient. The higher the speed, the larger the gaps that are necessary to facilitate turning movements. The larger the gaps that are necessary, the longer the red-light delays must be. The longer the delay at red lights, the more congestion created and the longer it takes to get to where you are going.

Drivers sit at red lights in order to earn the privilege to drive at unsafe speeds once given priority by a green light. If we designed streets for safe speeds, we would not need large gaps, drivers would not need to sit at red lights in order to create those gaps, and we could all get to where we are going sooner and with greater safety.

Imagine calling any system efficient that artificially generates congestion at one point while simultaneously leaving vast amounts of the system underutilized. That's not efficient; that's wasteful.

The system of traffic signals used within our cities is absurd during peak times. During off-peak times — which is most of the time — it is perhaps the greatest systematic waste of time and resources ever developed by humans. If you respect humankind, you should hate traffic signals, as I do.

Six Corners

In Springfield, six streets come together at one intersection known as Six Corners. From an urban design standpoint, these are the kind of gorgeous intersections that can define a neighborhood. They present opportunities for different views and powerful architecture. From a wealth-building standpoint, they are a goldmine — a great confluence of activity with three times the number of corner retail locations than a standard intersection of two streets. Piccadilly Circus in London, one of the world's most iconic gathering spaces, comes to mind as a prominent example of six streets coming together.

Springfield's Six Corners is no Piccadilly Circus. It has a couple of gas stations, a Dunkin Donuts, a fried chicken and pizza restaurant, and a parking lot surrounded by a chain-link fence. It is a very sad and unimaginative use of space, particularly given the potential.

Traffic engineers generally hate these kinds of intersections because, in the narrow rubric of automobile traffic, they are difficult to manage and control. Six streets merging in one location is complicated to properly signal. In modern times, these intersections tend to have a high rate of crashes, including serious collisions. The design manuals do not address them well because they are all subtly different and defy a rote standard.

I was once asked to be an expert witness for a case on a six-street intersection. The team wanting to hire me was hoping that I would support the need for a dedicated signal for bikes. Their client had been run over by a bus and seriously injured. I turned them down. The intersection was such a total mess of signals, signs, concrete barriers, and the like that it was almost impossible to figure out what was going on. There was no way I would ever suggest adding to the clutter with another signal, an act that would only make things more confusing, and thus more dangerous for everyone.

The way to make that intersection safe is the same thing that needs to be done with Six Corners in Springfield; the traffic heading into the intersection needs to be much slower so that that signals can be removed. The signals must be removed so that a humane interaction of life — along with capital investment — can return.

Six Corners is the intersection of six streets, not six roads. The objective of this intersection must be, as with all streets, to build wealth. The binary choice of sitting and waiting at a red light — which is, out of necessity, excessively long at these kinds of intersections — or driving at speeds that are the unsafe for a neighborhood, are both wealth-destroying options.

This is reflected in the development pattern, which compares in financial productivity to some of the lowest found in a Springfield neighborhood, that is, except for one corner, that of a pre-automobile building in the traditional neighborhood style. Today it houses a barber shop and a corner store. Instead of being set back with a large parking lot out front like all of the auto-era properties, the traditional building comes up to the edge of the sidewalk, framing the corner. It was a solid start, but the building is now stuck in the adolescent condition of what should have grown into Springfield's version of Piccadilly Circus.

To their credit, the city has recognized, to an extent, the damage the street design has done to this intersection. In 2020, they completed a $4.1 million renovation, removing the signals and installing a roundabout. It is a step in the right direction, and a massive improvement over what was there, but the design unfortunately still acquiesces to the prime engineering values of speed and volume.

According to the local paper, Mayor Domenic J. Sarno said that the reconfiguration of traffic flow at Six Corners is "key to the rebirth and revitalization of the neighborhood," and vital for public safety and improving the quality of life for residents and businesses in the area.[2]

The design does improve safety by slightly narrowing lanes coming into the roundabout, which should slow vehicles somewhat as compared to the speeds they would have with a green signal light. The crossings for people on foot are an improvement in that people no longer need to wait their turn, but a human in this space is still relying on drawing the attention of a driver who will be comfortably navigating the intersection in System 1.

As with most roundabouts built in North America, the curves are gentle, not sharp, allowing traffic to maintain relatively high speeds throughout the turning movements. Vehicles taking the next right are provided a massive curb radius, making that turning movement very easy, even at speed. The message the design communicates to the driver is that they exclusively own the space; it is built for them.

Traffic flow will benefit from removal of the signals, and that is a good thing, but the revitalization they are seeking here will almost certainly prove elusive. Despite turning two of the six corners into something of a park, this space is unlikely to attract people, and thus unlikely to attract significant investment. It is not human space.

It will attract automobile traffic, however, since drivers no longer must wait needlessly at traffic signals. At the grand opening, the mayor said, "I have driven through this roundabout numerous times and the improvements speak for themselves."[3] Instead of driving, I wish he had walked.

Shared Space Intersections

I try and maintain optimism by considering the proliferation of North American roundabouts to be a gateway drug of sorts for traffic engineers, the first step on their path to a Strong Towns approach. American roundabouts are almost always overengineered, with an emphasis on maintaining traffic speed and volume, but at least they come with some acknowledgment that a continuous flow intersection is better than a traffic signal, if only in that location. That is a significant step in the right direction.

If we can wean engineers off a propensity to place traffic signals on city streets, we can start to ask them to contemplate ways to build wealth along those same streets, particularly at intersections which are — from a visibility and access standpoint — a focal point for wealth creation.

To build wealth, intersections need to be places for humans outside of a vehicle. The way to make intersections great places for people to be while also accommodating traffic flow is to build what is known as a *shared space environment.*

With a controlled intersection, a red light means that someone else owns or dominates the space for a period while you wait for your turn. A green light means that it is now your turn to own and dominate the space while others wait their turn. A shared space intersection is one with no signals, no signage, and few pavement markings. Nobody owns or dominates the space; it is shared by everyone present. Functionally, a shared space intersection is the opposite of a controlled intersection.

For someone used to the rigid priority expressed in North American street design, viewing a shared space intersection can be disorienting. Vehicles enter the space and flow through to their exit. Bikes do the same. People on foot or in wheelchairs walk wherever they need, crossing on the edges or going through the middle. There are no raised curbs or separated sidewalks and no bollards or other delineations separating motorized vehicles from the nonmotorized. At first it may seem chaotic, but it quickly becomes quite beautiful. In fact, the word I would use is "humanized."

While a few have now been built in the United States, the only shared space intersections I have experienced are in Europe, where they are common enough to no longer to be considered a rarity.

I was fortunate enough to get to know the great designer Ben Hamilton-Baillie before he passed away in 2019. Among many other genius thoughts and insights, he introduced me to the shared space intersection he helped design in Poynton, England, for the A523 highway than runs through the center of town.

The A523 is a major highway accessed by roughly 25,000 vehicles a day. It runs right through the historic heart of Poynton, creating a functional moat that bisected the community, harming not only commerce but the spirit and sense of place shared by the people who live there. Park Lane intersects the A523 from the east and Chester Road from the west at a slightly skewed intersection known as Fountain Place. It is not as complicated as Springfield's Six Corners, but it is odd enough to present a major challenge to standard design orthodoxy.

Testimony of residents, along with video footage of the intersection, suggested a hostile environment before the shared space project. Multiple high-speed lanes entering the intersection along the A523 route necessitated traffic signals. Congestion levels were high. Safety was low, with serious crashes commonplace. The environment was loud and uncomfortable.

What struck me most was St George's Church, which occupies the southwest corner of the intersection. Completed in 1859, the church is the tallest building in Poynton and occupies its most prominent spot. The grounds include the graves of some Poynton residents, including the war graves of soldiers killed in World War I and World War II. This is important ground, yet the highway crowded right up to the edge of it, making the church and its related functions a kind of awkward nuisance to the primary purpose of the space: moving vehicles.

Transition to a shared space intersection began in 2011 with the narrowing of the approach lanes down to one in each direction. Traffic engineers and critics deemed this impossible because of the volume of traffic, but reducing from three or two lanes down to one was critical for slowing speeds well before drivers entered the shared space. Nearly 400 feet before entering the intersection, the street design changes, signaling to the driver that they need to shift from System 1 to System 2, slow down, and be aware that this place is different.

After traveling that 400 feet and entering the intersection, drivers are not stopped by traffic signals but instead flow freely into the space. So does everyone else, including those on foot, on bikes, in wheelchairs, and all others. The pavement is colored to give some suggestions for where people might drive or walk, but there are no signs, no hard edges, and no constraints on movement. Movement is continuous, but at slow speeds, with the space designed to be shared by equals.

For an American, the most astounding thing about the shared space environment is how people are treated as equals. As a driver in the United States, I am very used to people running across intersections, even when I am fully stopped and they obviously have the right-of-way. It is almost as if they recognize that they are interlopers in the space, that their choosing to cross in front of me is delaying me and, of course, the street is designed for the driver and not the person crossing on foot. Watch for this; it is a common American behavior that is nearly subconscious.

In Poynton, people feel free to walk. The drivers navigate between them. People seem to wave and acknowledge each other, both from inside and outside the vehicle. The slow speeds tame the environment, removing the aggression created in the traditional model. The reason for this is described well by Martin Cassini, an advocate for traffic system reform:

> "[With a shared space design], a new hierarchy emerges with vulnerable road users at the top. Pedestrians in the shared space scenario where there are no lights to dictate behavior are seen as fellow road users rather than obstacles in the way of the next light."[4]

In other words, we treat each other as humans. This is counter to how many have come to understand drivers — as speeding aggressors dominating the public realm. There is a reason for that impression, as current design practice creates that aggression, even in nonaggressive people. Cassini explains the subtle way that shared space intersections free us to become more humane:

> "There's a misconception that if you take away the lights people are going to drive fast. Actually, the opposite is true. It's the green light that encourages the speed, that licenses the aggression. If you take away the light and there is uncertainty at the junction, people naturally approach slowly and filter."[5]

Remember that this humane environment is happening in a place that is simultaneously accommodating a fairly high volume of traffic. The A523 is still moving over 25,000 vehicles per day. And most people actually get to their destination more quickly, despite the lower speeds.

Ben Hamilton-Baillie literally stood with his shared space designs. To demonstrate the high level of safety, he would blindfold himself and walk backwards through the intersection. We sat together while he showed me videos of him doing this, along with photos of him laying down in the middle of the intersection while cars, bikes, and people moved around him. Imagine doing that on any American street, let alone a high-volume intersection during a period of peak demand. It would be impossible, which makes shared space seem almost magical.

Only, it is not magic. It is the answer you arrive at when you recognize that streets are platforms for building wealth, that intersections are a focal point for wealth creation, and that humans are naturally humane until they are caged and treated inhumanely. As Hamilton-Baillie stated about the Poynton shared space project:

> What's often difficult to remember is now how much more space we have here. Taking out three lanes on the approach roads on either side before, now down to a single-lane approach. A lot of people at the time thought that was impossible. You couldn't cope with this volume of traffic with only single-lane approaches. I think what Poynton has demonstrated is that it is possible to create this continuous-flow, low-speed environment, still cope with pedestrian crossing movements, and most importantly recreate a space, a place outside the church and the center of Fountain Place here, which is part of the town. It is no longer merely an appendage to the highway.[6]

It is beautiful to see the wedding parties now able to stand in front of St George's in a place that celebrates them being there. The solemn gatherers at a funeral are now able to accompany the remains of the deceased to the vehicle that will transport them to their final resting place, with the intersection now an environment that honors their presence instead of being annoyed by it. The individual seeking a moment of peace need not navigate a long stretch of hostility to find it.

Fountain Place in Poynton is now a street built for people — a platform for building wealth. All that benefit, and traffic flows even better than before.

Willow Street and College Drive

Back in my hometown of Brainerd, the latest push is for a new traffic signal at the intersection of South 6th Street and Willow Street. It is undoubtedly a dangerous intersection. I personally know someone who has been in a serious crash there, and I have witnessed many near misses. Among council members and neighbors with whom I have spoken, there is universal consensus that a signal needs to be put in soon before someone is killed. I struggle with how to respond to their level of conviction.

South 6th Street is the old highway that runs through the center of town. Even before it was highway, it was the main north–south street through the city, passing by the grand hotel, theater, landmark water tower, and terminating at Gregory Square, the focal point of the community. This was the grand boulevard of Brainerd — a grandeur seen today only in historic photos.

Nearly all of those regal buildings are now gone, torn down and replaced with flat, modern buildings surrounded by large parking lots. Most of those have not fared well, especially since the highway was rerouted around the city two decades ago in a bypass that spawned a big box building boom in the neighboring city, along with all of the related fast food, strip malls, and gas stations. Since then, traffic counts through the city have been dropping in what has amounted to an exceptionally long game of bait-and-switch for all of those highway-oriented businesses that rushed in decades prior. We would love to have back what we gave up getting them.

A few years ago, the city was planning to do a full reconstruction of South 6th Street, tearing up the entire roadway to replace not just the street surface but the drainage, sewer, and water systems. As part of that process, the public was asked to weigh in on alternative designs. The city was pondering maintaining the existing five-lane highway (two lanes in each direction with a center turn lane) or downsizing to a three-lane stroad (one lane in each direction with a center turn lane).

This was a choice between "horrible" and "really bad," and so I put together a third option, a Strong Towns approach that was mostly two lanes but did include areas with some on-street parking, some separated bike lanes, and some expanded sidewalks within the core downtown. I proposed the intersections be shared space, open without any traffic signals. The head of the local chamber of commerce mocked my design, and the mayor, who called South 6th Street one of the "arteries of a community," vehemently opposed my plan.[7] South 6th Street carries only 12,000 vehicles per day, about half of what the A523 through Poynton carries.

The city ultimately opted to put back what was there, spending extra money to cling to the remnants of a development pattern in decline rather than spend less to rejuvenate the corridor. That is the story of South 6th Street.

Willow Street, the intersecting street where the signal is now desired, is its own sad tale. For most of my life, Willow Street was a local shortcut. My parents, who grew up in Brainerd and knew it well, would take Willow whenever we were driving to the ballpark, but few of my friends' parents ever did. I suspect that was because they were newer to town and did not know the route. Back then, Willow was steep, narrow, and poorly maintained.

Then, one day, the city rebuilt Willow Street in a manner I found completely bizarre. This little shortcut that connected another modest shortcut called College Drive to South 6th Street was rebuilt with two 20-foot-wide lanes. Willow Street was now a small highway to nowhere. I had no idea why this was done. It was baffling.

Then the reasoning behind this action became clear when the city reconstructed College Drive. Using state and federal stimulus funds appropriated in 2009, the local shortcut known as College Drive became a four-lane, major arterial projected to carry tens of thousands of vehicles a day. It was also the first roadway in the area to use roundabouts. There were three of them, and, like American engineers are prone to do, they are designed to sustain high speeds and volume through the intersection. One of these roundabouts funneled traffic to the new highway to nowhere I knew as Willow Street.

The latest traffic counts have 6,900 vehicles traveling on the oversized Willow Street intersecting with 12,900 vehicles traveling along the five-lane former highway of South 6th Street.[8] These volumes are extremely low for the capacity that has been built on these streets, but the ratios may trip a warrant and justify the installation of a signal. Despite the high cost of installation and ongoing maintenance, another traffic signal is what most people in Brainerd seem to desire.

Not me. The problem at this intersection is not the volume of traffic but the speed. South 6th Street is 70 feet wide. That is the total width of the travel lanes, the center turn lane, and the shoulders along South 6th Street. A person driving along Willow Street wishing to cross the old highway of South 6th Street must find a gap in traffic that allows them to travel that 70 feet unmolested.

Starting from a stop and accelerating at a rate of 4.7 feet per second-squared, it will take 5.4 seconds to cross South 6th Street.[9] Assuming that drivers are traveling 30 miles per hour along South 6th Street — that is the posted speed limit, but a high percentage of drivers travel faster — an intersecting car on South 6th Street will cover 240 feet in that 5.4 seconds.

So, if everyone is obeying the law, the person driving on Willow and wanting to cross South 6th Street will need a nearly 500-foot gap in the traffic stream for that to happen safely. Figure 7.1 illustrates the crossing of South 6th Street. If people are speeding, the gap required grows dramatically. During peak periods, that kind of spacing is rare, and so what happens is that people do dangerous things.

They accelerate too quickly. They cut into traffic and rely on other drivers to alter their course. They go halfway across the street and stop. And these are people in vehicles; people on foot are totally helpless in what is a near impossible situation.

Go back and consider my design for South 6th Street (Figure 7.2). Instead of five lanes, my design had only two lanes to cross, more than adequate for the traffic volume that is projected. In my design, the travel speed is 15 miles per hour, half of what is the currently permitted speed. To cross my South 6th Street from Willow Street will take only

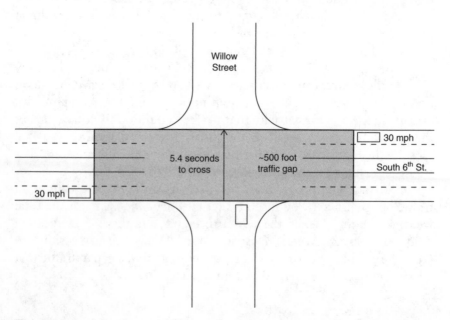

Figure 7.1   Necessary traffic gap for crossing existing South 6th Street.

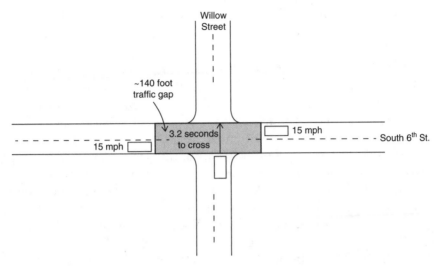

Figure 7.2   Necessary traffic gap for crossing redesigned South 6th Street.

3.2 seconds and require a total gap of merely 140 feet, a gap that will naturally occur far more frequently than a 500-foot gap.

And if people driving misjudge the gap, in my design there is the potential for a minor collision with a low likelihood of serious injury. With the current highway design, a mistake can too easily result in death.

The city overbuilt Willow Street. Then they overbuilt South 6th Street. Now, because of the problems created by these two overbuilt streets intersecting, they are going to be forced to build a traffic signal, not only at great financial expense, but at the cost of robbing people of even more time as they are forced to sit at red lights, earning the right to travel at dangerous speeds through town.

Through it all, the development in the vicinity of this intersection has struggled to thrive. We are moving cars through town, and we are spending huge sums of money to do it, but we are not building any wealth. We are not building a place. This is maddening.

The High Cost of Traffic Flow

I wrote this book during the 2020 COVID-19 pandemic. There are many memorable images from that year, but those of us who work in transportation will long recall the empty highways, vacant parking lots, and smog-free skies over major American cities, all due to a dramatic decrease in driving.

January 21 was the first confirmed coronavirus case in the United States.[10] By early April, vehicle miles traveled in the United States had dropped 46 percent from pre-COVID levels.[11] By June, most major U.S. cities experienced a recovery in traffic volumes, but by the end of the year, many remained below 2019 levels.

There were fewer people driving, but those who were traveling on the country's roads, streets, and stroads were dying at higher rates. In fact, the rate of crashes and deaths exploded, especially during months with the least amount of traffic. During the first three quarters of 2020, the traffic fatality rate jumped to 1.25 per 100 million vehicle miles traveled, up from 1.06 during the same period in 2019. In the second quarter, during the initial pandemic lockdowns and stay-at-home orders, the fatality rate hit 1.42, a terrible rate of carnage.[12]

This seemed to surprise safety officials, who came up with some rather incoherent explanations for the phenomenon. The National Highway Traffic Safety Administration (NHTSA) has issued a series of emergency reports highlighting a rise in what they call "risky behavior," including lack of seatbelts, driving under the influence of alcohol and drugs, and excessive speeding.[13] In a bizarre open letter to the driving public, the NHTSA chastises Americans for their sudden embrace of hedonism and recklessness:

> Most fatal crashes are linked to risky behavior. If you fail to obey the speed limit, to wear your seat belt, and to drive sober, your risk for a crash, and a fatal one at that, goes up. The law enforcement and EMS community across the country have made your road safety a priority—but they are already stretched thin and at risk. Please do not further burden them with your poor driving choices.[14]

It is as if the safety officials at the NHTSA believe that many Americans, in a bout of pandemic fatalism, decided to start drinking alcohol and doing drugs before going speeding in their cars without wearing a seatbelt. Here is more from the NHTSA's open letter:

> It's irresponsible and illegal to drive under the influence of drugs or alcohol, which not only puts your life at risk but the lives of others. Please wear your seat belt—it is the single most effective step you can take to protect yourself in a crash—and make sure your family buckles up and that children are in the right

car seat for their size. And please remember that most serious crashes involve excessive speed; speed limits are in place for the safety of all road users.

Driving is a privilege, and with it comes the responsibility of protecting yourself and those around you.

This response is appalling — almost a willful ignorance of what is actually happening, which is not difficult to discern. Traffic congestion has a calming effect on traffic. Sharing the road with many other vehicles forces a driver to slow down, either because they have to be prepared to react to more things going on, or because another vehicle is physically restraining them from full movement. Slowing down vehicles saves lives.

With the virus-induced drop in traffic volume, what is being revealed is the incredible level of overengineering and unsafe design that occurs throughout our entire transportation system. Remove the traffic congestion that routinely thwarts high speeds and drivers naturally feel empowered to utilize the full capabilities that have been engineered for them. Speeds go up, and so does the rate of fatalities.

It is not that more people are driving without seatbelts or choosing to drive impaired by drugs or alcohol. Those people have always been there. There is no reason even to suspect that the rate of them has gone up, that suddenly people have opted for riskier behavior. It is just that traffic congestion is no longer there to get in their way.

Instead of scolding the public, the NHTSA should ask some difficult questions about the time of day and conditions under which traffic fatalities occur. If they did, they would discover that most happen at nonpeak times and in noncongested areas. They would discover that the traffic fatality rate is much higher during periods of low congestion. This is not because aberrant members of the public time their trips to avoid congestion. It is because the transportation system is designed to be really dangerous, and traffic congestion, along with the slow speeds that result, is masking just how dangerous it is.

Turn this observation around and consider that, for times of the day when there is significant traffic, all of the investment in mobility is wasted. All of the extra lane width, additional setbacks, recovery areas, and the like provide no added value, despite their immense cost, because congestion slows everything down. We might as well have narrow, calming streets where people naturally drive slowly because, when we supposedly need the added capabilities of highly engineered streets, congested traffic conditions force people to drive slowly anyway.

And when we don't have traffic congestion, the overengineering is killing people.

The Strong Towns Approach

Traffic signals are the most mindless and wasteful thing Americans routinely install to manage traffic. Removing nearly all of them within cities would improve our transportation systems and overall quality of life.

The Dutch traffic engineer Hans Monderman said, "If you treat people like idiots, they will act like idiots." American intersection design starts with the assumption that people are idiots and must be treated as such. That is an incorrect assumption. The correct assumption is that humans are smart, intuitive, and thoughtful, and they should be treated that way.

Traffic signals do not improve the efficiency of transportation systems. They do the opposite, creating environments where drivers can either travel at dangerous speeds (green light) or must be stationary (red light). The result is a lower average travel speed, unnecessary and excessive delays, and more dangerous trips.

The result of traffic signals is an environment of aggression, where a green light licenses a driver to take ownership of public space to the exclusion of others. This is an inhuman approach that, on our streets, reduces the financial productivity and wealth-building capacity of cities.

Reducing street speeds can increase traffic flow and reduce travel time for most trips, especially when traffic signals are replaced with continuous flow intersections. There is little to no need to create gaps in traffic flow when speeds are low.

Continuous flow intersections, such as roundabouts, traffic circles, and shared space environments, must be designed for slow speeds. Features like right-turn slip lanes and wide curve radii are counter to this objective.

Intersections are a focal point for wealth-building. A shared space environment is the optimal way to build wealth and accommodate automobile traffic in the same space.

Photos and video of the intersections detailed in this chapter, along with other information on intersections and traffic flow, are available at www.confessions.engineer.

Notes

1. https://www.infrastructureusa.org/keeping-baby-boomers-mobile-preserving-the-mobility-and-safety-of-older-americans/
2. https://www.masslive.com/news/2020/09/rounding-off-the-corners-springfield-celebrates-completion-of-six-corners-roundabout-project.html
3. Ibid.
4. https://www.youtube.com/watch?v=-vzDDMzq7d0&t=292s
5. Ibid.
6. Ibid.
7. https://www.brainerddispatch.com/news/3706200-brainerd-city-council-public-weighs-south-sixth-street-reconstruction
8. https://mndot.maps.arcgis.com/apps/webappviewer/index.html?id=7b3be07daed84e7fa170a91059ce63bb
9. https://fdotwww.blob.core.windows.net/sitefinity/docs/default-source/content/rail/publications/studies/safety/accelerationresearch.pdf?sfvrsn=716a4bb1_0#:~:text=The%20recommended%20parameter%20values%20for, NCHRP%20Report%20383%20(13)
10. https://www.ajmc.com/view/a-timeline-of-covid19-developments-in-2020
11. COVID-19 Effect on Collisions on Interstates and Highways in the US. Bob Pishue, Transportation Analyst, INRIX.
12. https://www.wsj.com/articles/coronavirus-increased-rate-of-crash-deaths-on-u-s-roads-11601582215
13. https://www.nhtsa.gov/sites/nhtsa.dot.gov/files/documents/traffic_safety_during_covid19_01062021_0.pdf
14. https://www.nhtsa.gov/open-letter-driving-public

8

Transportation Finance

My current residence was built in 1914. It sits in the northern portion of the original plat of Brainerd, Minnesota. The house is on 4th Street, a designation shown in even the earliest maps of the city. Those maps also indicate a steamboat landing and a single railroad crossing of the Mississippi river, critical transportation infrastructure of an age long past. The pioneer settlers of my community mostly came to town on the Northern Pacific Railroad. They all would have known, or easily would have been able to find, the location of 4th Street.

One block east of 4th Street is 5th Street. The two streets run parallel and, in the original plat, are the same width and length. While there was no discernable difference between 4th Street and 5th Street back in 1914, and even today the homes and businesses along them are similar, the construction of the streets is now very different.

5th Street is a typical residential street, with parking, sidewalks, and trees on both sides. There is enough room for two-lane traffic, although when two cars meet going opposite directions — an uncommon occurrence because there is not much traffic — the drivers tend to operate them slowly to avoid a crash. There are a lot of stop signs along 5th Street that disrupt the traffic flow, slowing vehicles to a speed more compatible with the neighborhood. Grading on a curve, it is one of the city's more pleasant streets.

In contrast, 4th Street is a collector street, one designed to carry high volumes of traffic at speed. The width of 4th Street is not that much different than 5th Street, but parking is only allowed on one side. This is to give vehicles more room so that drivers never have a need to slow down. The stop signs have mostly been removed as well so as not to impede the flow of traffic. As a result, vehicles travel significantly faster past my front door than they travel past the front of my neighbors whose homes face 5th Street.

Why is my street designated for speed and volume and the street one block over is not, at least not to the same extent? It is not because a council member disliked me or the prior occupant of the house. In fact, I have spoken with several of our elected officials and they would like to see 4th Street changed. It also is not because my neighbors want it to be fast and dangerous; they also seem uniformly to agree that it should be more like 5th Street.

It certainly is not because there is a significant volume of traffic on 4th Street that needs to be accommodated. Hardly any cars pass at all; the most recent traffic counts show just 455 vehicles a day.[1] To give some context: If all of those vehicles passed by my door during the peak hours, between 7:00 a.m. and 6:00 p.m., that would be, on average, only one car every minute and a half. Minneapolis has alleys with higher traffic counts. So then why the different design for 4th Street? The reason is simple: 4th Street is a state-aid route while 5th Street is not.

The federal government provides states with money for transportation. Some of that money flows through to local governments for street projects "selected as to form an integrated network of highways and streets."[2] The city designates a limited number of qualifying local streets for receiving this aid. These then become part of the state-aid system and are eligible for federal and state funding for construction and ongoing maintenance.

That sounds great — what city does not want assistance maintaining their local streets? However, the program requires state-aid streets to meet minimum design standards, regardless of how much traffic they carry, what kind of neighborhood they pass through, or what those investments do to the overall prosperity of the community.

Even though 4th Street carries fewer vehicles each day than some single-lane, dirt alleys in Minneapolis, it is a state-aid route, and, therefore, must be designed to near-highway standards. It has wide lanes, broad recovery areas, limited parking, speeds above levels safe for neighborhoods, and few stops. My family and I live on a mini-highway, solely because of the way the United States funds transportation.

While the percentage of streets designated for state-aid in Brainerd is small, the amount of aid received is a significant percentage of the local street maintenance budget. That budget is stretched. The city already struggles with a large backlog of routine maintenance obligations on non-state-aid streets. By designating 4th Street as a state-aid route, the city government maximized the length of street that qualified for state and federal funding, freeing up local money for other projects.

If the mayor and city council agreed today that 4th Street is a platform for building wealth instead of a stroad for moving vehicles, they would need to remove it from the state-aid list, along with a significant number of other streets that form the "integrated network" of which 4th Street is a part. The city would then have the freedom to design the street however they wanted, but they would have to pay for that themselves. That would require some combination of an increase in taxes, a budget shift from some other fund to the transportation fund, and an increase in debt, growth of the tax base, or more deferment of the maintenance of other streets.

Most of the financial burden for a better 4th Street would ultimately fall on my family and our neighbors, few of whom are currently passionate enough about safety to fork out thousands of dollars for their share of the cost to forgo state aid. Instead, we take our chances with the fewer than 500 cars that pass each day.

In other words, the community is stuck. Pretty much everyone agrees that the design is terrible, but pretty much everyone also agrees that the city must have the state-aid money. We waste valuable resources overdesigning the street, making it more expensive to build and maintain than it should ever be, while also impairing property values. In the process, we make the street significantly more dangerous for everyone. This is all induced by state and federal transportation spending.

The street in front of my house is a state-aid street. So is State Street in Springfield, Massachusetts.

A Means to an End

In most years, the greatest source of state or federal assistance that a municipal government receives comes in the form of transportation funding. State-aid is just one of the myriad transportation programs used to funnel money to local governments. There are numerous local and regional agencies, consultants, contractors, and other organizations established across the country to plan for, lobby for, and receive this money.

The postwar American development model positions local governments at the bottom of a food chain of governments. In response to cash incentives, cities have allowed themselves to become the de facto implementation branch of state and federal policy. Instead of focusing on the urgent needs of their residents, municipal bureaucracies and local power centers orient around the capital flows that come out of Washington, D.C., Wall Street, and the various state capitals.

With transportation funding being the largest, most liquid, and most flexible source of capital, a disproportionate number of local problems are examined through the prism of transportation. This has had a profoundly distorting effect on the way local governments prioritize their time and resources.

A city wanting to experience economic growth could focus on lowering barriers for startup entrepreneurs, increasing connectivity between their existing businesses, or improving the quality of their workforce. These are all low-cost, high-return strategies with a great track record of success. Instead, they are far more likely to pursue a transportation grant for a new highway interchange, a costly venture almost guaranteed to have a net-negative impact on the city's overall financial productivity, but one where the funding is readily available.

A community looking to create jobs could follow any number of proven methods. In my estimation, the Economic Gardening program run by the Edward Lowe Foundation is the nation's top initiative, providing consistently high returns on modest amounts of capital. Since such a program would need to compete with other local sources of funding, the community is more likely to seek a transportation grant for a streetscape project, wrapping the installation of decorative lights and concrete pavers in the rhetoric of job creation.

America is suffering from a public health crisis, with obesity and lack of exercise being primary health risks. The city could support a culture of health by striping existing streets for bike lanes, creating a farmer's market, and loosening restrictions on walkable, neighborhood businesses. These are low-cost responses that can be done quickly and have other positive benefits beyond health. Instead, they are more likely to seek state assistance for a recreational trail or maybe a federal safe-routes-to-school grant to add a few blocks of sidewalk around a school.

Many believe that climate change is an existential threat to humanity — one that should prompt the nation to take aggressive action to curtail carbon emissions. Local politicians sharing this concern have all the tools they need to be leaders in carbon reduction. They can shift their local transportation investments from supporting automobiles to focusing on walking and biking. They could also loosen development regulations to allow the evolution of more walkable neighborhoods — places that could support financially viable transit. Instead, they are more likely to spend their time applying for funding through the Congestion Mitigation and Air Quality Improvement (CMAQ) Program, a federal program that adds highway capacity based on the absurd theory that doing so will reduce emissions.[3]

Many local leaders are focusing on social justice issues and want to improve racial equity within their communities. In my home state of Minnesota, the city of Minneapolis has struggled to find consensus on police reform, housing reform, and neighborhood empowerment, despite a sense of urgency following the murder of George Floyd in May 2020. In contrast, there is consensus on supporting commuter rail projects to some of the region's wealthier suburbs, support that is wrapped in the rhetoric of helping the disadvantaged, despite the tenuous connection to serving the impoverished.

Whether it is jobs, economic development, public health, environmental issues, social equity, or any other urgent matter that local communities struggle with, there is seemingly always a way to respond using state and federal transportation dollars. We frame so many of our struggles as transportation problems, not because that is the best way to approach them, but because that is where the money is.

This has induced an endless list of absurd transportation projects, endeavors that would never even be considered, let alone actually constructed, if it were not for capital that flows freely due to state and federal transportation spending.

For example, in 2009, the American Recovery and Reinvestment Act introduced Americans to the concept of a "shovel-ready project." These projects, which had completed all of the planning, environmental reviews, and design work and were stalled merely from a lack of funding, were presented as the best hope for quickly getting money flowing and people back to work.

In my experience, these were not the best projects; they were the worst. Having gone through the lengthy process of planning and design, when the moment of decision came, local leaders opted to accept their sunk costs and table the project because they could not justify spending local money on it. That is a bad project. Then overnight, with federal stimulus providing the option of using someone else's money, these projects suddenly became an excellent use of resources.

Every year since 2014, the Frontier Group, a research organization that is part of the Public Interest Network, publishes a report on highway boondoggles. These are all horrible projects, but they are also easy targets because of their size. Every city has multiple versions of 4th Street — small transportation projects that are overdesigned, overbuilt, and a waste of funding — which together represent death by a million cuts for our economy. Documenting them all would be impossible.

Even so, *Highway Boondoggles 4*, published in 2018, focused on a project I have become intimately familiar with: the I-49 Inner City Connector in Shreveport, Louisiana. While an egregious example of a transportation project shifting from being the means to becoming the end unto itself, it is worth examining because it mirrors many of the dynamics I have experienced with smaller-scale, more local projects.

It certainly reflects the kind of thinking that created the current version of State Street in Springfield.

Allendale Strong

The first time that I went to Shreveport, my luggage was lost by the airlines. I remember having that unkept feeling that comes with not being able to change clothes. For a Minnesotan, Louisiana is hot and humid, even during the winter. One of my hosts, a young engineer, local activist, and Strong Towns member named Tim Wright, walked with me to the Allendale neighborhood where I was scheduled to meet with some residents at a place called the "Friendship House." I was carrying an overloaded briefcase and was tired, sweaty, and wishing I could be somewhere else.

When we reached the neighborhood, the outward signs of poverty were clear. The houses were small. Many were in a state of disrepair, with some boarded up. There were numerous vacant lots overgrown with weeds. An old wooden retaining wall was crumbling and looked like it might give way in a hard rain. The streets were falling apart, clearly neglected for decades. This was a struggling place. I did not see a lot of hope and, in a bit of self-absorption, was wishing this meeting would be quick so I could collect my things from the airport.

I have a keen eye for neighborhoods, though, and I started to see things that did not fit the context, at least not the one I was imposing. A series of modest homes badly in need of paint but with freshly mowed grass and well-tended flower beds. A sign that kept repeating in the windows and on lawns expressing love and support for the neighborhood and the people who lived there. A group of men hanging out on the porch offering an unsolicited friendly wave and warm greeting to an obvious outsider. A little bit of public art — not graffiti, but something subtle and beautiful that a person driving through was not likely to notice, but a person walking by would enjoy. All of these little things started to cut through my impatience and alerted me that there was more to the story.

And then there was Ms. Rosie's garden, a humble plot that exuded a sense of neighborly love amid the modest beds of flowers. A few minutes after strolling through the garden, I would meet its creator, Rosie Chaffold, an Allendale resident who built it as her way of resisting the neighborhood decline.

After some drug dealers burned down her garage and shot out some of the windows in her house, she responded in a way that I, as a Christian, am called to do, but generally find too difficult to even fully comprehend. Here is how she described it in an interview:

> I felt like in some way, God was not going to let Allendale be lost. I asked a man who owned a lot here if I could use it to put in a garden. I have always loved flowers since childhood. They bring beauty and they give me hope and they would give me strength for the rest of the day. He said they have already burned your garage down and shot out your windows. Do you want them to kill you?
>
> I remember telling him that if I die trying to save this neighborhood, I am ready to go. And I meant it. It was too nice of a place to just let it go. I came early in the morning to work in the garden and the drug dealers would laugh at me and call me names. That went on for months and then some of them started to work in the garden.[4]

More would join in, and then a community group started to help, and ultimately the modest Allendale Garden of Hope and Love, as it is known, became a fixture of the neighborhood. And an inspiration. Allendale residents face their many challenges first with hope and love, and then with whatever else they can do together. I learned this at the Friendship House.

As I arrived, I was warmly greeted and welcomed in. In short order, I was seated awkwardly at the focal point of a circle of people who began to tell me the story of their struggle with something called the "I-49 Inner City Connector." These were obviously kind, generous, and thoughtful people, but as they spoke, I found their story increasingly difficult to believe.

Interstate 49 runs from Kansas City, Missouri, south to Lafayette, Louisiana. While important regionally, the roadway has a huge gap in Arkansas and another in Shreveport, an indication that it has long been a low priority from an interstate perspective. The people at the Friendship House told me how there was a plan to route the Shreveport section of this highway through their neighborhood, taking out many of their homes and businesses. The project was going to cost $700 million, an astounding sum for what I could surmise was only a modest improvement in travel time. The alternate route the assembled Friends preferred would avoid their neighborhood but would cost even more. The Allendale route was being advocated for by a local group of prominent citizens, ominously called the Committee of One Hundred.

I asked questions and they presented me with articles and brochures explaining the project, but I remember thinking that this could not possibly be the story. The federal government was paying to run a highway through a poor, disadvantaged, and almost exclusively black neighborhood? The plan would kick these families out of their homes, destroying whatever wealth they had built, tearing apart a tight-knit community? The project was being pushed by a group of local insiders calling themselves the Committee of One Hundred, a name that would only work in a large and smoke-filled room?

I knew that I was a long way from Minnesota, but this story was impossible to believe. I liked the people assembled at the Friendship House a lot, and I wanted to assist them if I could, but this was 2016, not 1966. Despite their warmth and generosity, I found their narrative improbable. That is just not how these things work these days.

I am deeply grateful for their patience with my naïve doubt because, of course, I was wrong. That is how things are still working in Shreveport, and far too many other communities. The Louisiana Department of Transportation, with the financial backing of the federal government, is preparing to build a highway through the Allendale neighborhood. The plan to dislocate the families that live there and destroy their homes hangs over the neighborhood like a Sword of Damocles, emaciating Allendale by starving it of needed investment capital. The lessons from heavy-handed government action in disenfranchised minority neighborhoods during the interstate-building era have been forgotten, smoothed over most recently during the project's environmental review process.

A large part of that smoothing has been done by the Committee of One Hundred. According to their website, the Committee is a Louisiana-based corporation. They support undertakings deemed, by the Committee, to promote the welfare of the region. Here is how they describe their membership:

> Members are required to be the highest-ranking local executive of business and professional enterprises transacting business actively in Northwest Louisiana. Selection for membership shall primarily be based upon proven community interest and leadership.
>
> The membership meets regularly to carry out its purposes and activities, with no non-member guests allowed at membership meetings with the exception of invited speakers to keep members informed.[5]

To keep the project moving, these local elites advocated for the preparation of a report touting the economic benefits of the project. The report, entitled "Economic Impacts of I-49 Completion, Inner City Connector,"[6] analyzes the project using methods that are standard industry practice.

Despite being widely used, these methods, at best, grossly misrepresent the benefits of transportation investments. At worst, they are a fraud, project propaganda that is accepted and never seriously questioned by industry insiders who receive tremendous benefit from perpetuating it.

The Fraud of Saved Time Calculations

In Chapter 4 of *Strong Towns: A Bottom-Up Revolution to Rebuild American Prosperity*, I wrote about America's Infrastructure Cult, the chorus of politicians, professionals, advocates, and media that reflexively champion infrastructure spending as a solution to seemingly every economic problem. I used to be one of them, until I stopped assuming that everyone else knew what they were talking about and started running the numbers myself.

The absurdity of what the Infrastructure Cult considers serious analysis is jarring to those who have not been exposed to it, raising doubts as to what is really going on. People hearing this for the first time often say, "This can't possibly be true," because it is so ridiculous. I am going to take it slowly and quote directly from the "Economic Impacts of I-49 Completion, Inner City Connector" report in the hopes that it will increase the credibility of these insights.

The first of three economic analyses put forward in the report is the most often cited for measuring the economic benefits of transportation spending, that being the value of saved time. Here is how I describe it in the book *Strong Towns*:

> A project is proposed to add a lane to a congested highway. The highway is carrying 100,000 cars per day. Each trip is projected to be 30 seconds quicker once the new lane is completed. Project advocates would then take those 100,000 trips, multiply that by 30 seconds of saved time per trip, and conclude that the project will save 3 million seconds – roughly 830 hours – of otherwise lost time each and every day.
>
> That's a lot of time, especially when you realize that the median worker in the market makes $25 per hour in wage and benefits. At that rate, saving 830 hours of time is equivalent to saving $21,000 per day.
>
> And when you factor in that there are 365 days in a year and that the added lane can be expected to last at least 50 years, all of a sudden saving each person a mere 30 seconds of time on their commute results in a total of $380 million saved. Do that calculation over thousands of different projects and it adds up to hundreds of billions of dollars. Now we're talking real money!

For the I-49 Inner City Connector, the amount of saved time for each person who drives the corridor is 3.2 minutes each day. The report suggests that this is worth 53 cents per trip, per day.

We could pause right here and raise concerns over the absurdity of paying for a project in hard currency and measuring the benefits in saved time; after all, none of us can pay our taxes with saved time. We could also point out how crazy it is to suggest that humans value their time in this way; that people driving this route will become 53 cents a day more productive instead of just getting an additional 3.2 minutes of sleep each night.

We could ponder that complex nature of traffic and rightly point out that any anticipated time savings is going to create system-wide feedback loops that are, at best, unpredictable, but typically result in greater congestion and increased delay.

We could do all of this and more, but the assertion of 3.2 minutes of time saved equating to 53 cents per trip in benefit is not the craziest section of the economic analysis. Usually when this kind of calculation is performed, there are tens of thousands — sometimes hundreds of thousands — of trips that, when multiplied by 53 cents per trip, make it seem like a big number.

Usually, but not always. As stated on page 5 of the report:

> In addition to daily commuters, the completion of I-49 will impact truck traffic and passenger traffic traveling through Shreveport in a north-south direction. The NW LA COG has estimates of this through traffic based on traffic counts. The 2015 estimate of north-south through traffic is 235 vehicles/day or 86,000 vehicles/year. The Inner City Build Alternatives is a shorter route for through traffic than the Build Alternative 5. The differential is 2.56 miles.

As reported, there are 235 vehicles that are projected to traverse the entire I-49 inner city connector each day. In addition, the report states, with an equally bizarre amount of precision, that an additional 3,374 commuter vehicles will travel to one of the planned interchanges. That is a total of 3,609 trips per day. Note: That is not a typo.

Pause and remember that the project is expected to cost $700 million. Shreveport's population is roughly 200,000 people. That is an investment of $3,500 per resident. At 53 cents per day, impacting 3,600 cars per day, it will take 1,005 years to make the investment back, and that is assuming the 53 cents a day is real, which it is not.

Even so, the report preposterously labels this saved time as "household income" and combines it with another estimation of money saved from reduced vehicle wear and tear to conclude on page 5 that "the aggregate savings for the first 20 years of the Inner City Build Alternatives is $45 million."

All of this is based on an underlying assumption that people value their time and resources the way that the model suggests. Joe Cortright, an economist at City Commentary, published an analysis examining a situation where drivers had a choice about whether to pay to cross a bridge that would reduce their travel time, or save their money and spend extra time in congestion. Despite Infrastructure

Cult assumptions, dramatically more people than the models suggest chose to sit in traffic rather than pay. Cortright estimates that about 80 percent of the value derived with this method is not actually there, even as abstract benefit:

> If travelers attach so little value [to] travel time savings, this calls into question the rationale for investing public funds in highway projects. Benefit-cost analyses used to justify highway projects count the estimated travel time savings, often valued at around $15 per hour, as the benefit of the project. If the real value of travel time savings is something like $3 an hour, that reduces the benefits by about 80 percent.[7]

If that were the case, and I think it might be too generous still, the time value provided by this $700 million project would be only $9 million. The 53 cents of estimated value per trip is reduced to slightly more than a dime.

Of the three economic analyses included in the report, the calculation of saved time, while absurd, is the most credible. The other two are simply make believe.

Make Believe Growth

There is a paradox internal to the standard financial analysis of transportation projects, one that ends in a cognitive dissonance that I have never seen acknowledged by any professional working on these projects. That paradox is this: The benefits of decreased travel time directly contradict the benefits of increased economic growth. The two cannot coexist, yet they are always calculated together. It is the transportation finance version of having one's cake and eating it, too, at least theoretically.

In the language used so far in this book, the benefit from reduced travel time assumes that the I-49 Inner City Connector is going to be a road, that there will be negligible friction conflicting with the desire to move traffic quickly from one place to another. The benefit calculated in the second of three economic analyses used to justify the project assumes that the connector is also going to be a street, a platform for building wealth.

And not just building wealth but building unprecedented levels of new wealth in a community that is experiencing economic distress and population decline. This is ridiculous because the project cannot both reduce travel times and create massive levels of new development, the latter of which will require several interchanges and friction points that are guaranteed to slow traffic.

One of the principal financial justifications for building the I-49 Inner City Connector is to improve travel time by completing a less-congested and more direct route for I-49. But why is there congestion there in the first place? It is because the highways previously built through and around Shreveport already have a tight series of interchanges where drivers enter and exit the system, causing backups and slowdowns each day during prime commuting hours. Shreveport has already leveraged federal investments in highways to spur local development. That is what they are proposing to do once again, only this time through Allendale.

Congestion is harming the Shreveport economy; therefore, a highway must be built to bypass the congestion. To justify the construction of the highway economically, new big box stores, franchise restaurants, strip malls, gas stations, and housing subdivisions must be built, creating congestion along the new highway. The argument is circular.

The report calls this "differentials in economic output from real estate development," which is a jargony way to say that, once new land is made accessible by the connector, it will be redeveloped to a higher level of intensity. Here is how this is stated on page 6 of the report:

> Highway construction that provides enhanced accessibility also provides real estate development opportunities that can stimulate economic growth. Those opportunities are governed by the future demand for real estate, as well as by the future supply of real estate.

Project proponents have set forth the case that there is going to be over $800 million in annual economic benefit from the Inner City Connector in the form of salaries and wages. What is immediately problematic about that number — $800 million — is that it sounds impressive but does not really communicate anything meaningful.

How much of this new economic benefit would have happened without the highway? Are these new jobs, or are they jobs simply displaced from other parts of the city? Are these good jobs that build capital and wealth within the community, or are they discount jobs where the profits quickly leave the community? Is this the best way to achieve a financial return on a $700 million investment?

There is no attempt to answer any of these questions in the report. Instead, through overly simplified spreadsheet gymnastics, the report merely assumes that the project area will get its share of growth projected for the region. This is all called a *shift-share analysis*, which is a standard tool for making (largely incorrect) macro forecasts. From page 7 of the report:

> The LWC and shift-share methods provide similar estimates of overall employment growth of about 10–13 percent over the decade.

There are a couple of problematic things right away with this analysis. First, over the last 25 years, the population of Shreveport has shrunk from 186,000 in 1990 to an estimate of 184,000 in 2017. A sudden counter-trend increase in employment of 10–13 percent is simply not credible. The report is projecting 30,653 new jobs just from this highway, and that is for a city with a population under 200,000. That is ridiculous, even ignoring the silly level of precision being suggested.

Again, the internal paradox of this approach shows up in the math. One spreadsheet in the report is projecting 3,600 trips a day. Another is projecting $800 million in economic benefit. If we assume that each of these trips is a new employee commuting to a new job, that is $220,000 in economic benefit per commuter every year. That is not a real number.

The report suggests that one in four of the new jobs will be in retail. Are the people of Shreveport suddenly going to start consuming more because of a new highway? Assuming that the people of Shreveport today are buying toothpaste, toilet paper, and other consumer goods, which they are, then where is this new consumption going to come from? Without population growth, what is driving this growth in jobs?

Project proponents would say that growth always follows new highway construction. Build some interchanges and good things happen. This is true on its face, but it is only part of the story. A more complete narrative would recognize that investments like these simply shift jobs from one place to another.

For example, the Shreveport area has 9 Walmarts. There are 14 McDonalds. One or more of those — the older ones that have gone past their short life cycle — can easily be closed with a new store constructed near one of the proposed interchanges in Allendale. Is that economic benefit? According to the parameters of this study, it would be.

To add insult to injury for the people of Allendale, on page 13, the report included this opaque statement, which I will subsequently interpret into normal English:

> The completion of the Inner City Connectors would provide substantially better highway access for commercial development in a large portion of the PSA. Moreover, the PSA has a plethora of adjudicated space owned by the City of Shreveport that should be redeveloped and brought back into commerce. The significant constraints on development are costs for raw land and for land assembly. The later constraint is due to the subdivision of the PSA into residential lots that must be assembled for commercial and industrial projects. This constraint could be reduced with a concerted effort to acquire and redevelop land within the PSA.

Here is what this says: Real estate developers, with Wall Street financing, love to develop at and around interchanges. The I-49 Inner City Connector project creates a number of those opportunities, especially since a significant amount of land in the project area has already gone back to the government through tax default, the inevitable result of the decline brought about by the Sword of Damocles the I-49 project creates over this neighborhood.

The government can sell, but most likely gift, this land to developers. The only potential hitch in this plan is the stubborn Allendale residents who are still there, dotted throughout the neighborhood. If they cling to their properties and refuse to sell, it will make it hard to develop the project area fully.

The city can nudge this process forward with, as they say in the report, "a concerted effort to acquire" the land. That kind of effort generally involves buying the lots or acquiring them through condemnation at the deflated, preconstruction values. When the city later sells them or gifts them to developers, the gains from the $700 million investment in the highway are passed on to those private corporations.

The Allendale neighborhood is being systematically devalued by public policy choices. This makes it easier for the city, on behalf of the public, to acquire the properties of Allendale residents for free or at greatly reduced prices. Once the project is built, the windfall gains will be privatized. It is the poverty of Allendale, not its development potential, that makes this entire project possible. What is happening here is immoral, an injustice the report's math cannot hide.

This section of analysis in the report concludes with an acknowledgment of sorts on page 13:

> This assessment provides a probabilistic rather than deterministic forecast.

The probability of the I-49 Inner City Connector creating 30,600 new jobs, opportunities that would not have simply occurred somewhere else, jobs that are not merely being shifted from one now blighted place to another, is precisely zero.

None of this is real. It is all make believe. Sadly, the third section of the report is even more ridiculous.

Fabricated Network Effects

In the social sciences, equations too often allow people to stop thinking. They give license to be lazy — to simply apply rote math to situations that are far more complex than the numbers suggest. Researchers can provide precision, such as the $62,118,727 of so-called agglomeration effect reported on page 40 of the report, which makes it seem like they know what they are talking about. They might even believe that they do.

The most insulting part of the economic analysis provided for the I-49 Inner City Connector project is the reported agglomeration effects in the third section. Again, this is standard analysis found in similar reports across the nation. Here is how this particular report explains agglomeration effects on page 14:

> Economists have recently recognized network effects and agglomeration economies as important factors driving metropolitan growth. The growth of new technologies since the 1980's have demonstrated the importance of network effects on production costs and output. Highways are an infrastructure asset with network effects. Improvements that speed up travel times eliminate congestion. If the improvements are within central nodes of a network, they can improve the efficiency within the entire network. The measurement of the network effects from transportation improvements is through the calculation of agglomeration economics.

And here is how the agglomeration effects are reported in the executive summary of the report, providing the simple equation that allows all critical thought to end:

> Increasing the speed of travel in the transportation network drives the expansion of the labor market. Increasing speeds by 10 percent has an effect of increasing labor productivity by 2.9 percent (Prud'homme and Lee 1999). Our analysis suggests that travel times for commuters are reduced throughout the Caddo Parish portion of the network from the completion of the Inner City Build Alternatives. The estimated agglomeration economies from this network change are approximately $60 million per year.

The equation: Increasing speeds by 10 percent creates increased labor productivity by 2.9 percent. That is a powerful correlation for an industry approach that values speed above all other considerations. According to something called Prud'homme and Lee, all that is needed to demonstrate large economic benefits is to show that people can get places more quickly, at least theoretically.

So, what is Prud'homme and Lee?

Two researchers named Remy Prud'homme and Chang-Woon Lee wrote an article entitled "Size, Sprawl, Speed, and the Efficiency of Cities" (Sage Journals, 1999). The two are from, respectively, the University of Paris XII and the Korea Transport Research Institute.

The article reads as if the authors are engaged in an ongoing conversation that they hope their peers expand upon. There is a lot of hedging and context provided, the kind of discussion that two researchers would have when exploring a hypothesis within a soft science. Prud'homme and Lee make it clear, in numerous places, that this paper is anything but a definitive study.

Speed is simply one aspect of the efficiency measurement that the two authors examine. In fact, even the title "Size, Sprawl, Speed, and the Efficiency of Cities" suggests, as discussed in the paper, that the size of a city and its concentration also have an impact on efficiency. Here is how they introduce their article:

> Some cities are more efficient than others. Why? At a time when most people live and most activities take place in cities, identifying the determinants of the efficiency of cities is of importance not only for city planners, but for also for macroeconomists. This paper considers three potential determinants of urban efficiency. . .the size of the city, the speed at which people and goods are moved in the city, and the sprawl or the relative location of jobs and homes in the city.

In the introduction to the paper, Prud'homme and Lee emphasize that size of an urban area has a huge impact on productivity. In a Strong Towns way, they point out that there are diminishing returns to outward expansion:

> The relationship between urban productivity and urban size has been recognized and studied for a long time. In a seminal contribution, Alonso (1971) developed a model that assumed that both benefits and costs increased with city size, with the benefit curve increasing less and less and the cost curve increasing more and more.

In other words: There are benefits for cities when they grow bigger, but at some threshold of outward expansion, the costs start to accelerate far beyond the benefits. Again, this is a basic insight analyzed at length in *Strong Towns: A Bottom-Up Revolution to Rebuild American Prosperity*.

The data Prud'homme and Lee rely on comes from 3 Korean cities (Seoul, Busan, and Daegu) and 22 French cities (unnamed, except a note that Paris was not included). I have unfortunately not been to Korea, but I have been to France many times. There are no cities remotely like Shreveport in France, especially in the applicable dimensions of "size, sprawl, and speed."

For comparison, the French city of Saint-Étienne is nearly the same population as Shreveport. Despite having the same number of people, Saint-Étienne is 30.9 square miles while Shreveport is 3.9 times that size, a total of 120.8 square miles.

Obviously, this is consequential, especially when relying on a rote correlation between increases in travel speed and increases in productivity. A French city with the population of Saint-Étienne/Shreveport is going to have a well-developed transit system. The Prud'homme and Lee paper was considering modest increases in the operational efficiency of transit systems moving people through a dense city.

Shreveport, by comparison, has a pathetic transit system. There is no rail. Bus service does not have the frequency to be considered reliable. It is a place overwhelmed — except for a short period of time in a limited space — with excess auto capacity. The idea that increasing auto speeds in Shreveport would have the same impact, or even anything near the same impact, as improving transit efficiency in a place like Saint-Étienne is ludicrous. No earnest and forthright person could read the Prud'homme and Lee article and conclude that it would apply to a place like Shreveport.

While the authors of the "Economic Impacts of I-49 Completion, Inner City Connector" report were eager to cherry-pick one correlation from the Prud'homme and Lee paper, they ignore another on page 10 that, while less helpful, would be far more applicable:

> When the average potential job-home distance increases by 10%, the effective size of the labor market decreases by about 11.5%.

In other words, the more you spread things out, the more difficult it is for people to get to work, a quite logical assertion for Prud'homme and Lee to make. This would have been included in the "Economic Impacts of I-49 Completion" study if the authors and project proponents were truthfully trying to discern the costs and benefits of the project. They were not.

What they were doing is what engineers, planners, and project advocates all over the country do when going after state and federal funding for their project: They create propaganda. This is how the system works, and everyone involved knows, understands, and accepts it.

They cite benefits from saved time that have no correlation to the way that people actually value their time while ignoring well-documented impacts of induced demand. They fabricate development impacts with wild assumptions that have no internal consistency while overlooking the adverse impacts of jobs that are merely shifted from one place to another. They cherry-pick correlations from a nonapplicable study while ignoring the more applicable — and damning — aspects of the same study.

This goes beyond a lack of rigor to something rightly thought of as *institutionalized dishonesty*, a ubiquitous deception made acceptable only by its broad adoption. It is immoral and it needs to end.

Reforming an Immoral System

All of this institutionalized fraud and elaborate self-deception is being done for the sole purpose of securing transportation funding. Whether it is pretending that 4th Street in front of my house is a critical part of Minnesota's transportation network, asserting that State Street in Springfield is a major traffic corridor for the region, or claiming that the I-49 Inner City Connector through Allendale is so important to our national interstate system that it justifies not only a $700 million public investment but the destruction of the Allendale neighborhood and the repeating of historic injustices toward disenfranchised populations, none of it would even be considered were it not for the federal system of transportation funding.

I want institutions that function on behalf of local communities. I want professional engineers and transportation planners to serve the common good. I want a system where politicians are rewarded for prudence and not avarice. All of these desires are deeply corrupted by the centralized and opaque way in which we have chosen to fund transportation investments. Decent people are turned foul while the corrupt are given wide latitude, all at great harm to our economic, civic, and physical health.

Such is my personal outrage. If I were the sole decision maker, I would rescind the national gas tax, close the U.S. Department of Transportation, and end the federal role in transportation spending. That would make me as radical as Canada, a country where one can safely and comfortably drive across an entire continent despite the lack of a federal transportation department. It would also force me to stand alone with my indignation because I do not know any credible politician or policy advocate who shares my view on this.

And so, the pragmatic part of me is forced to embrace some type of reform agenda. They are many good people working to reform aspects of this system. Unfortunately, they tend to fall into one of two different philosophical approaches.

The first is inspired by a progressive mindset, which tends to focus on the excesses of highway funding while being far less rigorous about similar financial frauds committed in pursuit of transit, sidewalks, trails, and other projects that they prefer. They make fickle allies from a Strong Towns standpoint because, when forced to choose, they tend to be willing to tolerate a lot of terrible transportation spending so long as their priorities are also funded.

I was invited to give a speech once to a group of advocates gathered in Washington, D.C. I did not know until I arrived that, right after my talk, the event organizers planned to march the group down to Capitol Hill, where they were scheduled to meet with legislators and lobby for more transportation funding. I scrapped my planned remarks and instead asked the hundreds of audience members how many of them were from New York or California. A sizeable contingent of hands went up.

I then pointed out that both New York and California sent substantially more transportation dollars to the federal government than they received back in transportation spending. If the New York or California legislative delegations wanted more transportation spending, as well as more control over how that money was spent, that could easily be accomplished by shifting the federal government to a maintenance-only approach for the interstates and devolving all other transportation authority back to the states. New York and California could maintain the same level of taxation and have at least 20 percent more funding.

That message did not resonate with the audience, a group somewhat predisposed to believe in the magic of centralized power. I am not part of that group, but neither am I fully comfortable with the other group actively pushing for reform, that being those with a more auto-centric, libertarian mindset.

People like Joel Kotkin and Randall O'Toole tend to fit into this category of reformers. I used to find them baffling until I stopped taking their arguments literally. Like the progressives, the auto-centric libertarians have their preferred subset of projects, only theirs involve automobile infrastructure. They get quite exercised over the way financial analysis is done on transit projects, but they do not apply a consistent critique to auto-oriented projects.

The key to understanding the incoherence of the auto-centric libertarian is to recognize that they equate the automobile with individual freedom. In that mindset, when the government spends money increasing the amount people drive, they are simultaneously increasing individual freedom, which in their eyes is the primary role of government. They will join in condemning boondoggle projects and pork-barrel spending, but they accept, and often promote, highway expansion as the proper role of state and federal governments. I find them to be frustrating allies for the Strong Towns cause.

Fickle or frustrating, there are at least allies with whom we can work. And so, while a Strong Towns approach is perhaps not a perfect fit for everyone, it may be a workable alternative to the impulse merely to build, build, build, build, and build.

Any federal or state level reform would start with a recognition that there is a difference between a road and a street. Roads provide high-speed connections between places and are not used to induce growth or development along a corridor. Streets are platforms for building wealth within a place, which is a hyper-local undertaking. The federal government should fund roads only; there should not be any federal spending building, expanding, or maintaining streets. All supporting documentation, environmental reviews, economic analysis, and the like should reinforce this shift in approach.

There is a role for the federal government, and especially for state governments, in funding stroad conversions, essentially attempting to fix the damage their prior policies have wrought. A program to eliminate stroads over the next two decades could redirect the current energy around growth-through-expansion to something more productive. In addition to funding, the federal government could nudge the professions to a Strong Towns approach by providing technical support and design leadership around stroad conversions.

This should also expand to urban highway conversions, which the federal government should also prioritize. The only new highway lanes we build in this century should be around cities, but only in conjunction with removing the highways that never should have been built through cities. Those latter urban highways need to be turned back into local roads and streets, reconnecting neighborhoods and restoring community.

Beyond these investments, the fix-it-first agenda should be the default, but the intention behind the rhetoric needs to be codified into policy. Many expansion projects are done under the banners of maintenance and safety, which is a small step intellectually when insiders believe that maintaining traffic speed and volume improves safety. No expansion of any type should receive federal funding in a state with a backlog of maintenance obligations.

The federal government should immediately place a lengthy moratorium on new interchanges and then reform the funding formulas to limit future federal contributions. Any interchange that is not part of an interstate-to-interstate connection should receive no federal funding unless the roads intersecting at the new interchange have no accesses within a mile of the crossing. There should be a prohibition on the use of federal funding for new frontage roads.

The base interstate system of two lanes in each direction can remain funded by the gas tax or other federal appropriation, but states should be allowed to use mileage charges, congestion pricing, tolls, and other flexible revenue approaches on the additional lanes to fund transportation. The federal match on new lane miles should be decreased to 50 percent, and no match should be given to states that are using traffic projections in the absence of a demand-based fee structure that proves the need for the project.

Local governments have responded to state and federal incentives by overbuilding their transportation networks. Correcting that mistake will be difficult because it requires local communities to expand their menu of possibilities for land use, zoning, taxation, civic life, and a variety of other issues that they control. At times, the necessary transition from municipal insolvency to a stable level of financial productivity will be painful. If there is a compulsion at the state and federal level to provide local governments with resources, give them cash instead of laundering assistance through a transportation program. If a transportation project is their urgent need, then they will have that option, but they will also have the flexibility to think more broadly and pursue other ways of building prosperity.

Transit is its own special circumstance, and I will devote the entire next chapter to it.

I do not have much optimism that the Strong Towns approach to transportation finance will be embraced by state and federal lawmakers, especially while they seem eager to embrace various economic experiments, theoretically to sustain us in a state of unsustainability. That leaves local mayors, city councils, professional staff, and civic advocates to buffer their communities from harm.

To that end, of all the advice and insights I have shared in this book, the one I would emphasize in this section is this: Stop looking at every struggle you face as a potential transportation project. If your community is working on a transportation project, delve deeper to identify the real problem — lack of jobs, the need to retain youth, to improve civic life, and so forth — and find other ways to solve it.

Transportation is a means to an end, so treat it that way, and never as an end unto itself. And never go into debt as part of a matching program for state or federal infrastructure dollars. You will find yourself the sucker at the card table, and your community will pay the price.

More information on transportation finance, including the latest information on the I-49 project in Shreveport and other similar projects, is available at www.confessions.engineer.

Notes

1. https://www.dot.state.mn.us/traffic/data/tma.html
2. https://www.revisor.mn.gov/rules/8820.0500/
3. https://www.transportation.gov/sustainability/climate/federal-programs-directory-congestion-mitigation-and-air-quality-cmaq#:~:text=The%20Congestion%20Mitigation%20and%20Air, attain%20national%20air%20quality%20standards
4. https://communityrenewal.us/project/i-became-a-target-but-that-didnt-stop-me/
5. https://www.committeeofonehundred.org/history/
6. http://www.i49shreveport.com/site/Assets/72/156/Shreveport%20I49%20Project%20Report%20V5%20January%202016.pdf
7. https://cityobservatory.org/what-hot-lanes-reveal-about-the-value-of-travel-time/

9

Public Transit

I walked to Springfield Union Station with Steve Shultis, a local Spanish teacher who also shares his passion for urban life on his blog, *Rational Urbanism* (http://rationalurbanism.com/). Steve was one of the earliest readers of *Strong Towns*, challenging me on several things but also being a strong voice of encouragement, something especially important to me in those tentative early days. Over time, I became good friends with Steve and his wife, Elizabeth Lawton. It was sitting in the guest room of their house that I first heard the news about a young girl, who would later be identified as Destiny Gonzalez, who had been killed on State Street.

Joining us on our way to the transit station was Laura Masulis, the co-founder of a makerspace in downtown Springfield. She and her colleagues were working to bring energy into the struggling downtown, incrementally pushing back against a pervasive mindset that seemed unwilling, perhaps even unable, the see the potential of the space. Downtown Springfield is a gem that has lost its luster under decades of neglect and bad policy interspersed with the occasional silver bullet project, efforts big on promises but small on results. Laura is a big part of the antidote to what ails the city.

The walk took us up Dwight Street, a three-lane stroad of one-way traffic dedicated to moving vehicles quickly into the core downtown. The further we went, the more denuded the landscape became. The final block before the train tracks is a perfect representation of Springfield's self-induced decline. On one side of Dwight Street is the Springfield State Office Building, a full block of classical architecture, stately yet simple. Opposite the stroad is an auto service station set back from the street and surrounded by parking. A Goodyear sign towers over the decorative lights, the latter suggesting a feeble attempt to address a belated sense of loss on the site.

To reach Union Station, the three of us were forced to walk the final block on Dwight Street through a lengthy tunnel. The abstract art positioned on the walls did nothing to alleviate the anxiety of walking narrow sidewalks a few feet from traffic moving at lethal speeds. We met some people traveling on foot in the opposite direction and had an awkward time of negotiating past each other in the confined space between the concrete wall and the traffic lanes. Nothing about this felt safe, let alone comfortable.

The other end of the tunnel opened onto Union Station, a stately building surrounded by numerous parking lots. The station opened in 1926. It recently underwent a $94 million renovation to restore the building and make it into a regional transit hub.[1] Many bus and rail lines converge on Springfield Union Station, reportedly making it the busiest transit station in Massachusetts outside of Boston.[2] My two companions were proud of it and wanted me to see what had been done.

I understand why they feel proud. Despite the desolation that surrounds it, Springfield Union Station is a gorgeous building, and I am happy for Springfield that it has been restored and put to good use. And, through the narrow lens of transportation, creating a regional transit hub improves convenience and operational efficiency. It is only three and a half hours from Springfield to New York City's Penn Station, a proximity to America's wealthiest and most global city that should have Springfield booming.

On paper, especially given all of the investment that has been made in Springfield, the economic winds should be at their backs. Yet both Laura and Steve fight a continuous battle against the forces of decline. They are both optimistic, and I can see the progress of which they are a part, but progress is different than momentum. There is no real momentum.

The brownstones a few blocks from this transit hub should be selling for four times what they are routinely listed at. The shops up the street should never have the prolonged periods of vacancy they suffer from. The parking lots should be filling in with new buildings, the real estate too valuable to sit empty as it does. Despite enormous public investments in transit connections throughout the region and to other major cities, the signs of decline are everywhere.

It is discouraging to see the disconnect between the busy regional hub of Union Station and the desolate quality of the blocks that surround it. It is discouraging because, when done correctly, public transit is a wealth-multiplier. When built as a road to provide a high-speed connection between places that people want to be, a transit connection magnifies the wealth of each connected place. When deployed to a street, public transit overcomes geometric limitations to allow more people to live and transact in an area than they would be able to otherwise. Transit is an essential part of maturing a street as a platform for building wealth.

Yet American public transit is rarely deployed in this way. Most transit systems I experience are set up like Springfield's. Enormous sums are spent on transportation infrastructure, yet next to nothing is spent connecting transit stops to the community. A great deal of resources is spent providing basic service to a broad area, but that service lacks the frequency or reliability to provide any real value to those who live there.

Instead of marrying people and place, it is as if the designers of the transit system focus only on the actual transportation device, not the experience of the rider and not the quality of the place being served. The typical North American transit experience can be represented by a cold metal bench placed on a narrow sidewalk between a parking lot and a stroad. It is the opposite of a positive experience. It is the opposite of building wealth.

The Purpose of Public Transit

Roads connect productive places, while streets are the platform for building wealth within a place. Our divergence from these simple principles has made our auto-based transportation system dysfunctional and the resulting land use pattern financially unproductive. Auto-based transportation investments are bankrupting our cities.

North American transit serves as an appendage to this dysfunctional system. In most places, it is merely a charitable overlay, practically an afterthought grafted on to the auto-based approach. As such, the advocates for public transit tend to define its purpose — and tout its benefits — by comparing transit to the automobile and by fitting its use into an auto-dominated rubric. This is utterly unconvincing.

For example, it is frequently asserted that a primary purpose of public transit is to reduce traffic congestion by providing an alternative way for commuters to get to work. The theory is that drivers, fed up with being stuck on congested roadways in a car, will opt to ride a bus or train, particularly one that can bypass the congestion. In practice, it is the wish of every driver stuck in traffic that the drivers in front of them would opt for transit, not recognizing that, if that somehow did reduce congestion, it would merely clear room for other discouraged drivers to use that capacity. In a hierarchical transportation system, there is no functional limit to the demand for more capacity.

Connected to reducing congestion, it is often put forth that public transit is necessary because it reduces carbon emissions by moving people from single-occupancy vehicles into transit. While I grasp the argument that twenty people riding together on a bus potentially emits less carbon than twenty people riding in individual automobiles, I am skeptical of the overall claim. I have never seen a study that credibly correlates increases in transit use with an overall reduction in carbon emissions, largely for the same reasons that increasing transit use, or building more road capacity, does not create a sustained reduction in traffic congestion. There is no functional limit to the demand for more capacity.

Some have argued that, while not the primary purpose of transit, there are health benefits related to public transit. I appreciate the correlation that, in cities with great transit, there tends to be better health outcomes, but those cities — New York, Washington, D.C., San Francisco, Boston — also tend to be more affluent, and affluence is even more highly correlated to positive health outcomes.

On the ground, I find the logic connecting transit and health benefits to be rather tortured. The pleasant and healthy walk one might have approaching a D.C. Metro station has no comparison to the despotic and dangerous walk needed to reach a bus stop in suburban Atlanta. It is not the transit that improves health; it is the walking. If the purpose of transit is to improve public health, we would see better outcomes focusing on making it safer and easier to walk. Not only would it be much cheaper, but it would also be far more effective.

Increasingly, investments in public transit are made to attract younger people who, it is suggested, prefer a transit lifestyle over other ways of living. Maybe in New York City, Washington, D.C., or San Francisco, where underground railways combine with an urban form to provide a North American version of a European city, but no millennial in Akron takes their date to the snowed-in bus shelter for the ambiance. Certainly, the neighborhood around Springfield's transit system — despite the grandeur of the renovated Union Station — is not attracting young professionals chasing an urban lifestyle. It is not attracting anything except for parked cars and the homeless.

This leaves the two most asserted purposes of public transit: to attract investment for the community and to serve the poor. The suggestions are that Americans invest in transit because it creates economic growth and because it helps people, especially those too poor to own and operate an automobile.

If economic growth and social equity are the purposes of transit, there is no evidence of that outside of Springfield's Union Station. The transit hub is surrounded by parking lots, which are the opposite of economic growth. There is not even an attempt to create economic growth in these vacant spaces, let alone a transit-based inducement for it to happen. In fact, the space devoted to parking is considered a feature of the design, not a flaw.

Connections to and from the site for anyone on foot are dangerous and despotic. There is no discernible attempt to leverage the $97 million invested in the building to improve the downtown or any of the surrounding neighborhoods.

What is discernible, however, is that there are lots of poor people in Springfield, many of them congregating at the transit hub, often taking local buses to and from the site. If helping these people is one of the primary purposes of the public transit system, it is not at all clear how that is supposed to work. The poor have little to no benefit from the parking lots surrounding the site. If getting them from the station to the downtown or any of the surrounding neighborhoods was the benefit, then there would be some equivalent investment in making that connection. There is none, as all of the money and right-of-way is being spent on increasing the speed and volume of the surrounding automobile traffic.

Assuming the poor and the economically motivated will overcome the disconnect Springfield Union Station has with the rest of the community and find their way across the dangerous stroads to the site, it is not clear how the actual transit service provided there is supposed to improve social equity or motivate anyone to invest in Springfield. The bus routes primarily cater to distant commuters and theoretical tourists, not the core neighborhoods of Springfield.

The most helpful route for improving mobility for the poor within the city — The Loop — departs from Union Station roughly every 40 minutes, a frequency not conducive to convenient travel planning. It passes through the core of the city and provides stops at such places as the MGM casino (twice), the Basketball Hall of Fame, and the LaQuinta Inn. The entire round trip is about 2.5 miles, which means that it is nearly always quicker just to walk to your destination rather than wait for the bus.

Whether the purpose of public transit is reducing congestion, improving the natural environment, supporting public health, attracting youth, inducing economic investment, or assisting the poor, it is broadly failing at all of them, in Springfield and in cities across North America.

Transit advocates tend to argue that this failure is because there is a lack of public commitment to these issues, and that more funding for our current transit systems would yield better results. I am sure that there are isolated instances where that may be true but, broadly speaking, there is no credibility to that assertion.

Transit in North America is failing because it exists without being tied to any discernible or measurable purpose. Like nearly all postwar transportation investments, it has moved from being a means to an end to being an end unto itself. And as an end, it is an afterthought, an appendage to a dysfunctional auto-based transportation system. If public transit is to have a real purpose it can fulfill, it must separate itself from the underlying auto-based system and stand on its own as the primary wealth accelerator for maturing urban areas.

How Transit Became the Lesser Partner

To review Chapter 2 of this book, a *road* is a high-speed connection between productive places, while a *street* is a platform for building wealth within a place. A *stroad* is a street–road hybrid, a transportation investment that attempts both to move traffic quickly and build wealth while failing at both, a combination that makes stroads expensive to build and maintain, low in financial productivity, and dangerous for everyone.

Historically, transit functioned as either a road or a street. Ships, barges, trains, trollies, jitneys, and wagons all served as transit in the past. These were mostly private endeavors that turned a profit for operators.

An easy way to think about transit functioning as a road is to consider a steamship or a train. In both instances, a person would board the transit system in one location and depart at another location, with a high-speed connection (by the standards of the day) in between. In such a system, transit provided an enormous value to both places by connecting people over great distances in ways faster than they could otherwise travel. This is the reason that the great pre-Depression cities of North America were on harbors, rivers, canals, and rail lines; these were the quickest ways to travel great distances.

My small town of Brainerd had a steamboat landing on the Mississippi river. Further upstream there was a railroad bridge, making the Brainerd train depot an important stop on the Northern Pacific line. Springfield is on the Connecticut river and, likewise, had a landing, a bridge, and a rail stop. Without these high-speed connections to other places, neither city would have grown and prospered as they did.

Once someone arrived by steamboat or train, they were in a place built on a network of streets. Modern Americans marvel at the grandeur of the architecture that even modest historic train stations had, but there is a very practical reason why these investments were made. For many people, that was the first impression of the community, a billboard of sorts advertising the quality of the place.

That positive messaging would be reinforced or undermined by what happened outside the door of the station as passengers emptied out onto the street and began to interact with the community. Amid the commercial establishments and residential homes, transit functioning as a street would have been everywhere, providing a convenient way to traverse the city at a pace slightly faster than walking. This could be a jitney or a wagon providing a lot of flexibility in route and destination, or it could be a trolley with the ability to hop on or off at will along a fixed route.

These street-based transit systems functioned quite differently than road-based transit because their purpose was different. Within a city, transit was not about connecting places across distances but in building wealth within a place. It was designed to make being in the city more convenient and comfortable. The wealthier and more successful the place became, the more the demand for street-based transit and the greater the intensity of the transit that could be provided.

Maturing cities everywhere had fixed-rail trolley lines connecting neighborhoods. While not necessarily fast, these systems made city living less burdensome by allowing people the convenience of riding instead of walking, which was especially helpful when transporting items. For cities with terrain, it made hills easier to traverse. Large cities had dense webs of this transit and even small towns like mine once had a trolley line that went from the downtown into outlying neighborhoods.

In the early part of the 20th century, as the automobile was becoming more widely used, the economics of transit within the city began to change. Many books and articles have been written about the villainous role of automobile manufacturers in the demise of private transit systems, but the reality is almost certainly less nefarious. Automobiles could travel faster and were more flexible than most local transit options, which reduced the demand for transit. Particularly for fixed-route systems where the underlying economics assumed a steadily maturing place, a sustained drop in demand meant a decline in service, delays in maintenance, and ultimately insolvency. For existing transit networks, widespread automobile adoption created a self-reinforcing downward spiral.

Yet many people depended on these systems to sustain their property values and to get around the community. There was pressure — along with some incentives from corporations looking to sell "modern" bus technology — for local governments to assume responsibility for the ongoing operations and maintenance of local transit. These governments inherited systems in distress, badly in need of investment at the same time demand for transit was declining.

The aggressive horizontal expansion of cities that would define North American development patterns after World War II was not preordained. Other countries integrated the automobile into existing road and street networks, learning lessons as they went. It was only in the United States, and to a lesser degree in Canada, that government investments in auto-based transportation became the primary mechanism to drive growth, improve social mobility, and codify what would become known as the American Dream.

In *Strong Towns: A Bottom-Up Revolution to Rebuild American Prosperity*, I explain how an economic model predicated on neighborhood stability and bottom-up wealth creation was, following the Great Depression and World War II, replaced by one emphasizing economic growth and transactions:

> With the world's reserve currency, abundant and cheap oil, and low individual debt levels, the United States serendipitously found itself with the ingredients it needed for rapid economic growth. What happened was a generation of American growth, two and a half decades of spreading prosperity that is still broadly nostalgized.
>
> In this period of time, Americans built the interstate highway system, the largest public works project in the history of mankind. These transportation investments broke the stability of high land values, making abundant raw land available to the masses at affordable prices. Investments in infrastructure systems accelerated. Through Urban Renewal initiatives, new planning theories were put into practice, remaking entire neighborhoods.
>
> Policymakers quickly discovered that the tools for fighting deflation in the Great Depression worked even better for expanding the economy during the postwar boom. Focusing again on housing, the FHA used the same approach of lowering down payments and insuring banks against default. This time it wasn't fighting a deflationary spiral; it was expanding demand for housing, dramatically increasing prices.
>
> Growing demand for new housing was a boom for the economy. Building this new version of America created millions of jobs, from carpenters and contractors to appliance manufacturers and door-to-door encyclopedia salesmen. A robust housing market created wealth in a growing middle class, a trend that became central to American self-identity. After things being so hard for so long, everything suddenly became easy.
>
> Generations of wealth incrementally built within America's cities had been destroyed in favor of rapid growth and economic expansion, an exchange with a naturally redistributive effect. Individual Americans had experienced how national growth solved their individual problems, a narrative they would never seriously question thereafter.

While many federal and state programs joined to make this growth machine possible, the uniquely American catalyst was the massive top-down investments in transportation, starting with the interstates but including the transformation of local communities around the automobile. For many decades, the easiest way for a local community to experience growth was to receive money for a transportation project.

Interstates made an incredible amount of land around cities accessible for development. By the laws of supply and demand, abundant accessible land on the periphery cratered land values within established cities, destroying the natural pattern of incremental redevelopment that had matured cities for centuries. This depressed property values in historic neighborhoods, further undermining transit economics, but it was a boon for the new American suburbs, which were explosive in their growth.

For these suburban cities, the recipe for short-term success became simple: Have the federal government fund a highway along with the necessary bridges and interchanges. Work with the state to fund frontage roads and an arterial stroad network. Tap into development fees and other growth-related revenue streams to pay for collectors. Then allow national developers and the centralized marketplace to provide everything from shopping malls, big box stores, and fast food to residential homes on cul-de-sacs.

The current narrative of this boom is that it built the middle class. The less common, but more accurate, insight is that government investments in transportation made many holders of formerly worthless land into instant millionaires while creating a way for communities to experience growth quickly and the macro economy to generate lots of financial transactions. The overwhelming liabilities to service and maintain all of this infrastructure would start to come due a generation later, but in the short term, especially in those decades immediately after the Second World War, it was seemingly a golden age.

From a transportation standpoint, the more of this new version of America we built, the more demand there was for auto-based infrastructure investments. That demand was easy to meet because, especially in the early days before the maintenance costs kicked in, the federal gas tax was a cash cow. So were similar taxes enacted at the state level, and most people were happy to pay them because they could see what they were paying for in the new construction that was everywhere.

As the postwar transportation system evolved, the quality gap between the auto-based transportation systems and transit systems expanded. Attempts to forestall decline in transit were wrapped in the language of modernization as many fixed-route systems were abandoned or replaced with buses. These became synonymous with the working poor. The economics of public transit, long tied to property values, no longer worked; with cities stagnating or in decline, the wealth just was not there. Transit became marginalized, forced to compete with other parts of the local budget for funding.

With state and local tax structures adapted to the new growth model, there were few mechanisms for cities to gain resources by building wealth in core neighborhoods. While the Housing Act of 1961 required mass transit to be included in comprehensive urban planning, it wasn't until the 1970s that transit advocates really began a push to access gas tax revenue by grafting their projects onto the automobile commuter model. Transportation planning from this era, projects that often took decades to see to fruition, began to include transit systems as a parallel commuting option, something designed to supplement the automobile-based systems.

This reimagination of transit happened simultaneously with the first wave of highway maintenance bills. Building new interstates, along with all of the accompanying local infrastructure, had a large economic multiplier, but maintaining them and even expanding them created no comparable gains. Yet it must all be maintained. Amid the energy crisis, high inflation, and economic malaise of the 1970s and early 1980s, the gas tax was not keeping up with mounting needs. Something needed to be done.

That something came in the form of a compromise in 1983 with the Surface Transportation Assistance Act. The Act increased the gas tax from four cents per gallon to nine cents, with one cent of that going exclusively for public transit. This buoyed beleaguered transit systems but ended the idea that highways should be paid by user fees in a pay-as-you-go system. It also married transit funding to an increasingly dysfunctional auto-centric transportation system.

It did not take long for transit projects to fall into the same false internal narratives that plague automobile projects, using phony numbers and specious correlations to justify massive investments designed to induce growth. Unlike auto projects, however, which have the ongoing backing of dedicated state revenues, the local match for transit projects was most often municipal debt backed by projected fare receipts. This made false projections extra harmful as shortages at the farebox had to be made up with service cuts, further undermining the entire model.

Enticed by the go-big-or-go-home nature of federal funding, transportation planners discounted their core ridership and embraced a build-it-and-they-will-come approach used in highway projection models. Expensive rail lines run to cornfields on the periphery of cities in the hopes of inducing a new place more often resulted in some niche apartments, a vacant coffee shop, and a lot of parking lots.

In my professional career, I have watched transit be plagued by two competing mindsets, neither of them helpful. The first is that transit is a core service for the poor, a charitable overlay to our insolvent auto-based system. The second is that, for transit to be successful, it needs middle- and even upper-class ridership. If these visions were even reconcilable, there is no way to fulfill either with transit stuck as the lesser appendage to a deeply dysfunctional auto-based transportation system.

Either as a charitable overlay or a lifestyle option for the rich and middle class, our approach to transit is incoherent, providing often intolerably poor levels of service at ridiculously high cost. Transit antagonists can rightly point out that, in most instances, it would be cheaper to buy every transit rider a car than to build and operate transit systems the way we currently do. Proponents then rightly point out that auto-based transportation systems are heavily subsidized and do not pay their own way, either, as if somehow pointing out that hypocrisy makes the case for more unproductive transit investments.

Antagonists will then suggest that our transit systems are poorly run with inconvenient and unreliable service, which is true in most places. Proponents will then counter that we could overcome these shortcomings if we only spent more money on transit, which may theoretically be true but, without reform of the current approach, only in a world with no resource constraints.

This debate will continue, both sides generally correct in their assertions yet speaking past each other, increasingly locked into partisan narratives that deny Americans the opportunity to see transit for what it really is: the greatest wealth accelerator our cities have.

Instead of trying to be a lesser partner in an insolvent and immoral system, public transit needs to become the lead partner for cities in building wealth.

Transit as Wealth Accelerator

The proper role of transit is as a wealth accelerator for local communities. The purpose of investments in transit is to support broad-based wealth creation within a city. Unlike auto-based transportation investments, transit can actually deliver on that purpose, and when it does, also provide many of the other benefits that transit is capable of providing, from a net reduction of carbon emissions to increased social equity and more.

Transit is a wealth accelerator when it is used in support of productive development patterns and is deployed to function either as a road or a street. Successful transit requires successful places, so if you desire transit, you must focus on building a productive place, somewhere where people want to be outside of an automobile.

The difficult thing for American transit advocates, who have been conditioned by current transit funding models to think only in terms of large projects, is to accept is that transit systems must be scaled to the intensity of the places being served. Rail lines to corn fields and commuter lots make great applications for federal funding in the current paradigm but produce systems that underperform and are expensive to maintain. A high-frequency bus loop is less glamorous and fundable but can reinforce a development pattern that drives investment.

Start with a place, then pick a transit option scaled to that place as a means to an end of making that place more financially productive.

For Springfield, Union Station is a place, albeit not a good one. At that site, there has been an overinvestment in transit and an underinvestment in place. Springfield should begin a strategy of turning the parking lots and derelict buildings around the station into productive development serving the needs of the people in that place.

That development strategy requires the city to recognize that the stroads around the building need to become streets, with an emphasis on slowing traffic and making it easier for people to bike and walk to and from the neighborhoods surrounding Union Station. This should begin, as detailed in Chapter 5, with a Street Design Team humbly observing where people struggle and then taking immediate, incremental, and ongoing action to address those struggles. This is the hard work of building a place that should be started long before a significant transit investment.

Springfield is burdened with having too much transit in a place that is disconnected from the nearby downtown, which is also struggling but has potential for more rapid returns. This is where The Loop should be reimagined, not as a route for tourists, but as the backbone of a transit system that serves local commerce.

All the public employees, lawyers, accountants, salespeople, clerks, and everyone else working in the core downtown should find it ridiculously convenient to board The Loop and get to wherever they need to be to conduct business in the core downtown. That means the service interval cannot be an impractical 40 minutes but a reliable 10 minutes. Springfield should not want anyone to have to think hard about scheduling their trips throughout the downtown.

To achieve a 10-minute interval will mean more buses, but it will also mean dedicating space on the streets for buses, giving them priority at intersections and making bus stops convenient and easily accessible. Do this and it reinforces the value of working downtown — if you are in that zone, you are connected to everyone — while also making it more convenient for those choosing to do so.

It is important to pause here and point out that transit is the only way to overcome the geometric space limitations of the street while still building wealth. In an auto-oriented model, the more cars that are there, the more space that must be given over to accommodating those vehicles. That means parking lots instead of destinations, driving lanes instead of sidewalks, which is the opposite of wealth-building. Auto-based development effectively puts a cap on the success of a place, a physical limitation for how many people can be in one place at one time and, subsequently, how much investment can occur.

Transit removes that cap. If the buses on The Loop are too full at 10-minute intervals, then surge to 5-minute intervals. If there is even more demand, make one of the street lanes bus-only. Widen the sidewalks and then allow buildings to expand and adapt, using the success of human congestion to drive investment. Eventually, the positive feedback loops of wealth creation will accelerate the shift from automobiles to higher levels of transit intensity until all that is left on the street from a transportation standpoint is people on foot served by fantastic transit. That will be a ridiculously productive place full of people deeply satisfied by the experience.

In Springfield, the extra buses for The Loop should come from redeploying all of the capacity that is squandered providing marginal commuter service to far-flung areas. These buses should be redeployed to The Loop as well as to improving the frequency and reliability of service throughout core neighborhoods. State Street should be a bus corridor, not with a strange collection of randomly timed routes that happen to use State Street as part of a longer trip, but as a fixed route with a predictable schedule, essentially a bus or series of buses that run back and forth all day.

The thousands of people who live within a few blocks of State Street should only have to walk to that street to quickly catch a bus that will take them directly downtown. Same for the return trip. As with The Loop, the buses should be given priority at intersections and the stops should be designed to be comfortable and convenient. State Street as a street, and all of the adjacent streets where riders will be coming from, are platforms for building wealth. Thus, Street Design Teams should be deployed to humbly observe where people struggle and then work to make those neighborhoods better places to live. That is what transit as wealth accelerator looks like within a network of streets.

For transit on roads, the approach to accelerating wealth is different. Roads are connections between productive places. For transit to work on a road, it needs two things. First, it needs productive places to connect to. Transit on a road must connect from one place people want to be to another place people want to be. Parking lots, the back of a big box store, and the roadside ditch are all common transit stops in the current model but should not be for transit on a road.

In Springfield, a reimagined Union Station — fully connected to the downtown and the surrounding neighborhoods by changes to the surrounding streets — is a great place for a road-based transit system to connect to. Penn Station in New York City is another. Much like how Springfield should push to keep its roadway connections to other regional centers from being degraded, a direct train from Springfield to NYC that did not stop along the route would be optimum. Such a service would create enormous wealth opportunities within Springfield.

Downtown Holyoke is another place that people want to be. Holyoke is not New York City, so the transit between there and Springfield Union Station should probably be a dedicated bus, one that travels back and forth between the two places, connecting their people and their economies.

After two productive places, the second thing road-based transit needs is the ability to arrive first. This is not a measure of speed but of comparative speed. The steamship that traveled up the Connecticut River was not fast, but in its day it was faster than all of the alternatives. A bus might not be fast, but if it is faster than traveling by car, especially during peak times, that transit connection will provide immense value to those connected places.

This means that, especially during congested periods, buses need to be given priority over other vehicles. A dedicated lane, or a lane shared with carpools or subject to congestion pricing, is necessary. This is not a system that prioritizes commuters but one focused on building local wealth, stability, and prosperity by prioritizing places.

Jarret Walker is one of the most innovative transit planners in North America. He has been instrumental in the reimagining of numerous transit systems in ways compatible with a Strong Towns vision. Walker's blog, Human Transit, and his book of the same name, have deeply informed my understanding of transit. Most notable of Walker's work is a reorganization of the Houston transit network. The project tripled the amount of frequent bus service without increasing operating costs.[3] In the nation's fourth largest city, this is nothing short of spectacular.

Paying for Transit

Most local governments have all of the tools they need right now to pay for successful transit systems. The key is to separate capital costs from operations and maintenance, funding them each in ways that create positive feedback loops.

Capital costs are investments in transit infrastructure, including trains and buses, but also transit stops, buildings, shelters, sidewalks, dedicated lanes, signage, and other things necessary to make the transit system work. Because a Strong Towns approach is both scaled to a place and designed to build wealth within there, capital costs should always be paid by capturing part of the wealth being created.

This can be done with a direct assessment, the establishment of some type of service district, or even a dedicated percentage of a property or land tax. The idea is that the investment in transit makes properties more valuable and a percentage of that value is returned to fund the investment.

This approach requires that transit systems be scaled to the destination being served, which generally means smaller and more targeted projects. That is a more difficult transition than it sounds because the advocacy energy in transit today is mostly focused on large, federal-backed, commuter-based investments. Their projects have been in the works for a long time, the federal funding is ultimately there in a pipeline, and big dreams are hard to walk away from, especially when land speculators have placed bets on future routes and have themselves become project advocates.

For transit to be viable, it is essential that it be scaled to the community so that it can be successfully operated and maintained with a high level of service. This should always be preferred over an oversized system that underperforms, one which the community will struggle to sustain. The goal of transit as wealth accelerator is to create feedback loops where a successful place creates demand for transit, which creates more demand for development, which creates demand for more intense transit, and on and on and on. The intensity of the place and the intensity of the transit should grow together so they will both always be viable. When transit jumps too far out in front of the place it serves, it is difficult — financially and culturally — to close that gap.

Operations and maintenance must be funded through the fare box, which should never be used to retire debt or fund capital improvements. Mixing funds between capital, operations, and maintenance makes internal accounting and management sloppy. We need transit systems to be well-run and responsive, which means the routine constraints of having to balance operations and maintenance with fare collection.

If there is a federal or state contribution to transit, I would like to see that go to retiring the legacy debts of transit agencies so that they can have a clean break with the auto-based system. I can also see a role for direct subsidy to riders lacking the ability to pay full fare, although that need not pass through transit agencies.

A Strong Towns approach requires transit advocates to give up on their dreams of serving low-density areas with publicly funded mass transit. We have built many places in this country that, for better or for worse, cannot be reasonably served by public transit. Our attempts to serve these places have not only squandered resources, but they also resulted in a level of service to those areas that is dehumanizing. If our goal is to help the poor, the standard American approach to public transit is a distraction.

Regarding the poor, just as we define so many of our local challenges in terms of transportation projects because that is where the money is, we have done likewise in our attempts to serve those living in poverty. I agree with the underlying motivation but find the toolbox of transportation projects to be far too limiting.

Transit as a wealth accelerator is a difficult concept for people accustomed to thinking of transit as a charitable service for the impoverished. Even though decades of being the lesser partner to an insolvent auto-based transportation funding model has not delivered quality transit to the poor, for some the idea of building wealth is off-putting. I see it as essential.

While there is wealth in Springfield, Massachusetts, in general the city is not a wealthy place. A bottom-up strategy to build wealth there broadly is, at its core, an anti-poverty strategy, one that focuses on the urgent needs of people and responds to their struggles with humility. A transit system with increased service on The Loop will benefit the members of the middle class who work downtown, but it will dispro-portionately benefit the poor who will also be able to reliably use it to get around.

Investments to connect Union Station to the downtown will attract investment and grow businesses, but it will also make it safer for the poor who predominantly use those streets. A culture of walking and biking, the culture of place that is a prerequisite for successful transit, is an egalitarian culture, one where the functional gap between social classes shrinks. Rich and poor alike walk on two feet.

A high-frequency service along State Street will serve neighbor-hoods that are dominated by low- and moderate-income residents, allowing many more to forgo the expense of an automobile. A bottom-up development strategy of incrementally building wealth will create low-income housing and small-scale business startup opportunities, inviting more people into those neighborhoods while allowing the added wealth to accrue to those already living in the community.

The Strong Towns approach to transit is about building wealth, and building wealth is about creating a stable and prosperous community. A system that is merely a charitable overlay to serve the poor in good times but is exposed to catastrophic cuts when it is most needed is not a successful approach.

The Strong Towns Approach

Public transit is a wealth multiplier. Deploying transit is a primary strategy for building wealth within a community.

Transit builds wealth when it is deployed as a road connecting two productive places or as a street as part of a strategy to build wealth incrementally within a place. Transit investments must be scaled to the places that they are serving, increasing in intensity as the place increases in productivity. Advocates who want to improve transit need to focus primarily on building a productive place.

For transit to build wealth on a road, it must be given space and priority to provide faster travel times than auto-based trips.

For transit to build wealth on a street, it must be given adequate space and receive priority at intersections. It must also be part of a reliable network of high-frequency service, making it unnecessary, and ultimately burdensome, to travel streets by automobile.

On streets, transit is used to overcome the geometric limitations of automobiles, allowing greater investment to occur on the same street framework. Successful transit provides a high level of service by crowding out the automobile and auto-related infrastructure. All transit trips are also walking or biking trips, so a transit strategy must emphasize building great streets. Use Street Design Teams to identify urgent struggles and respond incrementally.

Pay for capital projects with a direct assessment, the establishment of a service district, or dedicating a percentage of a property or land tax to transit. Operations and maintenance must be funded through the fare box, which should never be used to retire debt or to fund capital improvements. For the sake of stability and the need for positive feedback loops, there is no role for using sales taxes to fund transit.

Investments in public transit are an ineffective way to alleviate poverty. There are many helpful ways to support the poor that do not involve transportation. Considering only the transportation system, we best support the poor by making public transit an indispensable mechanism for building wealth within the community.

More information on the Strong Towns approach to transit, including a case study on reimagining the Houston transit system, is available at www.confessions.engineer.

Notes

1. https://www.masslive.com/business-news/2017/05/peter_pan_agrees_on_union_station_move.html
2. https://www.amtrak.com/content/dam/projects/dotcom/english/public/documents/corporate/statefactsheets/MASSACHUSETTS17.pdf
3. https://jarrettwalker.com/project/houston-2/

10

Transportation Technology and Fads

I am going to start this chapter by revealing to you an astounding transportation technology that has the potential to revolutionize your community. It has been shown to dramatically improve property values, both in commercial areas and throughout residential neighborhoods. It attracts business investment, especially in high-tech and other professional sectors, but also significantly in the retail and service sectors. It is a proven job creator. It has been tied to innovative breakthroughs in technology, mathematics, physical sciences, arts, and literature.

This amazing transportation technology serves nearly all ages, allowing a community's youth and elderly alike to be dramatically more mobile and self-reliant. In fact, cities where this technology is prominently in use disproportionately attract young professionals and high wage earners.

Moreover, the transportation technology allows hands-free use so that a person can talk on the phone, listen to music, or let their mind wander while in motion. It has even been demonstrated to improve mental health.

Additionally, adoption of this technology is also guaranteed to improve public health, with well-documented links to increased heart and lung fitness, reduced risk of heart disease and stroke, improved management of hypertension and high cholesterol, reduction of joint and muscular pain, stronger bones, improved balance, and reduced incidence of diabetes.

I will also suggest that, in my opinion, using this technology makes one look good. Tastes may differ, but I have found that people who use it are, in general, far more attractive than people who choose not to.

While no transportation option is completely benign to the environment, this amazing technology is very low impact, having negligible direct carbon emissions and requiring no fossil fuels to operate.

The most amazing part is that, for the user, the technology is virtually free. For the community, there are some modest infrastructure costs, but they can be phased in, replacing more costly and unproductive investments in many instances.

Almost everyone can use this technology, but those who are unable will greatly benefit from its widespread adoption. There is no need to worry about adverse impacts because, literally, the technology evolved over millions of years to match the very specific needs of humans.

The astounding transportation technology I am talking about is, of course, our legs and feet and the miracle of evolution that allowed humans to walk upright.

Our ability to walk does not feel astounding — we largely take it for granted and discount it — so I want to start this chapter by anchoring on walking as a measuring stick by which other technologies should be judged. It is hard to beat walking, no matter the metric used, because building a place designed for people who walk is the historic norm, not the afterthought that it has become in modern American cities.

For thousands of years, humans built their habitat around people who walked. As I wrote in *Strong Towns: A Bottom-Up Revolution to Rebuild American Prosperity*, these walking cities were evolving human ecosystems, finely tuned to our needs:

> That habitat helped people…meet their daily needs, but it also helped them raise their young, care for their elderly, save for the future, pass along their stories and culture, comfort their primal urges, and reach for higher truths by communing with the existential. In short: the city helped make them human.

We are compelled today to acknowledge that the wisdom contained in the cities our ancestors built, in the patterns and approaches they developed over thousands of years, exceeds our capacity to fully understand. There are deeper truths there than we will ever know, spooky wisdom that has co-evolved along with humanity itself, to serve our needs — known and unknown — in ways we have been far too eager to casually dismiss.

Humans are evolved to walk. To the extent that we understand human history, our earliest ancestors seem to have walked great distances on an almost daily basis. They gathered food, hunted, and sometimes migrated to distant locations, all by walking. It is not a stretch to suggest that our physiology is designed to walk, and, in some ways, our health requires that we walk regularly.

I walk a lot, partially for the health benefits but mostly because I enjoy it. That, and I am cheap. I save hundreds of dollars every month, not to mention hours of time, by arranging my lifestyle so that most of my daily routine can be done by walking, including taking phone calls and doing meetings while I am out for a stroll. If someone wants to visit me at the office, I usually ask if we can instead meet at the park and walk. My visitors seem to enjoy it.

I am also driving less. Now that my oldest daughter has her driver's license, I am rarely asked to drive her and her sister to the dance studio. Along with school, dance was one of two routine destinations not easily accessible by walking or biking. Both the school district and the studio owners were enticed to build in remote locations by cheap land and the ability to offload the cost of transportation onto their patrons. Without those trips, I now hardly drive at all.

Some might assume that this lifestyle is a function of privilege or affluence, but like many midwestern cities and most small towns, houses in my community near the walkable urban core are some of the most affordable. In my hometown of Brainerd, the walking lifestyle is available to nearly anyone, and while some of my neighbors are affluent, many of them are not. Most of the middle-class families that I know live on the periphery and are burdened with the cost of maintaining two cars along with the time loss from daily rush-hour commuting, not to mention the mental and physical toll of it all.

I will reiterate that I live in Minnesota, a state known for cold weather. The amazing thing about winter is that another revolutionary technology — clothing — keeps me warm when I go outside. Sure, there are days when it is really cold and I would rather not do the eight-block walk to my office, but I never regret it once it is done.

Humans can adapt to walking in just about any climate on earth, although our sensitivity to adverse weather seems to be heightened when we spend extended periods indoors where temperatures stay in a tight, climate-controlled band. Walking, like all habits, is self-reinforcing.

I once spoke to a pastor who told me how greater adherence to the Golden Rule — do unto others as you would have others do unto you — would alleviate, if not solve, most of the struggles he witnessed his parishioners experiencing. If people just practiced a simple form of kindness and decency toward each other, much of the world's suffering would disappear. He relayed how the mayor of his community made essentially the same claim; that much of what they spend time and energy on at city hall would go away if people treated each other decently. As an organizing function for society, the Golden Rule is an extremely powerful device, for Christians and non-Christians alike.

I have come to see walking in the same way. There are very few chronic problems plaguing society today that would not be allevi-ated, at least somewhat, if everyone walked a mile or two each day. Public health, from obesity-related ailments to mental well-being, are improved by walking. Seeing our neighbors in shared spaces would likely improve our social cohesion and sense of community. It would almost certainly make us care more deeply about the places outside our own door, giving us added impetus to work together.

It would make us more aware of the struggles of others in our communities, very real challenges that we have the capacity to do something about. In that sense, it would provide added purpose and a sense of meaning to modern lives that seem increasingly atomized.

A community of people who walk has a very different economic structure than one where everyone drives. It is more fine-grained and personal, where Adam Smith's invisible hand of the markets meets his insights on human behavior and our innate desire to be thought of as lovely to each other. Granted, such an economic ecosystem would be less efficient than our top-down, centralized marketplace, but it will still be a market — one that responds to supply and demand curves, has financial incentives, and rewards risk and innovation — albeit at a scale that is human.

I do not mean to suggest some Utopian outcome if only we all gave up our cars and walked, but who among us has not been advised by a doctor, or at least a loving parent, to eat healthy, get a proper amount of sleep, and regularly exercise. So much of what we do as modern Americans is made more difficult by our inattention to these basic needs.

So many of the transportation fads that we embrace are merely attempts to overcome the currents pushing against us because, unlike our ancestors and in sharp contrast to our basic physiology and mental makeup, we choose not to walk.

Making walking easier is one of the easiest and highest-returning investments a city can make.

Biking

It stretches credibility to include a device that has been around for two centuries as a fad, but biking is experiencing a resurgence in cities. That is a positive thing because, after walking, biking is the lowest-cost and highest-returning transportation option available to us.

Pete Adeney, also known as Mr. Money Mustache, is best known through his blog for retiring at the age of 30. One key to enjoying a life of leisure and contentment is to stop wasting money. Adeney calls the bike the "Greatest Invention of All Time" and writes:

> The Bike is simple with just a few moving parts, simple enough for most people to maintain entirely on their own without paying a mechanic.

> It is efficient in many ways: bikes weigh only 20–30 pounds, but they can carry ten times their weight in rider and cargo. They convert a slow human with a walking speed of 3.5MPH into one of the fastest creatures on land, with an easy cruise of 15MPH and a top speed of over 40MPH on level ground and 50+ downhill for athletic people. And the side effects are incredible ... vigorous biking can consume 1000 calories per hour, meaning you can burn off an entire pound of fat in one big 3-hour ride. This kind of exertion pretty much fixes up all the rest of your body for free too, clearing your arteries, polishing your kidneys and teeth, and giving you clean stylish hair and a better sense of humor, all after the first ride.

> But another side effect is that bikes are good for your wealth. Let's start with the bare minimum: any mileage you put on your bike instead of your car saves you about 50 cents per mile in gas, depreciation, and wear and maintenance. From this savings alone, doing a couple of bike errands per day (4 miles) in place of car errands will add up to $10,752 over ten years.

Adeney shares pictures of his bike trailer, which he uses to haul groceries but also an astounding number of other things, including furniture, a grill, and an oven.

I love to bike, but I had to quit biking to work because I got there too quickly. My ten-minute walk is just a three- or four-minute bike ride, hardly enough to have any deep thoughts. I still routinely bike to the grocery and the hardware store, which are just outside of the comfortable walk zone.

In a city of stroads like mine, biking can be dangerous, and in fact it seems far more dangerous than walking. Most places I walk are separated from traffic, albeit traffic moving at lethal speeds. While biking, I am part of that traffic, keenly aware that a moment of inattention by a driver will do disproportionate damage to my body.

I have been dragged into the debate within the biking community over whether bikes should have their own separated infrastructure or whether cyclists should be aggressive in asserting their rights within the existing stroad environment by what they call "taking the lane," being very visible while biking within the stream of traffic. While these are not generally incompatible positions, the passion of each group often crowds out reasonable discourse.

Given the speed of traffic on our local stroads, I tend to prefer separated infrastructure, but I will "take the lane" and ride visibly (automobile drivers might say "obnoxiously") in traffic when there is no separate space, or the bike infrastructure feels dangerous. I have taught my kids to bike in these conditions. Chloe, my oldest, does not feel safe and rarely bikes, while Stella, my youngest, seems more confident and willing to venture out.

I emphasize their reaction to the same environment because it is clear that we have a built environment where biking is an afterthought, a clumsy overlay to an auto-based system. A strategy that turned our stroads into streets will also dramatically improve the biking culture here, making it safe for people of all ages to "take the lane" and bike on the streets, where they should be.

On roads, or in places where we still have stroads in place, automobile traffic is moving too quickly for bikes to take the lane or even to have adjacent infrastructure like bike lanes or shoulders. In these places, there needs to be separate infrastructure for bikes. It is unacceptable for people to be expected to cycle a few feet from vehicles moving at lethal speeds.

Some last thoughts on bikes: First, while I enjoy bike share in many cities that I visit, the economics of it currently seems problematic in most cases. If my choice is to spend hundreds of thousands subsidizing a bike share program or spend that same amount of money making it easier for people who are currently biking to continue to do so, I am going to always choose the latter. The easier we make it for that next marginal cyclist to get on their bike, the more we accelerate a culture of walking and biking, the greater the return on our efforts. It is a less measurable outcome than the number of bike trips, but more meaningful.

Second, electric assist bikes are amazing, and I can see them being particularly helpful for the elderly and for people with disabilities. I have witnessed people using them obnoxiously, but always within an environment designed to be obnoxious for people not in a car or other high-speed vehicle. We need to resist banning or regulating these devices too much and instead focus that energy on taming the environment in which they are used.

Finally, I will just point out again that I live in Minnesota, where people bike all year.

Scooters

I rode my first e-scooter along a beach in San Diego in 2018. As a sometimes-clumsy man in his mid-40s, I found it delightful. It was intuitive, safe, and fun. It did not surprise me at all that they exploded in popularity in cities across the country.

It also did not surprise me that there was a backlash. On the beach, scooters were strewn about where people left them, often in the path of where one would normally walk. Young people on scooters would sometimes swarm sidewalks, forcing others to yield in ways that were not courteous. This felt like the early days of a product launch where the kinks needed to be worked out.

A few places reacted with bans and heavy regulation, but most cities figured scooters out. They found places to park them, made agreements with providers to keep them policed, and figured out where they could be safely used. Most importantly, the unwritten cultural rules developed, and people began to respond to ancient desires to fit in to a functioning civil society.

Scooters have almost all the upside of bikes in terms of range and accessibility, but also all the requirements for safe streets and, on stroads, protected infrastructure. An evolving Strong Town should have no difficulty embracing scooters.

Transportation Software

Innovations in computer software, including an explosion in phone-based applications, have changed how we use transportation, from maps with real-time traffic data to updates on transit arrivals. There are two that I want to highlight, both for the problem they solve and the controversy they create.

Monkey Parking (https://www.monkeyparking.co/) was an app that allowed an individual who was leaving a parking spot to alert other drivers that the spot was coming available. A frustrated driver looking to park could then bid on that parking spot. The individual leaving would accept the bid, wait for the bidder to show up, and then swap spaces. Monkey Parking handled the transaction.

I love this app, mostly because of what it reveals about the real value of free public parking. In my hometown of Brainerd, as with most American cities, there is such a bizarre amount of free public parking that nobody would ever use Monkey Parking, but in cities like San Francisco — where the app was first launched— free parking is a scarce public good created and sustained at taxpayer expense yet given over for the private use of a few. Monkey Parking was designed to take this windfall and put a dollar amount on it.

This was offensive to many who felt that the people using Monkey Parking were somehow exploiting a public good. They apparently prefer their exploitation of a free public good to happen without the taint of a financial exchange. San Francisco city attorney Dennis Herrera said Monkey Parking created "a predatory private market for public parking spaces,"[1] as if people parking their private vehicle for extended periods in an expensive parking spot provided courtesy of the taxpayer was not predatory.

Monkey Parking revealed an arbitrage opportunity in the market for free public parking. In markets with a scarcity, parking has a high value, but the city was giving it away for free. The just thing for tax-payers would have been for the local government to recoup the public's expense by charging a market rate for the parking. Instead, the city banned Monkey Parking and any copycat apps, choosing to protect the fringe benefit of free public parking provided to a small and random percentage of city residents.

Monkey Parking has reinvented itself as a service for private parking spaces.

The wayfinding app Waze (https://www.waze.com/) has similarly generated controversy for exploiting an undervalued public good, although it has proven more difficult to shut down. Wave is a navigation software that uses crowdsourced information to improve travel times. Users can submit information such as crashes, traffic jams, and speed traps, that are then used to reroute drivers in real time. Waze was purchased by Google in 2013.

The most vocal controversy I have experienced with Waze comes from people who live on shortcut routes that Waze has discovered. Instead of having a sleepy street used primarily by a few locals in the know, they are now inundated with swarms of rush-hour traffic. The desire to have one's shortcut and reserve it too is irrational, but that does not prevent people from blaming Waze.

Again, the fix here is relatively simple: Make the street into an actual street instead of a stroad. Use the design to slow traffic to a neighborhood speed. Put in stops and other friction points so that the value of the shortcut is lost, and the real value of the place is improved.

Instead, I get frequent requests for Strong Towns to join efforts to have Waze banned. The app is doing a public service by using data to identify the worst stroads in each community. Fix the stroads.

Rideshare

Uber was founded in 2009; Lyft in 2012. Before these rideshare services, people were forced to hail a cab without using their phone. They were also forced to pay something closer to a market price for the ride, albeit in a vehicle generally lacking in luxury. The transaction would have happened in cash or, if the passenger really wanted to be annoying, by credit card.

With rideshare, we now schedule and pay for our rides on a phone without having to speak to anyone. Our rides are subsidized by a stock market bubble that has lasted more than a decade now. In 2019, Uber lost $8.5 billion dollars subsidizing our rides[2] and another $5.8 billion through the first three-quarters of 2020,[3] but investors rewarded it by increasing its share price 24 percent from $42 at its May 10, 2019, initial public offering to over $52 at the end of 2020.

Our rides are also subsidized by rideshare drivers themselves, who are general contractors paying for their own vehicle, gas, insurance, maintenance, and self-employment taxes. Pete Adeney, Mr. Money Mustache, suspected that this was not a great deal for the drivers, and so to test his hypothesis, he became one himself. Meticulously tracking his time and expenses, he found that he made roughly $7 an hour, and to maximize his take he was choosy about what trips he accepted.[4] A less discriminating driver would likely make less.

Markets can stay irrational for astoundingly long periods of time, and in a market that devalues labor, there will seemingly always be individuals willing to work a side hustle to make a little bit extra. At the end of the day, rideshare is merely a taxi service using an app with a business model that exploits excess market liquidity and Americans who are bad at math. Those realities may conspire to keep rideshare viable for some time, but I would not count on it to be a transformative presence in a future city.

Self-Driving Vehicles

No transportation technology has more hype or mystique for Americans, especially engineers, planners, and other transportation professionals, than the self-driving car. For many, it is the solution to all of the problems of the automobile. Here is how the *Washington Post* summarized the impact in a feature article in its transportation section:

> Not since the Model T replaced the horse and buggy have transportation and cities faced such an extensive transformation. Many planners say they see an opportunity to prevent — and correct — the 20th-century mistakes of the auto's reign: congestion, pollution, sprawl and roads designed to move vehicles rather than people.[5]

While the technology is impressive, recognize that the only difference between a self-driving vehicle and a taxi is the driver. There are instances where replacing the driver with a computer can bring about significant savings — long-haul truckers and bus drivers being two obvious examples — but the single-occupancy vehicle commuting into the office is not one of them.

The idea that people will pay thousands of dollars for the novelty of a computer driving their vehicle so that they can watch a movie, read a book, or catch up on their email seems more hype than reality. The modest shift from driver to computer bringing sprawl, pollution, and congestion to a halt also seems more fantasy than reality. The idea that cars will park themselves in remote locations to be summoned when needed is nice in theory but does not seem likely to reduce congestion or even passenger stress.

There are two significant changes that self-driving vehicles make possible, both with potential for positive but also severely negative impacts. The first is in reducing the cost of transportation by eliminating human labor, and the second is in improving safety by eliminating most driver errors.

It takes a special kind of person to be a long-haul trucker. I have known a few and they have unique lives with long stretches of both travel and time at home. It is one of the better-compensated blue-collar jobs, with the median pay for a truck driver at a little over $45,000 annually.[6] The *Wall Street Journal* quoted a report by a sociologist, Steve Viscelli, who wrote *The Big Rig: Trucking and the Decline of the American Dream* (University of California Press, 2016), that 294,000 trucking jobs will be lost to automation over the coming two-and-a-half decades.[7] That is a lot of jobs and a lot of potential savings.

The same economics applies to mass transit, where bus and train drivers make up a significant percentage of the ongoing operating costs. Replacing them with a computer could create a significant amount of savings. It would also make deploying more transit a simple matter of acquiring vehicles and dedicating the space instead of needing to hire, train, schedule, and coordinate a workforce.

The technology already exists to do this automation safely on our nation's roads. Right now, self-driving trucks could travel the nation's interstates — particularly overnight — in almost complete safety, arriving on the outskirts of their destination city before rush-hour commuting begins. The same with buses and transit systems that operate on roadways. These simplified environments are ideal for automation, especially if the deployment is tied to a remote monitoring system and a rapid response is in place to handle anomalies such as maintenance problems.

This shift to automation would be a tremendous improvement in safety. Computers do not get tired. They are not distracted. They feel no compulsion to speed or cut corners or do anything that might compromise safety. They are perfectly accountable, with all of their decisions traceable and capable of being learned from. Despite the loss of jobs, the gains should compel us to move ahead rapidly with deploying this technology on our roads.

All of this changes once self-driving vehicles leave the simplified environment of the interstates and begin traveling on the nation's stroads and streets. In these complex environments, self-driving technology is not ready, and it is difficult to predict when it ever will be ready to be deployed.

In a sense, stroads are the reason why we do not already have automated vehicle technology. On a stroad, vehicles are traveling at high speeds. At 30 miles per hour, a vehicle travels at 44 feet per second. At that speed, it takes 43 feet to come to a stop.[8] That is physics; even a computer cannot react any quicker.

I have seen fantasy simulations where vehicles fly through uncontrolled intersections at high speeds, only a couple feet between bumpers with computers handling the flow as if they were routing elections through a switch. What is always missing is the randomness of a city.

For instance, in any transition to automated vehicles, there will be a long period of time where some vehicles are computer driven and some are human operated. Those human drivers will do things that are unpredictable, like randomly stopping, or turning, or changing lanes without signaling. Physics will dictate wide buffers between vehicles, which human drivers will fill, forcing the automated vehicle to create more buffer. In these environments, self-driving vehicles will likely induce more collisions than they prevent.

Ultimately, however, society will reach a condition where all vehicles must be computer driven. There will be a ban on human driving. This will not eliminate the complexity, however, because on our stroads and streets there will still be people biking. There will still be people walking. There will still be the person in a wheelchair or a scooter crossing the street, the kid chasing the ball who runs out into traffic, or the dog that gets loose and is chased by their owner. At present, human drivers handle this kind of complexity better than any computer that could be placed in a vehicle.

Some argue with that assertion, and I have had a number of people suggest that the errors of computers in this environment are tolerable, especially when compared to the errors that humans make. It might be tolerable in an actuarial sense, but not in a social sense. While a person may be able to call their friend being killed in a car crash an "accident," they will not likely be able to forgive a computer that makes a similar error.

Even if computers become better than humans at driving in complex environments, there will still be random mistakes where computers kill humans. I do not see how this will ever be acceptable, so one of two choices will need to be made.

The first is already being proposed by the self-driving vehicle companies as a solution to their coding problem, and that is to simplify the driving environment so that streets are as predictable for the algorithm as a road. In practice, that means erecting a fence along the side of the street so that the computer can safely ignore anything outside of the traffic stream. The fence would be automated to open when red lights stop traffic and allow humans to cross safely.

The second alternative to making self-driving vehicles a reality is to convert stroads to streets and slow all traffic on those streets to safe neighborhood speeds. At 10 miles per hour, breaking distance is just 11 feet for a computer, compared to 43 feet at 30 miles per hour. And someone hit at 10 mph is unlikely to die or even be seriously injured.

Here is the catch: If to bring about a self-driving vehicle revolution you find yourself willing to address safety concerns by fencing off humans from the public realm or dramatically slowing vehicle speeds, what is it about the computer driver that is so enticing? I think fencing off streets would be horrible for cities, but it would solve our safety problems right now, even with human drivers. And if you are willing to slow speeds for computers, then why not for humans? It would bring about the same improvement in safety and we could do it right now.

What I consistently find is that advocates for self-driving cars are enamored with the technology, not the way it will be used or the impact it will have on cities. For them, the self-driving car is the end, not the means to an end. That should scare anyone who cares about the future of cities and it should remind students of history of the early days of automobile adoption, where centuries of accumulated wisdom on city building and humanity were abandoned in pursuit of a shiny object.

There is a chance that I am wrong and that the geniuses working on self-driving vehicles will find a way to have them operate at speed in urban environments, despite the complexity. We will be able to have urban life, including walking, biking, shopping, kids, the elderly, and all the messiness that goes with humanity. It will be perfectly safe, with automated vehicles able to react, maybe even anticipate, and compensate for any potential safety problem. What happens then?

If I know the self-driving car will stop when I step out into the street, I am never going to wait at a stupid traffic signal again. I am never going to stand in the pouring rain waiting for the light to turn. I am never going to stand on the curb in subzero temperatures, wind whipping at my back, hoping for a gap in the flow of traffic. I am just going to step out into the street because the self-driving cars will stop.

I cannot imagine the people of New York, who barely wait on the curb now, standing patiently for their turn when they know for certain the traffic will automatically stop for them. Now we are back to fencing, or policing, or worse scenarios, all because of a fetish with technology.

If you want self-driving vehicles, you can have them right now by limiting them to our nation's roads. That would be a huge advancement. If you want them on our streets, there is a chance that they will work if we eliminate stroads and slow vehicle speeds, although do that and the self-driving vehicle becomes mostly unnecessary.

Boring Technology

On December 17, 2016, Elon Musk tweeted:

> Traffic is driving me nuts. Am going to build a tunnel boring machine and just start digging. . .[9]

It has been difficult for me to get beyond Musk's frustration as I frame my understanding of his tunneling venture, the Boring Company, and the related technology he proposes for it called the hyperloop. Building a tunnel to bypass traffic must be every billionaire's dream — that and a helicopter — but it is a rather bizarre way for a society to fight traffic congestion.

From a practical standpoint, a tunnel has vastly more expense than a surface highway with far less capacity. While hypothetically one could put as many tunnels as needed to handle all possible vehicles, each of those tunnels would need to be maintained over time, something more expensive, not to mention prone to catastrophic failure, than surface roadways. Except as a bypass for the elite, it is unclear what tunnels would accomplish for commuting culture.

The simulations I have seen have a Tesla, an electric vehicle with no emissions, driving through a tunnel. To meet an acceptable metric of human mobility, the people boarding these automobiles at a station are carpooling four to a vehicle. How do they get to this station? Where are their cars parked? Why are they changing to a tunnel carpool? If people are riding together, why use small cars and not just a larger bus with quicker loading and unloading? What do they do once they get to the other end of the tunnel? These questions are rhetorical; this all seems like hype around another technology solution seeking the right problem to solve.

Boring technology has had a revolution over the past two decades. In the late 1990s, I needed to run a pipe under a state highway and, because boring was so expensive, opted to do an open trench, then install a casing pipe with my pipe inside it, then make costly repairs to the highway my project was damaging. If I were engineering this today, boring would by far be the lower-cost option.

The Boring Company is taking these significant advances in engineering and pairing them with other advances in electric vehicles. This is innovative, no doubt, and the cost reductions seem promising, but it is unclear how this is a transportation revolution, let alone useful beyond a niche market. For decades, airports have used driverless trams that operate in tunnels. Beyond industry-wide cost reductions that should continue to make tunneling a more widely available option, there is nothing new here.

People hoping boring technology will allow their city to have subways — underground roads — still have the challenge of building two places that people want to be if they want the connection to be financially viable.

The Hyperloop

The *hyperloop* adds another layer of engineering advancement onto that of the reduced-cost boring by making the tunnel into a large vacuum tube that can transfer a passenger container at high speeds. For short distances, the transfer times are likely to eat into any significant time savings making hyperloop, at best, a marginal improvement over more proven technology. Over long distances, however, it has the potential to be revolutionary.

Perhaps the most significant barrier to constructing high-speed rail in the United States is securing the land to build it on. While boring a tunnel for a hyperloop is far more complicated than building a machine and starting to dig, from a regulatory standpoint and in terms of overall impact, it should be way easier than anything else we might build above ground to achieve similar performance. The ability of hyperloop to be run above ground as well gives it even greater flexibility, especially within existing transportation corridors.

I have traveled from Minneapolis to Chicago many times. Driving, it takes around six hours, assuming there are no major delays. I rode Amtrak a couple times and, discounting the four to eight hours the Empire Builder was late in arriving, that trip took around six hours as well. Flying is even quicker, but with time going through security at the airport, it will be at least two and a half or three hours. Hyperloop could theoretically make the trip in 35 minutes, perhaps an hour counting loading and unloading. That is game-changing.

Hyperloop fits well into a Strong Towns approach as it is designed to function perfectly as a road. There are no stops, interchanges, or other obstacles that would reduce the capacity of moving from one place people want to be to another place that people want to be. It becomes most viable financially at moderate distances like Minneapolis to Chicago (400 miles) where the time for air travel is mostly spent loading and unloading and not in the air. For a trip across the continent, like New York to Los Angeles, airplanes would still outperform a hyperloop, although the latter would be competitive for time and potentially a lot cheaper.

There is every incentive for the private sector to lead on hyperloop. If the technology is viable, the land development potential at the stops is astounding and should cover all of the capital costs. That will likely not prevent companies from asking for subsidies, nor cities competing against each other to hand them out. As always, the best Strong Towns strategy is to build a productive place and use that success to attract investment. There are reasons to be excited about hyperloop, but I would not want my community to be first.

High-Speed Rail

A high-speed rail line between downtown Los Angeles and downtown San Francisco would be an amazing transit road that would provide tremendous value to both places. To build such a connection, the politics of transportation funding requires the state of California to instead build a stroad, adding fourteen stops so that there are enough partners supporting the project to make it politically viable. The reality of modern America is that even a high-speed rail project with the right funding in place is not likely to work.

Many books will be written on the failures of California's attempt to build a high-speed rail between their two largest cities, a project that was initially estimated to cost $34 billion and be operational in 2028 but is now estimated to cost near $100 billion and take until 2033. It seems likely that the only part that will ever be operational is the segment between the mid-size cities of Bakersfield and Merced, cities separated by only a two-and-half-hour drive. Depressingly, despite the extraordinary investment, there is little that can be done without a car at either end of that trip.

Many transit advocates lust for high-speed rail, treating it as a shiny object, something that could be obtained if Americans were not morally and culturally defective, held captive by the oil industry, or just plain addicted to automobiles. Nationwide high-speed rail is a centerpiece of the Green New Deal, the New Deal–inspired legislation sponsored by Rep. Alexandria Ocasio-Cortez (D-NY) and Sen. Ed Markey (D-MA) meant to address climate change, and a variety of other challenges. I appreciate that many people share this dream, but I am not one of them.

While I believe in grand visions — Strong Towns is a grand vision — I do not believe in shortcuts. More specifically, I believe that broadly shared prosperity, the kind that is stable and enduring, is something that must be built together from the bottom up, not something a charismatic personality can impose from the top down by sheer strength or force of will. In a democratic society, it takes humility to co-create something with those around you, especially if that thing is worthy of our aspiration and enduring affection. High-speed rail in America is the opposite of humility, which is why it fails to deliver on its many promises.

We could build high-speed rail if we were willing to become a less democratic society. We could build high-speed rail if we were willing to crowd out more productive activities to make it happen. We could build high-speed rail, but as with all transportation investments, does it serve us, or do we serve it?

If we want high-speed rail, we need to first become competent at the critical aspects of running a low-speed rail system, including how it is financed and sustained over the long term. On this, we are not even close, and so a little like the toddler learning to walk but wanting to run and play with the big kids, we have some maturing to do first. Acknowledging that is not a sign of failure but of strength.

I suggest that we start by building two places worthy of a high-speed rail connection. I suggest we start by building some Strong Towns.

Flying Cars

We were promised these back in the 1950s. Americans are still waiting. I suspect that we will be waiting a long time still. That is not a bad thing, especially considering how much work we must do just to make our cities comfortably walkable. After all, even if we can someday fly around in personalized jet cars, we are still going to need to walk once we arrive at our destination.

Let us do what we can with what we have to make our places more walkable. Everything else we want or need in our cities can build successfully on that, and we don't even need to be able to predict the future to start working on it now.

Notes

1. https://www.strongtowns.org/journal/2014/7/23/the-monkey-parking-arbitrage.html
2. https://www.theverge.com/2020/2/6/21126965/uber-q4-earnings-report-net-loss-revenue-profit-2019
3. https://sf.eater.com/2020/11/6/21552733/uber-eats-earnings-postmates-lossess
4. https://www.mrmoneymustache.com/2017/11/22/mr-money-mustache-uber-driver/
5. https://www.washingtonpost.com/transportation/2019/07/20/city-planners-eye-self-driving-vehicles-correct-mistakes-th-century-auto/
6. https://www.bls.gov/ooh/transportation-and-material-moving/heavy-and-tractor-trailer-truck-drivers.htm
7. https://www.wsj.com/articles/self-driving-technology-threatens-nearly-300-000-trucking-jobs-report-says-1536053401
8. https://nacto.org/docs/usdg/vehicle_stopping_distance_and_time_upenn.pdf
9. https://twitter.com/elonmusk/status/810108760010043392

11

The Routine Traffic Stop

"I submit to you we are one incident away from a powder keg blowing up here in the city of Springfield."

Rev. Talbert Swan, president of the Springfield NAACP[1]

On May 25, 2020, George Floyd was killed while he was being arrested by police in Minneapolis, Minnesota. The incident was recorded by onlookers at the scene. Videos of the white police officer kneeling on the neck of Floyd, slowly choking the life out of the Black man in his custody, were painful to watch. The death of George Floyd sparked protests and rioting across the United States and, to some extent, around the world.

One of the places that experienced demonstrations was Springfield. The protests and marches there were peaceful, with residents voicing their fears and concerns over the police use of force and public officials acknowledging their frustration. A demonstrator, Zulmalee Rivera, was quoted as saying:

"It's like we're fighting a war that we don't know about and it makes you question like if I get stopped by the police like, should I stop or should I just keep going because I probably have a better chance of living running from them than to comply."[2]

183

Springfield has experienced tension between its mostly white police department and the city's minorities and ethnic communities. Nearly a fourth of the city's population claims Puerto Rican descent, while around one in five identify as Black. One Black man, Tony Taylor, relayed his frustration to local media during a demonstration:

"It's 3:00 in the morning, and a cop will stop me and ask me what am I doing out. I'm a grown-ass man. And this stuff has to stop."

One of the gathering spots for demonstrators was Nathan Bill's Bar and Restaurant, an establishment named after a former Springfield park commissioner, Nathan Denison Bill, who served in that capacity for 28 years beginning in 1899. The restaurant is a focal point for demonstrators because of a 2015 incident where four Black men were beaten by off-duty police officers. Indictments against the officers for assault as well as perjury, filing false police reports, and misleading investigators took four years to bring forth.

Six weeks after the George Floyd incident, the Civil Rights Division of the Department of Justice issued a report on their investigation into Springfield's police department. It cited numerous incidents where officers used excessive force, took steps to cover up their actions, and were not held accountable. From the report:

Following a thorough investigation, there is reasonable cause to believe that Narcotics Bureau officers engage in a pattern or practice of excessive force in violation of the Fourth Amendment of the United States Constitution.

Specifically, our investigation identified evidence that Narcotics Bureau officers repeatedly punch individuals in the face unnecessarily, in part because they escalate encounters with civilians too quickly, and resort to unreasonable takedown maneuvers that, like head strikes, could reasonably be expected to cause head injuries. This pattern or practice of excessive force is directly attributable to systemic deficiencies in policies, accountability systems, and training.[3]

The report recommends changes to how officer use of force is reported, how cases are reviewed, how officers are trained, and how the department is held accountable. A particular recommendation stood out for what it suggested about the problems discovered.

New training curricula should explicitly address the importance of avoiding fist strikes to the head, neck, and face area, and avoiding kicking suspects.

Springfield is a difficult place to be in law enforcement. Various rankings put Springfield in a category of "most dangerous" city, something many residents will dispute but for which there is statistical evidence to support. Both violent and nonviolent crime in Springfield is consistently above both state and national averages.

The flash point for much of this crime is the routine traffic stop. I reviewed a week of Springfield's arrest reports and found that, of the 42 individuals arrested, half of them were charged with some traffic-related offense or were booked simultaneously, and with related charges, to someone who was.[4] It seems reasonable to assume that the latter were likely passengers in the same vehicle.

The charges include things such as concealed licensed plates, unlicensed operation of a motor vehicle, driving with a suspended license, crossing marked lanes, speeding, failure to stop or yield, lack of insurance, and lack of registration, but they were typically accompanied by other offenses — things most people would deem quite serious.

For example, one individual booked on September 6, 2020, was charged with operating a motor vehicle with a suspended license. Simultaneously, they were also charged with multiple drug possession charges, including one distribution charge, along with a charge of receiving stolen property.

A few days later, an individual was charged with crossing marked lanes, operating a motor vehicle with a suspended license, lack of insurance, and lack of registration. At the same time, the same individual was charged with drug possession and purchasing sex.

Most dramatically, near the end of the week, an individual was booked for operating a motor vehicle without a license and having license plates that were concealed. They were also charged with multiple firearms violations, including possession of a machine gun, along with assault with a deadly weapon.

The process whereby a traffic stop turns into an arrest varies but is familiar to anyone who has watched an episode of the show *Cops*. A driver of a motor vehicle violates a traffic law or does something suspicious. This is noticed by a police officer, who pursues the driver and has them stop their vehicle. As the interaction between officer and driver unfolds, the officer's suspicion is confirmed, and illegal activities are uncovered.

This report of an incident by WWLP News gives one rendition of this process. I have removed the name of the suspect because it is not important to this narrative.

> A Springfield man was arrested Thursday night after officers conducted a traffic stop on Walsh Street and seized a loaded semi-automatic large-capacity firearm.
>
> According to Springfield Police spokesman Ryan Walsh, officers saw the driver of a pick-up truck, 37-year-old [suspect], speeding on Walsh Street and then

run a stop sign while turning onto Wilbraham Road. Officers then stopped him on Archie Street when [suspect] got out and allegedly started running. Two passengers were still in the truck.

Walsh said while [suspect] was running he dropped a bag in the backyard of a home on Archie Street. Inside the bag, officers seized a semi-automatic large capacity firearm loaded with 15 rounds in the magazine as well as a bank card belonging to [suspect].[5]

To catch a criminal in this way seems like a triumph of law enforcement. It is undoubtedly brave, the officers clearly endangering their own lives by giving chase to a desperate individual, one with a high-capacity weapon. Yet few police interactions are this dangerous. Even in a city like Springfield, only a small percentage of all traffic stops end with even an arrest or any serious charges.

Go back to Tony Taylor, the Black man who relayed his frustration to local media.

"It's 3:00 in the morning, and a cop will stop me and ask me what am I doing out. I'm a grown-ass man. And this stuff has to stop."

To the extent that there is a powder keg ready to blow in Springfield, the powder has accumulated largely from thousands of routine traffic stops, incidents where no serious charges were filed or arrests made. These often small slights and seemingly random indignities add up, creating a shared experience among Springfield residents that is affirmed by official reports of police abuse.

If that powder keg finally blows, the spark that lights it will almost certainly be an incident that begins with a routine traffic stop.

Traffic Stop as Pretext

I ran my own planning and engineering firm for a dozen years starting in 2000. One day, one of my colleagues named Tim Schmidt returned from a site visit in a visibly agitated state. He was slamming things and raising his voice, behavior quite out of character. Tim had gotten pulled over by a police officer for rolling through a stop sign in the neighboring city of Breezy Point. He received a ticket for the infraction.

"The crazy thing is, I had come to a complete stop," I remember Tim saying. Based on my experiences in Breezy Point, I believed him.

Years prior, I filled in as the interim city administrator for Breezy Point while they were searching for a permanent replacement. In that capacity, I had a chance to meet with the police chief. He was a nice enough guy, and certainly well-liked in the community, but his approach to law enforcement made me uncomfortable.

He told me that he instructed his officers to be aggressive in pulling people over. He told me that they would look for any reason to make a stop and then use that interaction as a stepping-stone of sorts to look for bigger things. Did the driver sound a little strange? Get them out of the car for an intoxication test. Run their license and check for warrants. Pry around and see if you smell marijuana (or something like it) to justify a more comprehensive inspection.

The chief bragged that they had nailed a lot of bad people this way — individuals who had warrants or other red flags on their records. Often, they would be able to seize the vehicle or other property and sell that at auction, with at least part of the proceeds retained by the police department through a process I still do not fully understand. In the short time I was there, whenever the police chief wanted a new piece of equipment and there wasn't money in the budget, he would seek authorization to use the asset forfeiture fund, which was off budget and had an unknown balance (at least to me — and I tried to get access).

So when my colleague said that he was pulled over for no reason, I had little difficulty believing him. I had been pulled over myself in Breezy Point on a few occasions. One instance was for a taillight being out. A mouse had chewed through the wires in my car and I spent hundreds of dollars trying to get it fixed, but there was something loose that we could not isolate and repair. When the bulb went out, if I pounded on the light in the right place, it would flicker back on. I told this to the officer, and he allowed me to perform that trick if I would also open the trunk so that he could see inside. My light back on and my trunk voluntarily searched, I was allowed to go on my way without a citation.

I have experienced what I am sure is a disproportionate number of interactions with the police. One time, as a way to shame me as a hypocrite for something I said about slowing down traffic, someone looked up my driving record and posted a screenshot on social media. The online trolls taunted me because I had seven moving violations, but I knew that was only the tip of the iceberg.

During my consulting days, there were years when I put 50,000 or more miles on my car driving all over the state of Minnesota. A high percentage of these miles were late at night in rural areas, places where the local police officer was often waiting for the infrequent car to drive through the 55 mph to 30 mph transition on the edge of town. From a design standpoint, these are classic speed traps. The only notable characteristic of these transition zones is a sign with a new speed limit, which is seemingly random given the lack of change in the roadway or anything adjacent to it that might signal the need to slow down for an approaching civilization.

I once got a speeding ticket for going 40 in a 30-mph zone. When I drove past the patrol car, he rapidly turned around and I acknowledged his presence by immediately pulling over to the side of the road. Right in front of my parked car was a sign indicating a 55-mph speed limit. When the officer informed me that I was going 40 mph, I pointed to the sign.

"Right there, the sign says 55," I protested.

"You can't go 55 until you get *to* the sign," he informed me. I remember I received a ticket on that one.

I had a long streak where I would not get a ticket when I was wearing a tie, which I frequently was because I was heading home from a meeting in some small town somewhere. When I was not wearing a tie, it seemed like an automatic ticket. So I bought a clip-on tie and kept it close at hand. At the first indication of flashing lights, I would reach for my tie. If I was wearing a coat, I would make sure it was unzipped and open so my professional status was overt.

Once, my best friend Mike Tester and I were leaving Moondance Jam, a music festival where a band we were part of was serving as the regional host band. I do not drink alcohol, and Mike had not been drinking either, but traveling 60 mph in a 55 zone (a speed generally slower than traffic) gave the officer an excuse to pull us over and check. He asked us numerous times if we had been drinking, a reasonable presumption given where we were coming from. "We weren't drinking; we are musicians," Mike offered from the passenger seat, an unhelpful testimonial that has become a recurring punchline in our friendship. I got a ticket for speeding that time too. No alcohol, but also no tie.

It is worth noting that, in all these interactions I had with police officers, I was breaking the law. None of these officers were wrong in pulling me over. By the letter of the law, they were justified each and every time. Even my colleague, Tim Schmidt, who I am sure came to a stop, at least in the manner we might all commonly understand, probably technically broke the law in not having arrested all forward momentum for a sufficient length of time.

It is also worth noting that, while these traffic stops were legal and legitimate, the primary reason for them was never traffic safety. It was never about enforcing traffic laws specifically as a way to ensure the general welfare.

I also do not believe that these stops were about raising revenue or seizing assets, although I understand the bad incentives and outlier examples that lead many to such cynicism.

No, the traffic stops were always a pretext for something else. They were a way for police officers to make contact with humans, something police and security officials have found necessary throughout the entire history of organized human settlement, yet is impossible to do in modern times while vehicles are in motion.

The Investigatory Traffic Stop

There is widespread nostalgia in the United States for the concept of cops walking the beat. We like to think of law enforcement of the past as having an opportunity to know their rounds and the people in their direct care intimately. We intuitively understand that this is better than a system where the people enforcing the laws are nameless, faceless, and live apart from the places they serve.

Radley Balco writes in *Rise of the Warrior Cop*:

> In the United States, early police officers were nominated by ward leaders and political bosses, then appointed by the mayor. Cops were required to live in the wards they patrolled. All of this tended to make early police departments more like service agencies than law enforcement bodies. Since ward leaders were elected, they found they could pressure local commanders to prioritize police duties in ways that would help them get reelected. In some neighborhoods, police officers ran soup kitchens and homeless people were given shelter in police stations to sleep.

Getting to know the normal rhythm of a neighborhood allows a police officer to work proactively. The vehicle backed up to the front door of a house might be there because a new family is moving in, or it could be that the family is out of town and someone is stealing their stuff. The anonymous police officer patrolling in a vehicle is less likely

than the officer who walks the neighborhood to be positioned to proactively discern the difference.

Of course, discernment requires an officer to use their knowledge
and understanding to make inferences about what is going on. If the
vehicle being loaded looks like a moving van and the people doing the
loading wave to the officer in a friendly manner, all seems well, even
though it might not be. If the vehicle is not typical for the neighborhood and the people loading it seem startled or in a hurry, all could be
fine, but a closer look may be warranted.

This is called *profiling*. We are evolved to be a very social species,
and so humans make these kinds of judgments all the time. In our
past, there were enormous advantages conveyed to those of our ancestors who were perceptive, particularly about the intentions of other
humans. The modern human brain has inherited these traits and is
naturally wired to make snap decisions with only scant information.

We expect police officers to profile — to be on the alert for that
which may be problematic — because we want them to prevent crime
from occurring. We make heroes out of police officers who, acting on
a hunch, took some decisive action to foil criminal behavior. There
is a long list of novels, movies, and television dramas based on this
very premise.

Even so, in a society dedicated to free and equal treatment for
all under the law, profiling can also be deeply problematic. Should
police officers profile people based on their race? Most of us, I believe,
would say that they should not. How about an individual's social class,
something often projected in the make of automobile a person chooses
to drive? This also seems coarse and distasteful, yet it also seems very
reasonable to infer that an older white male, in a high-end car, driving
slowly, late at night, through an area known for prostitution, might be
up to something nefarious. Would we discourage a police officer from
acting on their intuition because those insights are primarily based on
race and class?

It is important to note that, in the instances I have described where
I was pulled over, I was also profiled. Driving under the influence is a
serious problem in rural Minnesota. More so than during the middle
of the day, a higher percentage of vehicles driving into a small town
after 11:00 p.m. on a weeknight are likely to be driven by someone
who has had too much to drink. The police officer sitting on the edge
of town, at that time of night, pulling over speeders, is simply acting
like a grizzly bear at the edge of the river during a salmon run; they

know where and when to be positioned to have the highest likelihood of finding what they are after. "Late Night Driver" is a profile.

Profiling is also why I rarely received a citation. Once the police officer determined that I was a professional wearing a tie on my way home from a meeting, that I was not slurring my words or otherwise disoriented, I ceased to be interesting. I clearly was not a drunk driver. Like a grizzly reaching for a salmon and instead grabbing a stick floating in the stream, it is best to throw your catch back and try again. With me, the officer did not find what they were looking for. "Professional Driving Home" is also a profile.

In the urgent quest to reduce drunk driving fatalities, the police officer was using the pretext of a legitimate traffic stop to fish for drunk drivers. If this were truly about traffic safety, the police department would continually post an officer at the edge of town, literally all day, to pull over drivers because a very high percentage of cars that pass such places are driven faster than the posted speed. No police department does this because the investigatory traffic stop is not about traffic safety. It is not related to some theory of public well-being that correlates broken taillights and lapsed registration with traffic deaths. The investigatory traffic stop is about using traffic laws to stop a vehicle in order to make contact with the humans inside.

Enforcement is Discretionary

Philando Castile was shot dead by a St. Anthony, Minnesota, police officer during a routine traffic stop on July 6, 2016. The pretext for the stop was that the taillight of Castile's vehicle was allegedly out, but the officer, Jeronimo Yanez, also made this statement to dispatchers:

> "The two occupants just look like people that were involved in a robbery. The driver looks more like one of our suspects, just because of the wide-set nose. I couldn't get a good look at the passenger."[6]

Traffic regulations provided the legal pretext for making this stop, but Yanez was fishing for a robbery suspect. He thought Castile and his passenger, a woman named Diamond Reynolds, might be the robbers (they were not). Before he approached the vehicle, Yanez radioed another squad car and told those officers that he wanted to check the identification of the driver and passenger. It all went terribly wrong. Yanez ended up firing into the vehicle seven times, killing Castile while Reynolds and her 4-year-old daughter, who was in the back seat, escaped injury.

Castile was only 32 years old when he died, but he had already been pulled over by police 49 times.[7] This might suggest that he was a reckless or dangerous driver. Upon closer examination, it is clear that he was repeatedly profiled, with traffic infractions being the pretext for an investigatory stop.

Here is how this was reported in the *Minneapolis Star Tribune*:

"Castile had been stopped before, when officers spotted him not wearing a seat belt, or when an officer ran his plate number and found his license had been revoked for not paying an earlier fine. Numerous stops came after he didn't use a turn signal. A few came after he was speeding. He was stopped for rolling through a right turn on a red light, having window tints that were too dark, and at least twice for not having a rear license plate light. He was rarely ticketed for the reason he was stopped."[8]

Many have argued that Castile was profiled solely because of his race. There is certainly statistical evidence supporting the contention that police departments have a disproportionate number of interactions with Black populations. A counter narrative suggests that police go where the crime is, and that Blacks are disproportionately targeted because Black neighborhoods have a disproportionate amount of crime. There is a circular nature to these two arguments, particularly when it comes to traffic enforcement.

The many infractions that Philando Castile was pulled over for are things that most of us do on a daily basis. Rolling through a right turn is a good example. Slightly speeding is another. With our roads, streets, and stroads designed using the principles of forgiving design, most people feel safe, and in fact are safe nearly all of the time, operating a vehicle outside of what is strictly proscribed by law.

Park a police cruiser in an upscale suburban neighborhood, and that officer could continuously conduct investigative traffic stops based on the violations they observe. And when they pulled people over for minor infractions, if they were tenacious and so inclined, they would occasionally uncover evidence of more serious criminal activity. Soccer moms rolling through stop signs or driving a few miles over the speed limit are not perceived as warranting this kind of policing, and that has nothing to do with traffic safety.

Almost all American drivers have experienced a point where the vehicle they are in is passed by a police cruiser, the officer exceeding the speed limit to do so, only to witness that vehicle pull into a café or coffee shop parking lot where other officers are gathering for what is clearly not an emergency situation. In 2013, ABC News did a segment on speeding cops and showed numerous examples where police officers drove at excessive speeds — sometimes 25 miles per hour or more above the legal limit — to nonurgent destinations such as Dunkin Donuts, without any sirens or flashers.[9]

It is easy to call these officers hypocrites, and ABC News did confront many of them in cringe-worthy ways, but I hesitate to call them all reckless, especially those traveling within the flow of traffic. There is a scene from a YouTube video called "Speed Kills Your Pocketbook" where a police officer using a radar detector notes that every driver on a busy roadway is speeding.

> "Everybody's been speeding. We haven't seen a single person that's been doing the speed limit here."[10]

If traffic laws are about public safety, police officers would not frequently and casually speed. If public safety is simply about enforcing the law, then police officers would just pull people over continuously. Our streets are designed to facilitate speeding, and they generally succeed. Police departments could do nonstop enforcement of traffic laws as drivers everywhere are continuously breaking one of a myriad of traffic-related regulations. They do not do this.

The decision by a police officer to intervene is then, nearly always, completely discretionary. The officer decides when, where, and under what circumstances they will enforce traffic laws. This makes traffic enforcement arbitrary; a random occurrence that is largely unrelated to safe driving.

Efforts to build safe transportation systems are undermined by this approach to policing. The irony is that good policing is likewise undermined by our approach to transportation.

An Impossible Situation

We have put police officers in an impossible situation. Since the widespread adoption of the automobile, changes to American cities have tended to isolate police officers physically from the populations that they serve. Sequestered in a vehicle, increasingly surrounded by electronic devices, officers must base their human hunches on only a few data points, many of which seem, intentionally or not, to reinforce stereotypes based on race and class.

We then ask them to police neighborhoods where the layout and design of the place they are policing induces residents to commit minor infractions continuously. Traffic laws are constantly being broken; taillights go out unexpectedly, drivers fail to come to a complete stop, and people improperly use their turn signals, to name just a few common instances. While nearly all of these laws have some basis in safety, it is rare that they present an urgent threat to the public.

In a community of near continuous breaking of minor codes, police officers must decide which of these nonurgent laws to enforce and when to enforce them. It should surprise nobody that police departments have chosen to use this discretion to pursue more serious criminals — those who pose an urgent threat to society.

To find these dangerous individuals, law enforcement uses their discretionary authority to target areas with high crime or areas where criminals are believed to pass through. They use minor traffic infractions as a basis for pulling people over and having human interaction. The higher the volume of people pulled over, the greater number of serious criminals the department is going to apprehend.

Yet the higher the volume of people pulled over, the greater the number of non-criminals with whom the police are going to have interactions. For the driver being pulled over, traffic stops can be terrifying. For the safety of the officer, the driver is treated as dangerous until proven otherwise. Bright lights are shined in their face and normal movements such as reaching for a license or registration can be misinterpreted as aggressive action.

Add to that the sheer indignity of being treated like a criminal in a public space while friends and neighbors pass by and take notice. Police officers are the only members of society authorized to use lethal force, a monopoly on violence that creates a massive imbalance in power in these exchanges. For the driver, these interactions can be traumatic experiences, even when the police officer is friendly and no citation is given.

None of this is to suggest that these are pleasant experiences for law enforcement. The routine traffic stop is one of the most dangerous duties a police officer performs. John Gnagey, executive director of the National Tactical Officers Association, was reported as saying:

> "Traffic stops and domestic violence are the highest-risk calls. You have no idea what you're walking into. If I had to rank them, I'd rank traffic stops first and domestic violence second."[11]

The National Law Enforcement Officers Memorial Fund tracks the number of officers who are killed in the line of duty. Their reports contain statistics, but also case studies detailing the experiences of officers being assaulted, shot at, shot and killed, run over with a vehicle, smashed into while still inside their vehicle, and other acts of violence while conducting traffic stops. One of their reports indicates:

> Traffic Stops continued to be the most common self-initiated incident that led to officer fatalities, accounting for 38, or 52 percent, of all 73 Self-Initiated Activity cases examined. The public encounters law enforcement officers most often during these stops for traffic violations; therefore, it makes sense that these stops are the independent enforcement action with the highest number of law enforcement fatalities.[12]

This entire approach has created a series of negative feedback loops our society is struggling to address.

Police target areas they perceive as high crime. When they discover criminal activity, which they inevitably do given the approach, it reinforces the initial perception. There is no control group receiving equally aggressive policing to create comparable statistics.

People living in targeted areas feel under siege. Each time they are pulled over for frivolous infractions, it affirms their correct perception that they are being treated differently than others within society. Occasionally, their understandable frustration turns into belligerence.

When suspects act belligerent during a traffic stop, police rightfully fear for their lives. The officers are carrying weapons, after all, and if they are not careful those weapons can be taken and used against them. The presence of a firearm creates tension and the possibility for rapid escalation, regardless of the intentions of any of the parties involved.

Repeat this pattern over and over thousands of times a day across the country and it is statistically inevitable that a tragedy will result. People pulled over in traffic stops will be killed by police. Americans have become acutely cognizant of this recurring phenomenon. And police will be killed by people they pull over, a frequent occurrence about which law enforcement officers are keenly aware.

Worse, honorable people will be able to look at many of these incidents and come to radically different interpretations of what occurred.

There is only one way to arrest this cycle and fix what is a seemingly impossible situation: We must end the routine traffic stop as a law enforcement technique.

A Safer Alternative for Everyone

If we want to keep police officers and the public safe while reducing the number of negative interactions with law enforcement, and if we desire a country where the rules not only matter but their enforcement is fair and equitably applied, then we need to end the routine traffic stop.

If we want to experience safety on our roads and streets, then we need an approach to safety that does not burden law enforcement officers — the only members of our society given the authority to use lethal force — with nonserious matters. We need to stop asking law enforcement to compensate for our negligent approach to design.

Traffic enforcement is important. It is too important to be discretionary and too important to be entangled with wider law enforcement objectives. We must create an enforcement response where nonurgent matters are handled differently than those where we have immediate fear for the public's safety.

There is entire list of technical violations that should never meet the threshold for a traffic stop. Driving without a seatbelt, a busted taillight, expired registration, failure to come to a complete stop, modest levels of speeding, and a long list of other violations of the law do not rise to the level of requiring immediate police contact.

These infractions need to be enforced, but that enforcement should happen electronically without direct contact. With the number of cameras and the amount of electronics in a typical police cruiser, it would be a modest exercise to establish a system for officers to document verbally the infraction and then send whatever video they have to a clerk who can issue the citation. The documentation can be appended to a file that could be reviewed by a judge should the citation be challenged.

We should reserve traffic stops for violations that pose an immediate threat to public safety. Driving more than 10 miles per hour over the speed limit, running a stop sign or a red light, or having reasonable cause to suspect a driver is under the influence are all serious threats that require immediate action. Let us reserve our most dangerous tactic, the routine traffic stop, for these situations.

All the violation data needs to feed back into a planning and design prioritization system. We can no longer ask law enforcement personnel to risk their lives to compensate for poor engineering. That means if a design is not achieving the desired outcome, that design needs to be changed.

If a high percentage of people are speeding along a stretch of road, either the speed limit is wrong, or the road design is wrong. There is no viable third option. We do not live in a society of deviants, so if a design is inducing people to break the law, that design must be fixed.

For widespread speeding on a street, there are not even two options. If a significant number of drivers on a street are speeding, the design is wrong and it must be changed. The design team must continue to iterate until the 85th percentile speed is below a safe speed. Only then can law enforcement be properly deployed to handle the real deviant behavior.

The city's design team needs to monitor the data and identify situations where people are running red lights, making illegal or improper turns, or performing other dangerous maneuvers. Where there are trends indicating high levels of lawbreaking, something is wrong with the design that should be given attention.

Once these systems are in place and there is a process for law enforcement and engineering to work together to fix designs, reduce the number of violations, and allow law enforcement personnel to focus on the most dangerous infractions, then the community is prepared to have a discussion on deploying cameras.

I have saved a discussion on cameras for last because, in my experience, it is the most difficult part of the enforcement conversation for people to think clearly about. I have found that most people have strong opinions on enforcement cameras.

There are those who believe that they are essential to creating safe streets and that the presence of red-light cameras or cameras to catch speeders improves safety. For reasons that prior chapters have hopefully made clear, I do not believe this to be true, although I am sympathetic to people who do. In the absence of a true commitment to safety, installing cameras can feel like some action is being done, that people are being punished for breaking the law. We need to move beyond this and build a real culture of safety.

There are others who believe that cameras are something synonymous with a police state, or that they are used merely as a mechanism to raise revenue. I will admit to being more sympathetic to this point of view, particularly as I have witnessed cameras be deployed across the country. One particularly egregious example I am familiar with is in Cedar Rapids, Iowa, where the police department is raising millions for their police fund through camera enforcement.

A January 10, 2020, news article from the *Cedar Rapids Gazette* reports that an average of 756 automated traffic tickets are being issued each day.[13] The city estimates that $11.4 million in fines will be issued during the year. That is $209 per household in this city of just over 133,000. A police captain was quoted in the article as saying, "Way too many motorists have been speeding." Yet, with the number of citations increasing, it is difficult to argue that these cameras are doing anything but generating revenue for the city. Without a response beyond the cameras, the public safety argument lacks credibility.

The way to give an automated ticketing program validity is two-fold. First, there must be a design response committed to reducing the number of violations over time. We do not run public safety as an Internet company might, inducing people to take an action and then acting as rentiers when they do. Using the cameras to gather data and set design priorities is essential. In places where speeding is the norm, it is unethical to use speed cameras to entrap people with bad design.

Second, the cameras must be deployed based on road and street design characteristics, not neighborhood demographics or other social factors. If there is a problem with speeding near highway interchanges, then all such places should have a camera installed simultaneously. The affluent person in their high-end vehicle must have the same opportunity to become a data point as the poor person with the old rusty car.

There are good reasons to consider ways to assist poor people who are caught in a cycle of fines and penalties, but if we're deploying cameras primarily to improve safety, then gathering driver data needs to be treated as a scientific pursuit, as blind to non-safety factors as possible.

Ending the routine traffic stop and replacing it with a commitment to addressing bad road and street design is the way we prioritize safety in a Strong Town. It also happens to be the way we build a more just society.

A Strong Towns Approach

We need to recognize that getting people out of their vehicles is the greatest thing we can do to improve public safety. The more that people walk and bike instead of drive, the safer we all become. More people biking and walking is also the most important thing that we can do to reduce tension and increase understanding between law enforcement and the people they serve.

We must divide our traffic enforcement response between serious and nonserious situations.

Serious violations should continue to utilize the traffic stop. Nonserious, nonurgent violations should be processed through a system where infractions are documented, and the owner of the vehicle notified by mail. This is similar to the approach used in other aspects of law enforcement, such as parking meter violations.

Violations data should be actively shared with engineering and design personnel. There needs to be a program for responding to places where violations routinely occur. The goal of a response program must be to use redesign techniques on the road or street to reduce the number of violations over time.

When such a program is in place, only then can automated enforcement devices be deployed. Their deployment should be in locations identified by traffic data or design characteristics. Where an excessive number of infractions occur, the sending of citations should be suspended until the problematic design features are corrected.

Recognize that law enforcement cannot compensate for bad road and street design. Most people will obey traffic laws when those laws are in harmony with the design. Traffic stops are dangerous for everyone and should be reserved for only the most serious offenses.

The latest from Strong Towns on traffic enforcement and routine traffic stops is available at www.confessions.engineer.

Notes

1. https://www.nepm.org/post/weekend-protests-common-message-wildly-different-tactics#stream/0
2. https://www.westernmassnews.com/news/demonstrators-gathered-in-springfield-to-protest-the-death-of-george-floyd/article_7a3a279a-a1e2-11ea-b8a9-ff04d15841f0.html
3. https://assets.documentcloud.org/documents/6983670/Spd-Investigative-Report-7-8-20-Final-Version-0.pdf
4. https://www.springfield-ma.gov/police/fileadmin/Police_Dept_files/arrest_logs/2020/arrestlog_2020_09_12.pdf

5. https://www.wwlp.com/news/crime/springfield-man-arrested-after-traffic-stop-loaded-firearm-seized/

6. https://www.startribune.com/police-audio-officer-stopped-philando-castile-on-robbery-suspicion/386344001/

7. https://www.nytimes.com/2016/07/17/us/before-philando-castiles-fatal-encounter-a-costly-trail-of-minor-traffic-stops.html

8. https://www.startribune.com/castile-lived-in-a-cycle-of-traffic-stops-fines/387046341/

9. https://www.youtube.com/watch?v=GieR7zepu5M&feature=emb_title

10. https://www.youtube.com/watch?v=2BKdbxX1pDw&t=1s

11. https://www.orlandosentinel.com/news/os-xpm-2010-12-09-os-traffic-stops-deadly-20101209-story.html

12. Making It Safer: A Study of Law Enforcement Fatalities Between 2010–2016. https://www.hsdl.org/?abstract&did=809129

13. https://www.thegazette.com/subject/news/government/cedar-rapids-traffic-camera-tickets-declining-but-on-pace-to-double-revenue-projection-20200110

12

Reforming Transportation Professions

In the winter of 2015, I received a notice from the board of licensing that a complaint had been filed against me regarding my conduct as a licensed professional engineer. The complaint indicated that I had engaged in "misconduct on the website/blog Strong Towns" for things I had written critical of the engineering profession. The board, which oversees licensing for a broad range of professional pursuits, has the power to sanction licensed engineers with reprimands, censure, significant fines, and suspension. It even has the power to strip an engineer of their license.

The complaint against me was filed by a former fellow of the American Society of Civil Engineers, an organization about which I have been an outspoken critic. At the time, he was also an active member of Move MN, a transportation advocacy coalition of contractors, engineers, trade unions, bike advocates, and others in my home state. Move MN was lobbying the legislature to approve a large increase in transportation funding. I was an opponent of Move MN and had written many columns questioning the proposed legislation.

The complaint against me alleged that my writing and advocacy was in violation of Minnesota rules governing the conduct and behavior of licensed engineers. If that allegation surprises you, if you believe my right to state my opinions publicly is protected by the First Amendment to the U.S. Constitution, then you are not aware of the way that state licensing boards, and the process of licensure or certification, are routinely used to silence dissent.

Here is what Minnesota Rules 1805.0200 requires for the personal conduct of licensed engineers:

> A licensee shall avoid any act which may diminish public confidence in the profession and shall, at all times, conduct himself or herself, in all relations with clients and the public, so as to maintain its reputation for professional integrity.

This is the law in my state. Most states have adopted similar language. States require engineers to conduct themselves in ways that maintain the reputation of the engineering profession, but what does that mean?

Clearly, conduct like cheating clients or committing fraud during the practice of engineering should be grounds for some kind of action. Signing plans or validating work that is outside one's area of expertise is another area where a sanction is likely warranted. As an engineer, I want complaints of negligence or incompetence of fellow engineers investigated, especially when people's lives are in danger. All of this relates to the board's role in protecting the health, safety, and welfare of the state's residents.

Yet, the law, as written, is broad and open to much interpretation. For example, will this book diminish public confidence in the engineering profession? I am positive that it will, at least in the short term, although not in the same way that an engineer committing fraud or displaying incompetence as part an actual project would.

Does my vocal opposition to the way the United States currently funds transportation undermine the reputation of the engineering profession? I suspect that it does, at least to a degree. Those who have read this far in this book are likely to be at least skeptical, if not hostile, to the notion of pouring more capital into subsidizing stroad construction, highway expansion, or unproductive transit systems.

So, I am, as the complaint alleged, conducting myself in violation of state law, but who is this law designed to protect? Does it protect society at large, or does it protect the engineering firms who have thrown their weight behind efforts to secure more transportation funding. Does it protect the vulnerable, or does it protect the engineer who does their work with confidence that industry standards will shield them from liability, regardless of the outcome?

Since I started Strong Towns, more licensed engineers than I am capable of recalling have told me privately that they support what I am doing but are afraid to say so publicly because of fear over their license. They fear having a complaint filed against them, of being reprimanded, censured, or even losing their license. This fear is so pervasive that my colleagues and I were compelled to create space for engineers to share their opinions anonymously through the Strong Towns website. The columnist "R. Moses" is a compilation of anonymous engineers sharing their insights and opinions in a way that does not threaten their livelihoods.

These are not unfounded fears. The complaint filed against me in 2015 was a clear attempt to discredit or silence me, as well as a push to intimidate others who might be tempted to join me. The licensing board found "no violation" but warned that my file could be reopened "should additional evidence warrant" doing so. Others have not gotten off so lightly.

The most high-profile recent example is that of Mats Järlström, an engineer living in Oregon whose wife received a red-light-camera citation that prompted him to investigate the ways that signals are timed. Järlström discerned that the equations used to time yellow light intervals were wrong because they failed to account for human behavior. He communicated his findings with state transportation officials and, when they were unwilling to consider adjustments, began to speak publicly about it.

This is when Järlström drew the attention of the state licensing board. As reported by the Institute of Justice, which helped bring a lawsuit on Järlström's behalf against Oregon's engineering board:

> After a two-year investigation, the board fined Mats $500 and said that he could not talk about traffic lights in public until he obtained a state-issued professional-engineer license. If Mats continued to "critique" traffic lights, he would face thousands of dollars in fines and up to one year in jail for the unlicensed practice of engineering. The board also said that Mats could not call himself an "engineer," even though he has a degree in electrical engineering and decades of engineering experience. Like most engineers in Oregon, Mats is not a state-licensed "professional engineer," and state law provided that only licensed professional engineers could legally use the title "engineer."[1]

The judge ruled in favor of Järlström, restoring to him his First Amendment rights to speak freely on the matter. I do not make a living as a professional engineer, and while my license provides me credibility in some circles, it is not necessary to do the work I undertake. I can risk being sanctioned in order to say things that must be said because, in doing so, I do not also gamble with my livelihood. It is a problem that all licensed engineers are not as secure to speak their minds.

While professional licensing and the state-appointed boards that oversee the process can serve a valuable role, they too often are used as tools merely to wield and maintain power. My book *Strong Towns: A Bottom-Up Revolution to Rebuild American Prosperity* is about shifting power from top-down systems to an approach that does a better job of understanding, reflecting, and serving the needs of people. This book expands on that power dynamic.

What needs to be clear to everyone is this: engineers and transportation planners serve society, not the other way around.

Thwarting Public Will

As a professional engineer, I was both angry and ashamed to read the 2019 letter from the Springfield Director of Public Works, Christopher Cignoli, to council members Jesse Lederman, Marcus Williams, and Andy Gomez (first referenced in Chapter 4). In asking for a signalized pedestrian crossing in front of the library, the council members were responding to the legitimate concerns of their constituents regarding safety on State Street. These elected officials were frustrated, and rightly so; many prior attempts to raise concerns over State Street and seek some remedy to improve safety were met with intransigence and inaction by the city's staff.

To have some relief, these council members were attempting to do the job their transportation professionals were unwilling to do and identify a remedy to an urgent problem. In the written response from Cignoli, they received no acknowledgment of their legitimate concerns. Instead, they were subjected to a litany of insider jargon and circular reasoning. It was condescending. The letter made clear throughout that their nonexpert opinions were not only unwelcome, but they were also unworthy of even being taken seriously.

Sadly, this practice is not uncommon. The letter from Cignoli contains four methods that I have frequently witnessed traffic engineers and transportation professionals use to assert their power to thwart the will of elected officials and the public. They are all unbecoming of a profession that is supposed to be about public service.

The first is a focus on process instead of outcomes. Time and again I have watched engineers and planners talk down to public officials, minimizing their concerns by pretending that some long and sanctified process of deliberation goes into every prior action taken. The Cignoli letter is overflowing with such condescension, starting in the second paragraph, where it says:

> "While this item has been discussed for a number of years, I will again provide all of the necessary background information and design issues that have been considered in the past."

Cignoli's irritation is barely subtext. In professional-speak, he is saying, "You annoyingly simple people, must I explain myself yet again?" I touch on this aspect first because the arrogance deeply bothers me. Safety on State Street keeps coming up because people keep getting hit, people keep being killed, and those responsible for an obviously dangerous situation, those like Cignoli who could do something about it, have shown themselves unwilling even to acknowledge the problem. Whatever discussion has taken place over the years, it has not produced a satisfactory result. People have been elected because they said they would find answers.

Way too many engineers and transportation professionals fall back on the assertion that extensive deliberation is de facto evidence of a good approach. There is no such correlation; the world is full of examples where people met extensively and repeatedly yet still made poor decisions. Even so, by making the assertion of extensive prior discussion and suggesting that this is somehow comprehensive, Cignoli can dismiss the council members' concerns without having to address them fully.

That is a shame, because even if past decisions did stem from quality deliberation, cities are not static places. Engineers tend to view cities as a collection of streets, pipes, and other infrastructure systems that can be managed like a machine, something they are uniquely able to fine-tune to optimum conditions. This narrow frame of reference fails to acknowledge that cities are complex human habitats, places that evolve, where new patterns and responses emerge over time regardless of how the infrastructure is planned and constructed.

Times change. Councils change. Priorities change. It is never wrong to question the status quo, especially when it comes to traffic engineering. The assertion that "smarter people than you thought about this for a long time" is the ultimate false flag. It intentionally diverts decision-making authority away from elected officials to the engineer, using the opaque backdrop of years of deliberation as a rhetorical shield.

The second common method engineers use to assert power and thwart public will is to give accepted industry standards and practices primacy over observation. An engineer working for their own priorities, instead of the priorities of the elected officials or the public at large, will quote industry standards as if they are inviolable laws instead of what they really are: guidelines for the typical scenario. They will suggest that, regardless of what may be clear or obvious, the standards constrain their actions. The letter from Cignoli includes many examples of this, including the following:

> Another option that was discussed in the past was the use of Rectangular Rapid Flashing Beacon (RRFB) (See photo). When this product was introduced into the industry a number of years ago, the Federal Highway Administration (FHWA) and the Manual on Uniform Traffic Control Devices (MUTCD) issued guidance on where these types of units should be installed.

The Manual on Uniform Traffic Control Devices is a favorite for engineers to cite when claiming an inability to act, but in a unique situation like that being examined along State Street in Springfield, the rote standards do not cleanly apply. Engineers and transportation professionals are supposed to think, to use their professional judgment, in places where it is warranted. That is not an opinion on my part; it is exactly what the MUTCD suggests should be done. Here is a quote from Section 1A.09 of the general provisions.

> The decision to use a particular device at a particular location should be made on the basis of either an engineering study or the application of engineering judgment. Thus, while this Manual provides Standards, Guidance, and Options for design and applications of traffic control devices, this Manual should not be considered a substitute for engineering judgment. Engineering judgment should be exercised in the selection and application of traffic control devices, as well as in the location and design of roads and streets that the devices complement.[2]

Statements providing discretion like this are found in every engineering manual, yet too often engineers pretend as if they are required to apply the directions of others mindlessly instead of providing their own professional judgment. In a unique situation like State Street, where, it should be reiterated, multiple people have died, citing standards as a reason to do nothing is not merely wrong; it is malpractice.

The third way that I have experienced engineers working to thwart public will is by asserting their own values into design decisions and then holding them up as indisputable truth when, in fact, they are a subjective ordering that should be made by elected officials — the decision to prioritize traffic flow over safety, for example. Another is the decision to establish a design speed incompatible with the neighborhood. As discussed in Chapter 1, these decisions are made without presenting them as options to elected officials, even though they are an assertion of values, not truth.

Cignoli's letter is full of the engineer's values being asserted as truth. As an example, consider this statement from the letter:

> Due to the volume of traffic at this location on the corridor, the current traffic signal cycle lengths (the length of time for all approaches to cycle through green, yellow, red sequence) at both of the signalized intersections are very long, in excess of 1½ minutes. Based upon the current long length of the two locations, when the [crossing] system button would be activated, there could be a significant amount of time (possible in excess of two minutes) until the pedestrian would be able to cross the road. Based upon data from the FHWA, the longer the wait period for pedestrian crossing, the more chance that a pedestrian will try to cross the road prior to the proper signals being activated.

The very first segment of this paragraph asserts that the signalized intersection must be designed to prioritize the volume of traffic. That is a value statement. Everything that follows it builds off that assertion of values. The volume of traffic must be accommodated; ergo the signal sequence must be long, ergo pedestrians must wait a long time to cross, ergo pedestrians will not wait and will choose to put their lives in danger anyway, and therefore the crossing system would be useless.

If instead human values were prioritized over the values of the engineer, this entire line of thinking would be turned around. We want humans to be safe, ergo the crossing signal sequence must be short, therefore the traffic volume on this street must be reduced. This is perfectly acceptable reasoning, yet it is not presented as an option by the engineer to the elected officials. It is their choice, but the framing of the decision by Cignoli robs Springfield's elected leadership of their agency.

The letter references "traffic queues" and "Level of Service" as if they were self-evident truths, not merely a set of values being asserted by the Public Works Department. As discussed in Chapter 4, Level of Service (LOS) is a term used for highway design and is not applicable local streets. Here is how, without presenting any alternatives, Cignoli's letter assumes that traffic queues and LOS are the primary values to be considered:

> Also, based upon the traffic data provided as part of the Casino project and volumes during the peak period, and based upon our experience, introduction of a [crossing] system would cause an additional increase in traffic queues by at least 25%, causing the Level of Service (LOS), currently C, D, E, and F, to deteriorate ever further to full failure of the intersection.

And that paragraph concludes, once again, with a false statement built on a scaffold of engineering values asserted as truth:

> This would result in vehicles being trapped within the intersection while cross traffic is trying to get through.

No, it would not. Or more precisely: it need not. What is being suggested here is that traffic queuing and Level of Service cannot be compromised under any circumstances — even to save human lives — and therefore, if forced to install a mid-block crossing (while maintaining queues and LOS), vehicles will be trapped in the intersection. Vehicles would not need to be trapped if queuing and LOS were adjusted, but that is not an option the public works department allows the elected leaders of the community to consider.

What we witness in these paragraphs is that the engineer's values are not open for discussion, regardless of human life and regardless of what elected officials are asking for. The engineer is taking options off the table, limiting the capacity of city council members to respond to the concerns of their constituents.

The fourth way that engineers routinely thwart the will of elected officials and the public is to assert that they are powerless; that ultimate authority does not reside with the professional engineer or even elected officials but elsewhere. Layered on this assertion of powerlessness is the implied threat that the real governing authority is somewhat despotic and vengeful and will likely react poorly if provoked by the silly requests of elected officials representing an unreasonable public.

Invoking empathy while deferring to the potential scorn of an absent authority figure is a tactic commonly used by babysitters trying to get unruly children to comply. It is commonly used because it is effective, especially because there is an asymmetry of information between the babysitter and the child. Here is how this tactic is used by Cignoli in his letter:

> If designs were to be presented on the installation of a [crossing] system, submission to MassDOT would be required as it would be a modification of a previously approved Traffic Control Agreement. MassDOT would then review the design and possibly reject the installation, or place significant additional roadway related improvements as a requirement at the expense of the City.

In other words, the city could go through the process of getting a crossing, but the state is going to create a lot of barriers to doing that and, ultimately, might not even let it happen. If they do, Cignoli suggests that they are going to make Springfield pay a heavy price. The subtext here is that the engineering values already asserted in the letter are universal, including at the state department of transportation, and that the situation on State Street that everyone else understands to be exceptional is actually just a straightforward technical exercise in applying rote standards.

Of all people, politicians should understand this to be false. None of these decisions are merely technical; they are all somewhat discretionary and, thus, political. This is especially true in a unique situation like State Street, where multiple deaths have occurred. It is a stretch to suggest that reasonable action here might require the state board to provide some type of waiver, but it is absurd to suggest that the city could not make a compelling case if they wanted to.

Cities are not powerless. Great local engineers who want to assert the values of the community, instead of opposing them, can become strong advocates for the community with state appeals boards. This is especially true when lives have been lost, as they have on State Street. A good engineer in this situation is going to say, "How do we solve this problem?" instead of giving all of the reasons why a problem does not exist and, even if it did, why it cannot possibly be solved.

All four of these common methods of thwarting public will are merely assertions of power. The engineer has knowledge and access to information that elected officials and the public do not. This makes the engineer a gatekeeper. Being a gatekeeper does not make an engineer uniquely bad; it merely makes them human, subject to all of the ordinary blind spots and personal failings that gatekeepers tend to develop.

There are many ways to deal with this problem, most of which involve shifting power away from the engineer and the systems that empower their values. As discussed in previous chapters, handling street design challenges with teams that empower nontechnical professionals is an important step. Redirecting funding away from a specific department and towards these broadly constituted teams is another.

In situations like State Street, seeking a second opinion from transportation professionals outside the city is a prudent step. City council members should not be proposing specific solutions; they should be asking for a menu of viable options and then choosing from among them. An outside advisor will have the freedom to greatly expand that menu.

I am also going to point out what I think is obvious: There are many engineers who should lose their jobs. If I were an elected official, I would not tolerate a senior staff member who worked to undermine the initiatives that a majority of elected officials were trying to accomplish, especially when human lives had been lost and more were at stake. In more than two decades of leadership, I have always welcomed dissenting opinions as part of a collaborative process, but I do not tolerate multiple agendas, especially when any of them conflict with the goals of the organization. Public servants need civil service protections to shield them from the nastiness of local politics, but the authority given to senior staff to manage the levers of government power require them to be directly answerable to elected officials. There can only be one agenda, and it must be that of the duly elected officials.

There are many great engineers out there ready to prioritize public safety over traffic speed and neighborhood prosperity over traffic volume. There are a lot of engineers ready to step out from behind the shield provided by industry standards and fulfill their ethical obligations to use their professional judgment in service of the public. Any city council wanting to can find these people, empower them, and then support them so that they can do great things.

Can the Profession Reform Itself?

While there are many great individuals who are engineers and transportation professionals, I have found the internal dialogue of the profession to be stuck in a place of comfortable tension for a long time. There is comfort in the sense that those working on transportation projects have a degree of credibility and prestige earned during the highway-building era, privilege that is kept alive by established bureaucracies and large budgets.

The tension comes from a growing realization that the golden age of massive engineering projects has passed, and what is left is an unfulfilled promise of prosperity now encumbered by decades of accrued maintenance liabilities. Engineers two generations ago inspired a nation by building interstates across a continent, constructing landscape-transforming dams, and erecting iconic bridges. Today's engineers are simply asked to maintain it all, a task far more challenging yet much less glamorous.

The profession's comfortable tension manifests in an internal conversation that is often asking good questions but nearly always landing on the wrong set of answers. For example, the May 2012 edition of *PE* magazine, a publication of the National Society of Professional Engineers, led with this provocative statement:

> In the 20th century, U.S. engineers became known for creating much of the basic infrastructure that helped propel the country to economic success. Now in the 21st century, the country is struggling to keep that infrastructure from falling apart. What happened?[3]

What happened? This is a great question. The many discussions that make up an answer should prompt a lot of soul-searching among my fellow professionals. When I started reading the article, I was naively optimistic that it would include some mention of the return-on-investment problem with most infrastructure projects, the lack of value capture as a mechanism for funding capital improvements, and the perverse incentives of the gas tax.

I thought it might touch on the distortion contained in standard cost/benefit analyses, the poor applicability of the standard approach to depreciation modeling, the failure to make maintenance a priority, or the politicization of the capital improvement process.

The article could have examined the profession's blind adherence to standards, the related propensity to overengineer, and the lack of knowledge within the profession when it comes to land use context and creating total value. *PE* magazine could have looked at the perverse incentives within standard engineering contracts or any of a myriad of problems that lie within the day-to-day practice of engineering as a profession.

These are all things that, for the most part, engineers directly control or can heavily influence. Such introspection should be an ongoing facet of any great profession, especially one in crisis. Unfortunately, years of plenty, and years of dominance where few challenged their advice, has not only weakened the internal dialogue of the nation's engineering profession but has created a nasty echo chamber — one that is inhibiting reform. The story in *PE* magazine is a vivid example of this echo chamber.

According to the article, there are two simple answers to the question of what happened, both centering around the unquestioned premise of needing more money for infrastructure. First, engineers were so successful at taking care of society's every need that Americans now take them for granted and, subsequently, do not give them enough money. Second, society is just too shortsighted and cheap to fund infrastructure properly. These answers are embarrassingly self-serving and delusional.

The first assertion starts with the fiction that engineers are so good at solving problems that their accomplishments are invisible to society. From the article:

> "As long as the commode works when you flush it, people aren't worried about spending money on infrastructure," says Bill Fendley, P.E., F.NSPE, who chairs NSPE's Legislative and Government Affairs committee.
>
> "It's just not visible," he continues. "We're spoiled in this country. You're used to being able to turn on the faucet and getting water, getting on the road and going and not having to worry about congestion, potholes, et cetera. It's just people assume. . .that all that should come naturally."

Is it really this simple? Can it all be reduced to an assertion that Americans are just spoiled? A country of people who seemingly understand that a car requires fuel, oil changes, air in the tires, and all kinds of ongoing work are just not capable of grasping the concept of paying for maintenance? In a nation where most families own their own home — a long-term investment that requires an enormous amount of ongoing maintenance — are Americans really incapable of grasping the idea? That is ridiculous.

What is more likely is that the ways that infrastructure systems are funded — systems established hand in hand with engineers and continually promoted by their advocacy organizations — cloud the relationship between the infrastructure being provided and the long-term cost for that infrastructure. More compelling is an observation that our infrastructure funding mechanisms are great at building a lot of new stuff but not so great at finding an equilibrium between demand and willingness to pay for ongoing maintenance. Americans are not spoiled; they are human.

This was alluded to in the article, although not in terms of changing the system but in getting more money for it.

> AASHTO polls show voters believe the gasoline taxes and water tap fees they pay go a disproportionately long way to funding the upkeep and expansion of infrastructure systems and therefore do not need to be expanded, especially in a limping economy, he says.
>
> As prices for repairs and materials increase, and charges like gasoline taxes fail to keep pace, such payments do less and less to maintain an increasingly costly infrastructure.
>
> "Most citizens have no clue what is needed in terms of cash flow in a given state to maintain highways, bridges, and other transportation," he says.
>
> Those voters also overestimate what they already pay for infrastructure maintenance and expansion. Combined, the viewpoints mean most voters believe there's enough money in federal and state budgets to adequately maintain roads, bridges, and other infrastructure even though groups like AASHTO and ASCE have identified massive spending deficits.

PE magazine would have us believe that, because the gas tax is opaque and distorts public perception of the costs and benefits of transportation infrastructure, more gas tax revenue is needed. That is not just incoherent, it is self-serving in the extreme. These funding systems funnel large amounts of money into infrastructure projects, many of dubious value that nonetheless generate tremendous demand and compensation for engineers. If the engineering profession were serious about discerning what happened and not merely focused on enhancing their own revenue streams, they would focus on reforming funding systems to be more responsive, not merely expanding them.

The second assertion of the article, that society is just shortsighted and cheap, is even more demeaning than the first. From *PE* magazine:

> Taxes are immediate, and infrastructure's returns are long-term. Therefore, an infrastructure tax, whether for a sewer system or development of a port, is viewed by most taxpayers solely as a cost to avoid, not an investment, says Andrew Herrmann, P.E., president of the American Society of Civil Engineers. And when taxpayers are still feeling the effects of a down economy, any new tax, and many existing ones, is the target of voter ire.
>
> More investment in infrastructure could boost the amount of tax revenue coming into the system, Herrmann says. His group's 2009 Report Card for America's

Infrastructure, the most recent, showed an increase of over 243,000 jobs if infrastructure investment is increased. Transportation costs for many industries would decrease, improving efficiency and, hopefully, productivity. Without needed infrastructure repairs and maintenance, quality of life, productivity, air quality, and ultimately employment, would all continue to decline.

Getting politicians and voters to think beyond the next month or next election is tough even with data like that, he says.

"It seems like a no-brainer, but it's hard to get people to understand," Herrmann says.

The *American Infrastructure Report Card* (https://infrastructurere-portcard.org/) recommends trillions in spending on infrastructure and a major part of their argument is that it will create 243,000 jobs. Beyond the mere absurdity of such a precise estimation of such an abstract projection, it is difficult to explain just how ridiculous this assertion is.

I am writing this chapter during what seems to be America's second wave of the COVID-19 global pandemic, an event that has destroyed millions of jobs. Looking back to pre-pandemic statistics, a weekly fluctuation of 250,000 jobs was a normal event. The suggestion that it is a "no-brainer" for Americans to spend trillions on infrastructure in the anticipation that it will create a number of jobs that is roughly equivalent to the estimation error of weekly job creation is absurd.

The condescension in this article comes from ignorance and the ignorance comes from the self-reaffirming echo chamber in which the engineering profession resides. NSPE, along with their more propaganda-prone cousin, the American Society of Civil Engineers (ASCE), can continue with these delusions, insisting that the profession's heyday of the 1950s can be recaptured if spoiled Americans simply stopped being cheap and agreed to spend more money on infrastructure. If they stick to that path, they will merely increase the disconnect between their members and the public that they ostensibly serve.

Or these organizations can start a dialogue within the profession, a conversation that questions the systems engineers have set up and perpetuated, the funding mechanisms on which they rely, and the standards that they have developed. If they take this less comfortable approach, they can become true leaders in restoring America's competitive position. I believe that they will also greatly benefit their members and the profession.

If taken seriously, the umbrella question of "what happened" should prompt many follow up questions. Strong Towns, the Congress for the New Urbanism, and a handful of other non-insider places are asking and answering these questions, with significant contributions from dissident engineers. Here are 11 questions that begin to properly examine what happened, as well as what can be done now that it has. For those who have progressed to this point of the book, the answers are hopefully self-evident.

1. Does the body of knowledge gained in highway construction (forgiving design) really apply to the construction of local streets and rural roadways, or should other models be considered?
2. Can we really build our way out of congestion, or have budget constraints now forced us to consider other alternatives?
3. Does the hierarchical road system really work, or does it create disproportionate obligations on older parts of the system in favor of modest levels of new growth on the periphery?
4. Do engineers have an ethical obligation to consider, during initial project planning, whether infrastructure improvements are financially viable over a second life cycle?
5. Do feasibility studies need to consider long-term financial feasibility as well as simple engineering feasibility?
6. Should advocacy organizations within the engineering profession oppose the gas tax and instead support transportation funding mechanisms that more closely correlates the demand for transportation improvements with society's willingness to pay, even if that means less money for engineering projects?
7. Does the standard approach to cost/benefit analysis accurately represent the long-term costs and benefits a project has for society, or has it become a tool for obtaining funding for marginal projects?
8. When planning projects, do engineers have an ethical obligation to consider the intricate relationship between land use and transportation, or do engineers simply continue to react to what they perceive to be "the market" for new infrastructure?
9. What should be the substantive difference between a licensed, professional engineer and an unlicensed engineering technician when it comes to the application of industry standards?
10. How distorting and corrupting are contracts that compensate engineers as a percentage of the total project cost?
11. Does the engineering profession share any of the blame for America's failing infrastructure and, if so, what should be done to prevent that from continuing?

Learning from Biology, Not Physics

In the 20th century, a lot of the challenges that engineers, planners, and other city-building professionals faced seemed simple and straightforward. They were almost one-dimensional in nature, or they could at least be credibly reduced to one dimension.

Consider traffic congestion. If a street has too much traffic and drivers routinely experience significant delay and unpredictable travel times, the one-dimensional answer was to build more capacity. In the decades immediately after World War II, there was not only the budget for this kind of response, but the systems of governance also gave engineers wide latitude to execute their plans without interference from a public that might not fully agree. If building more capacity meant tearing down half the businesses along Main Street or taking out a neighborhood's sidewalks, trees, and crossings, then that was the price paid for what was perceived as progress.

Large budgets and unchecked authority provide the luxury of being able to see a problem like traffic congestion, or even transportation in general, as one-dimensional. It allows the professional to approach the practice of engineering as if it were a mathematical equation to be worked out, one with a single, definite answer. This is an approach similar to Newtonian physics, where equations are used to derive insights that can then be verified through simple experimentation.

In general, engineers feel most comfortable working in cities when they can treat them like a physics problem. Professional engineers are unparalleled in their capacity to solve problems that are presented to them in this way. They have manuals, charts, codes, and other guides to help them apply best practices. They confidently project what traffic will be in 20 years based on their measurements of traffic over prior decades. They know what will happen when that new housing subdivision goes in, or a new traffic signal is installed, because they have equations that (they believe) tell them exactly what will happen.

This was all fine when society could ignore the problems that arose in the wake of bad engineering practices, when we had abundant resources to throw at every complication that arose, or at least the ones we cared about. That street expansion to cure congestion may have destroyed the downtown business community, but we can tell ourselves that there are now jobs to be had at the big box store on the edge of town. We can provide aggrieved citizens some tax rebates and tuition subsidies to adapt to the new reality, which also now includes the low, low prices that our economic models suggest are optimal.

As we continue to fight congestion in one dimension, we develop more and more narratives to explain away the problems that were building up. Suggestions that Americans are spoiled, politicians are cheap, and engineers are underappreciated are all narrative coping mechanisms for professionals conditioned to work in only one dimension.

Over time, the ignored or discounted problems become increasingly difficult to suppress, especially as our resources simultaneously become stretched. Ultimately, the urgent problems we face in our cities, such as congestion but also many more, stop presenting as something akin to physics but instead act more like biology, where many complex variables interact to create an emergent and largely unpredictable order. In biological systems, there are no simple solutions, or even simple explanations, only complex feedback loops that drive adaptation or failure.

Of course, cities have always been complex, adaptive systems. In *Strong Towns: A Bottom-Up Revolution to Rebuild American Prosperity*, I called cities "human habitat" and noted:

> Such systems are experienced as emergent. Their order is not imposed; it just appears, as if by magic. Each interaction may be understandable on its own, but the complexity of interactions makes the entire system unpredictable. Everyone learns from experience, adapts their individual behavior and, in doing so, continuously impacts everyone else.
>
> We often think of evolution as a process that happens incrementally over time. That's close, but the full reality is more like how Hemingway described bankruptcy: gradually, then all at once. Traumatic events, large and small, force both adaptation and failure. The combination creates the learned wisdom that is passed on to subsequent generations.

Regardless of what happens in the coming decades, two things seem abundantly clear for our broader society, but specifically for city engineering and related professions. The first is that we are very unlikely to return to the approach of the 1950s where complex problems could be grossly simplified so that they could be overcome with seemingly unlimited budgets and latitude. Our cities have taken on too many liabilities, and they lack the necessary financial productivity for that approach to be repeated, even if a more informed and actively involved society were to allow it.

The second is that these urgent financial constraints will force engineers to adapt, to develop new approaches to what are really an old set of problems. If it is to be relevant, the practice of engineering must expand beyond the rote applications of standards and equations to a deeper understanding of complexity. Psychology, sociology, behavioral economics, and many other pursuits that engineers tend to consider softer sciences, and thus not worthy of serious study, are essential for those working with cities as human habitat.

Engineers will need less of a physics mentality and more of a biological approach.

It is unclear if engineering professions can do this on their own, and I suspect that we may end up with a large knowledge gap between two distinct types of civil engineers. The first type will be those who are comfortable with standards, equations, and a more rote approach. Some of these professionals may make good mid-level managers, but they will be overwhelmed by tomorrow's problems (or dangerous if given too much authority and budget).

I hope this first type of engineer will end up working for the second type, the true problem solvers. These are people who are able to humbly grasp the overwhelming complexity of human habitat and work, as an expert but also as a servant, to nurture — I almost want to use the word "birth" — approaches that address localized challenges in co-creation with the people they are serving. I have met this kind of engineer and they are astounding people, but they almost always struggle within the current system because the business model of engineering lavishly rewards the first type of engineer. That must change.

Local leaders can encourage that change by rejecting rote engineering approaches and simplistic solutions to what are clearly complex problems. Even more proactively, they can structure engineering contracts and engagements to reward value added instead of merely the size of project. We should reject contract approaches that compensate professionals as a percentage of the project size or for studies that merely recommend more engineering work. We should pay engineers a premium when they use their skills and expertise to solve problems while also reducing costs and building long-term wealth and prosperity within the community.

Yet Another Complaint

This chapter on reform was to end with the prior section, but during its writing I received notice of a second formal complaint against me with the licensing board. As with the first, this one focuses on my writing and speaking as the inspiration for the offense, but it makes a new, more serious, allegation of fraud and misrepresentation.

In Minnesota, an engineering license runs for two years. Every other year, I receive a renewal notice, which is my reminder to go to a website, submit my continuing education credits and fee, and renew my license. I did this in June of 2016, and the following month we moved homes. In the move, I forgot to update the licensing board of my change of address.

I am license number 40142, but I rarely refer to that number because it has been more than two decades since I have signed a set of plans, specifications, or even a study as a licensed engineer. It has been more than a decade since I have done any consulting or performed any work that would constitute practicing engineering. So, when my license expired in 2018, without my receiving any notice or reminder, I did not remember to renew it.

There is a two-year period after expiration where an engineer can renew their license without having to take any relicensing exams or do any extra work beyond paying a late fee. During that window, I realized that my license was expired and, on the day that I found out, I paid the late fee and renewed. I was reissued my license, and everything seemed fine.

Six weeks later, I received notice that a complaint had been filed against me by a colleague, another professional engineer. The complaint alleged that I committed fraud by referring to myself as a "licensed engineer" and a "professional engineer" during the period when my license had lapsed. Here is what this fellow professional wrote in his complaint:

> Mr. Marohn talks about being a policy expert, the type that reads law and ordinance. It is not reasonable to assume that Mr. Marohn was not aware that use of the term Professional Engineer, PE, or other similar representations while not licensed, is a violation of law. It is also clear that both Mr. Marohn and Strong Towns, through speaking tours and fundraising activities, benefit from using the claimed licensure. I urge the board to investigate as it sees fit, and to send a clear message that frauds of this sort are not to be tolerated.

I responded to the complaint in writing and explained the timeline of what happened. I apologized to the board for my oversight but noted that it was unintentional, that I corrected my mistake immediately when it was discovered, that I was not practicing engineering and so had not been representing myself as a professional engineer in pursuit of engineering work during the gap in my licensure, and that I had paid my late fee while successfully renewing my license.

I assumed that would be the end of it as it all seemed innocent and straightforward on my part, with the complaint being obviously motivated by issues other than concern over the practice of engineering. To my surprise, months later I received another letter from the board, this one demanding that I agree to a censure, a reprimand, a $1,500 fine, and to take extra ethics courses. If I did not agree by signing what they called an *Order and Stipulation*, I would face a contested case hearing in front of a judge, which seems more than a little ominous. The letter from the board suggested that I had violated state laws by committing fraud because I intentionally misrepresented myself as a licensed engineer.

I was not expecting this at all. As cynical as I may be at times, this is not behavior I expected from a group of fellow engineers, particularly not in Minnesota, where I would like to believe we are better than this.

After months of letter writing with the board, I was forced to retain an attorney to advocate on my behalf. She was able to secure a meeting with the violations committee, where I was able to present my case and answer their questions. Unfortunately, this was not productive.

The chair of the committee, a geologist named Keith Rapp, indicated that he knew of me and my work at Strong Towns. He specifically cited a speech I gave for the *American Conservative* magazine. In his capacity as the chair, he made lengthy statements giving his opinion on what he felt I had done, which was quite negative, turning his opinions into a question for me to respond to only after being prompted to do so.

Another member, Eric Friske, an attorney who is a public member of the board, asked me if it was my opinion that anyone could start a podcast or write a blog and claim to be an engineer so long as they didn't perform any engineering work, as if the difference between me — a fully-qualified professional with a civil engineering degree, decades of experience, and a license to practice engineering, albeit with a temporary and inadvertent lapse in licensure — and your standard blogger is inconsequential to the board.

Paul Vogel, a land surveyor on the committee, made a lengthy statement suggesting that I had potentially impacted the public health, safety, and welfare by allowing people to believe, when they listened to me speak and read my writing, that I was a licensed engineer whose utterances could be relied upon. This suggests that somehow my competence in the field rests on the timing of my paperwork instead of my knowledge and expertise.

Some of this may simply be petty people flexing their narrow authority in the manner that those who serve on such boards sometimes do, but it's hard not to read more into their actions. They have ample discretion to drop the matter and move on, but they have stubbornly refused, insisting — as part of any final resolution — that I admit to being dishonest and intentionally misrepresenting myself to the public. If board members are not sympathetic to those trying to use this process to slander me, they are eagerly doing their bidding.

Regardless of whether the committee members are pursuing the agenda of my detractors within the profession or are merely their pawns, I am not willing to accept any judgment where I am forced to admit to dishonesty, fraud, or misrepresentation. Doing so would be dishonest, and so I am prepared to go to a contested case hearing if it comes to that. In my response to the board, I wrote:

> For the sake of my professional colleagues who may someday find themselves subject to such an inquiry merely for expressing their views and opinions, I cannot submit to the Stipulation and Order you have forwarded to me.

As this book goes to print, my case is still unresolved. Any updates will be shared on the website www.confessions.engineer.

Notes

1. https://ij.org/press-release/oregon-engineer-wins-traffic-light-timing-lawsuit/
2. Section 1A.09 of the General provisions https://mutcd.fhwa.dot.gov/pdfs/2009r1r2/pdf_index.htm
3. *PE* magazine, May 2012.

13

My Confession

He liked Elvis. And what's not to like? Although the King had died when he was only four, he had grown up loving the music. And that hair. What he wouldn't give to replace the pipe cleaners on his head with the cool, black waves of Elvis.

He could afford idle thoughts like this today. What a great day. A factory-installed speaker sat under the console in his brand-new SUV, pumping out the bass line for "A Little Less Conversation," the juiced-up version remixed by Junkie XL. He had it cranked way up, the thumping of his seat amplifying his satisfaction with the world.

A little more bite and a little less bark.
A little less fight and a little more spark.

Just two weeks earlier, a truck had pulled out in front of him, and he had smashed his little Toyota coup into the side of it. The little car crumpled like an aluminum can. There had been no way to avoid it. He had smashed his knee pretty bad and, thanks to some mice eating through the wires in the little car years earlier, the airbags hadn't worked, so he had knocked his head a little too. All in all, it could have been worse. The car he hit didn't have insurance, but he did. And now he had a brand-new SUV.

Baby close your eyes and listen to the music, Drifting through a summer breeze.

This was his second new car. He preferred new, having grown up in a family where old, junky cars always quit on you at the worst possible time. And while he might be able to coax an old-timer car into running with a screwdriver and a can of HEET, the newer models weren't so easily hacked. He was a professional now, running his own company no less, and he needed something completely dependable.

He was a father now too. His little girl was just eight weeks old. The Toyota was a great college commuting car, but his wife had made it abundantly clear to him that their baby wasn't going to ride in it. Too small. Not safe. He disagreed, but he was fast learning that you don't win an argument with a mom.

It wasn't clear whether the accident that totaled the car proved her point or his. He could see it both ways. He survived just a little bruised, but while the tank of a vehicle he hit barely suffered a scratch, his car couldn't even limp off the field under its own power. He liked that little car, especially the gas mileage. He could drive it hard and still get 34 mpg. While the new SUV had been near the top of its class in fuel efficiency, he was never going to get much over 24 now.

But the stereo was sweet, the ride comfortable, and, as the October breeze cooled his face through the open window, he thumped the pseudo-cowbell that was his new dashboard. He could definitely live with this compromise.

A little less conversation, a little more action please.
All this aggravation ain't satisfactioning me.

People who live through traumatic events frequently talk about how time seems to be suspended; how the event is perceived at a different speed than real life. It isn't clear whether the hyperactivity of the moment actually allows the otherwise sleepy brain to take in and store more information or whether the brain fills in the details later during the act of reliving the ordeal. Either way, only time can dull such vividness.

In the opposing lane of the two-lane highway, a car was stopped. It was preparing to take a left turn across traffic. Having been hit from behind, and having made the innocent and rarely costly mistake of having the wheels turned in anticipation, the driver and her young son were prematurely propelled on their desired course.

As they crossed the centerline and entered his lane, he saw them clearly. Their faces. The panic in their eyes. The driver looked like she was in her forties, although her face had the kind of early aging one gets from smoking for too many years. She covered it with her right hand as if the little bit of flesh, muscle, and bone could somehow prevent the inevitable.

The passenger was worse. The boy's eyes were wide as if he had just woken up in the middle of the night, walked downstairs for a drink of water, and stumbled sleepily onto a television showing a steamy sex scene, the tired, cloudy, and innocent mind registering a mix of shock, confusion, and disbelief. I'm not supposed to be here, but here I am, through no fault of my own.

Acting on instinct — the furthest reaction from heroism, although it likely saved lives — he banked hard to the right to avoid the car in his path. It couldn't be completely avoided, however, his brand-new SUV traveling at highway speeds and the distance simply not enough to avoid contact. At a slight angle, he hit her car, knocking him further to the right — uncontrollably — and sending her and her son spinning.

Come on baby I'm tired of talking.
Grab your coat and let's start walking.

The brain should be excused for doing strange things in a moment like this. If shock is an evolutionary response to trauma, one that enabled early humans the momentary strength needed to flee to safety when injured, the gallows humor that frequently accompanies such situations also likely has evolutionary origins.

As the SUV crossed the shoulder and departed the roadway, he momentarily laughed out loud as he performed an act that he had simulated with matchbox cars dozens of times as a boy; he ran over the stop sign. It could not have been any more perfectly lined up in the center of the grill. Bam. It was gone. Flattened. It was beautifully thrilling.

Then the vehicle was airborne, a fact not fully appreciated until it hit the ground on the far side of the ditch. One hop and then, as symmetrically as the stop sign had aligned with the axis of the car, so did a tree. Only, the tree didn't give way.

Pop. All of a sudden, the thousands of crash test dummy simulations he had seen in those boring car commercials they play during NFL games had some meaning. His body propelled forward, the seat belt caught, his head snapped into a balloon that had been inflated with a force greater than his own, and everything went black.

Darkness. Darkness. Black.

Why is the horn blaring? Who has their hand on the horn? THE HORN IS SO DAMNED LOUD!!!

He realized that it was his horn. He tried to press it as if pressing it would somehow un-press it and end the noise, but the airbag made that impossible. Then the smell — sulfur, something burning — and the song, much louder now that the car had stopped moving. He thought of how cars blow up in the movies. That doesn't really happen, does it?

A little less conversation, a little more action please.
All this aggravation ain't satisfactioning me.

He couldn't breathe and he started to panic. With his left hand he reached down, popped the seat belt and then, with no shame or ceremony, rolled out of the car onto the ground. He crawled around waiting for the air that had been forced from his lungs to finds its way back in. While he had experienced getting the wind knocked out of him before, there was an edge of terror that accompanied these frantic gasps. And the blaring horn. Would the music ever stop?

A little more bite and a little less bark, A little less fight and a little more spark.

As the air began to find its way back in, he found himself being dragged away from the car. Someone propped him up against a nearby tree.

"You okay?"

The horn. The music.

"Stay right here. We've called for help. It's going to be okay."

That horn is so loud. And the music is going to keep playing because the song is on repeat. He starts to feel shame as he realizes that these people are going to think that he listens to one Elvis song on repeat, over and over, day in and day out. Who does that?

He forces himself to get up and walk to the car. It is smoking out of the front end, which is bashed in a good 24 inches. The axles are destroyed, a fact made obvious by the tires being near parallel to the ground. The doors are open — they don't look closable — and airbags litter the front dashboard. If he could just shut off the radio.

Then someone new is moving him away from the car, someone with less panic in his voice, someone of authority. They help him to the ground, lay him on a blanket, and then cover him with more blankets. The cloth is heavy and thick like an old rug. These people talk to him, reassuringly, check his body for injury. They shut off the radio and the horn. First responders.

"What's your name?"

"Chuck."

"Okay. Chuck what?"

"Um … Marohn. Chuck Marohn."

"Okay. Stay still. An ambulance is on the way. We're going to get you to the hospital."

An ambulance? He doesn't need an ambulance. Someone who can walk doesn't need an ambulance. The stubborn pride of his upbringing rears its head. He reaches into his pocket and pulls out his phone. While it would take months for him to be able to process numbers reliably, the concussion symptoms persisting longer than he was likely even aware, his home is on autodial, so no deep cognitive function is necessary.

"Can you come and pick me up. I got in a little accident."

Ten minutes later his wife arrives, their infant buckled up in the back seat. She has driven the same road he had, the road they both have driven hundreds — maybe thousands — of times before. The road they would continue to drive. With their baby girl. And soon a second. And like all of those times except his most recent, there had been no accident, no small quirk of fate that had nearly ended a life.

In that she was lucky. And they have both been lucky ever since. High-speed traffic combined with stopped and turning traffic is a guaranteed recipe for tragedy. What happened that day wasn't an accident. Accidents are random and not foreseeable. What happened that day was the statistically inevitable outcome of that place. Of that design. Of rolling the dice over and over and over hundreds of times a day until the inevitable straight flush of tragedy poured out of the cup.

He got in the car, the pain throughout his body now becoming very real, and he looked at his wife. As she drove him to the hospital, all he could do was shake and sob.

That day in October 2004 was one of the worst of my life. The collision totaled a new car, one with slightly more than 500 miles on it. When I went to the salvage lot to get my Elvis CD and other belongings out of it, I saw the full extent of the damage. The front of the car was smashed in where I hit the tree, rolling up the engine block, thrusting against the hood that would never again shut. The front wheels were bent nearly 90 degrees on their axles, the force of the landing turning the wheels on their sides. The doors were open, unable to shut or latch as the force of the impact had buckled them.

My parents were there with me. We all looked at it in stunned silence, the wreckage suggesting a crash of such force as not to be survivable. My mother wept.

I had some deep bruises that took weeks to heal, some burns on my wrists from the airbag that hurt worse but healed more quickly, and then months of fog from a severe concussion. I am lucky to be alive.

Years later, on a similar stroad just a few miles from my house, there was another terrible collision that was eerily like mine. A car heading in one direction and another car stopped in the opposite lane waiting to cross. The waiting car was hit by another driver who did not anticipate the stopping. Four people were injured and one killed. One of the injured had to be airlifted to the hospital. I know that none of their lives will ever be the same.

This follows another incident that happened a little further up the same stroad. A cyclist riding along the wide shoulder was hit by an intoxicated woman who was also texting while driving. The biker, a neighbor of mine who was a very decent man with a wife, kids, and grandkids, was killed.

I drove by the tire tracks of that scene for weeks until they faded away. They lasted longer than the formal consternation over the incident. The official accident report compiled human lives into tidy statistics. Cause of accident: Driver inattentiveness. Alcohol. Improper signaling. These are the checkboxes that document human nature. People being people.

Life. Normal life.

I am certain that our descendants will be bewildered by the fact that modern Americans accept a lot of unnecessary suffering, injury, and death as part of a normal life. That we do it in service of an approach that gains us so little for all our efforts will only add to their puzzlement.

Vehicle speed and traffic volume are not values that transcend time. We abhor the slavery and inhumane conditions of ancient

Egypt, Greece, or Rome, but appreciate that their sacrifices were made producing timeless pyramids, monuments, and temples. For what particular greatness are we sacrificing our people? The misperception of a few saved seconds? To save ourselves a short walk? For the chance at a drive-through hamburger? This is senseless, beneath any nation that considers itself great, even if were not so destructive.

When we mix high-speed cars with stopping and turning traffic, it is only a matter of time until people get killed. That is an undeniably true statement that confronts every transportation professional who designs such environments. The inevitability of death and suffering cannot be explained away by blaming drivers for being human.

Yet that is what we do. We wring our hands and wish people would drive more safely. We put our faith in better technology and more enforcement because that kind of faith provides us comfort. That kind of faith absolves us. That kind of faith bridges lament to empathy, reconciling any lingering feelings of urgency with the promise of a more hopeful future.

We may get serious enough to create a goal of reducing death on our streets and roadways. Some may call it "vision zero" inspired by the notion that nobody should die from the transportation system. Others, less idealistic, may simply say "towards zero deaths," like it was a New Year's resolution to eat healthier or work out more.

Do these slogans provide you comfort? They do nothing for me.

Nearly all of us are merely one degree of separation from the human tragedy that has played out on our roads and streets. Most of us know someone — or many people — who have been killed. We may even know someone who survived while others did not. We may even be one of them.

I obviously never met Destiny Gonzalez. Of the more than 3,000 children who are killed each year on American roads and streets, there is no reason why I would have ever heard of her. I certainly would not have had I not been in Springfield the night she was killed, had I not visited the dangerous crossing on State Street that very day.

It has given me a degree of guilt that, while I have been deeply moved by Destiny's story, I am not able to sustain anywhere near the same level of empathy for even the dozens of similar stories people send to me each year. And they are but a small fraction of cases in this ongoing tragedy. I wish I had it in me to tell their stories.

The death of Destiny Gonzalez stayed with me for many reasons. I already mentioned that her age is very close to the age of my daughters. My kids loved to read, and I can picture a late night at the library, getting in that one last book before bedtime. The bright eyes and toothy smile of her photos give the impression of a seven-year-old I would have enjoyed.

Beyond that, the tragedy happened at Christmastime, a sharp contrast to the joy and rebirth of the season. That left a mark in my memory. Thanks to my Facebook feed, every year I am reminded of what happened. Some years I click through and move on. Some years I pause and wonder, "What is my responsibility?" Some years I say a prayer.

Those prayers always include Destiny's mother, Sagrario Gonzalez, who has been forced to bear a heavy burden. I was hoping to meet her before finalizing this book, but COVID-19 travel restrictions made that impossible. By all accounts, she and her husband Luis are very private people, devoted to and supported by a large family. Please, pray for them.

In 2016, Sagrario and Luis attended a book drive at Destiny's school, Elias Brookings, that was done in Destiny's honor. The local paper included this report on the event:

> For Destiny's mother, who still works at Brookings as a paraprofessional, every day without her daughter is a missed opportunity to share a joke, hear a story or read one of her journal entries.
>
> "I still have all of the little drawings she would make and the books she would create. She was a beautiful little girl and the light of our lives," she said.
>
> She credits her husband, her children and everyone at Brookings for helping to keep the memory of her little girl alive.[1]

More than anything, I want Sagrario Gonzalez to know this was not her fault. She did nothing wrong.

Relatedly, I also feel a deep amount of empathy for Sandra Zemtsova, to the point where I almost did not include her name in this book for fear that she might be negatively impacted. She is the woman who was driving the vehicle that killed Destiny Gonzalez. She was intoxicated at the time. Zemtsova ultimately plead guilty to motor vehicle homicide.

In my life, I have chosen not to drink alcohol or use drugs. The major influence on that decision is the recognition that many people

I love, admire, and respect have done great harm to themselves, and to others, through drug and alcohol use. Occasionally, this harm involved the use of a motor vehicle. I would never excuse them or suggest that they should not be held legally accountable, but I do recognize a certain statistical randomness in those unfortunate outcomes.

While Zemtsova absolutely did something wrong, my empathy is a recognition that she must now live with what happened. We have all had low moments in life, but few of our tragic failings — even those who have driven under the influence — have resulted in the death of another. It is hard for me not to have empathy, especially understanding how those involved in designing transportation systems shift an inordinate amount of blame for tragedy to those who make common mistakes.

The cost of a personal failing should not be so high.

Yet it is that high, at least for some unlucky enough to be that statistic. I have heaped a lot of blame on engineers, planners, and other transportation professionals for what I see as their willful ignorance. I do not know any who accept the harm that our transportation systems routinely inflict on society, but I know few that deeply struggle with it.

Most seem more comfortable with shifting blame to others; whether politicians who will not allocate all of the funding or discretion they desire, citizens who make demands for access or increased speed, or people who make mistakes while driving.

My confession is that, for many years, I was one of them. Not only was I one of them; I was very good at it. I designed and built dangerous stroads, all while convincing myself that I was making things safer. I pushed politicians to spend more, using my insider knowledge to limit their options and force their hand in pursuit of what I felt was the greater good. I allied with those who wanted wider streets, faster speeds, and greater volume because we had shared interests that I believed were enlightened.

The composite conversation I shared in the introduction to this book was easy to write because those thoughts are in my head. I was not indoctrinated; I readily adopted them and took comfort in the trappings of a profession that gave me power and authority, at least in one realm where I was an expert.

Even worse, despite considering myself a public servant in pursuit of the greater good, I joined with others in my profession to ridicule and marginalize those who disagreed with the standard industry approach. I was not open to criticism, reassuring myself that any truly valid critique would come from within the professions.

This was all wrong, and I am deeply ashamed of the many years I spent pursuing this approach. This book is the byproduct of countless hours of research, discernment, and dialogue that have given me a new perspective. Even now, I know that there is more to uncover, and more people who have important insights to add.

I have not written any of this to absolve myself. In my faith, we begin our services with a penitential act, one where we ask for forgiveness for things we have done as well as things we have failed to do. My list is long.

This book will not make up for the damage I have done, but I hope it begins to make amends. While I want engineers, planners, and others who work in transportation professions to read it, they are not the target audience. They are not the ones I am trying hardest to reach.

I am trying to reach the person who knows something is wrong but just can't put their finger on it. I am hoping they read this book, talk to their friends and neighbors, and become part of a new consensus on how transportation should work.

I want that mayor or city council member who doesn't like the options offered, but who doesn't have enough knowledge to know what to ask for, to read this book and have a better sense of what is possible. I want them to have the confidence to communicate that vision and demand action.

I want that local shop owner frustrated by the street design in front of their building not to fear change. I want that small developer whose neighborhood is being forced into decline to know that there are other options. I want the transit rider to know why they are treated like a second-class citizen and that it need not be that way.

I want the person who cares about their neighborhood to know that it should also care for them. I want them to know that they don't need money or power to make things better. I want them to know that prioritizing their quality of life over the speed and volume of their traffic is what a decent human is supposed to do.

And I want that parent walking with their young child to know that they need not accept a city where they are afraid to cross the street.

Maybe one of these is you? If it is, share what you now know with someone else in your community. Join with others who share your vision. Do what you can, with what you have, to start building a strong town. If you do, I promise you will find you have everything you need.

Note

1. https://www.masslive.com/news/2016/06/daughter_best_friend_avid_read.html

About the Author

Charles Marohn, known as "Chuck" to friends and colleagues, is the founder and president of Strong Towns. He is a professional engineer and a land use planner with decades of experience. He holds a bachelor's degree in civil engineering and a Master of Urban and Regional Planning, both from the University of Minnesota.

Marohn is the author of *Strong Towns: A Bottom-Up Revolution to Rebuild American Prosperity* (Wiley, 2019). He hosts the Strong Towns Podcast and is a primary writer for Strong Towns' web content. He has presented Strong Towns concepts in hundreds of cities and towns across North America. Planetizen named him one of the 10 Most Influential Urbanists of all time.

Marohn is a long-time commentator on KAXE Northern Community Radio. He currently co-hosts KAXE's *Dig Deep* program, a monthly examination of public policy issues affecting Minnesotans.

Chuck grew up on a small farm in central Minnesota. The oldest of three sons of two elementary school teachers, he joined the Minnesota National Guard on his seventeenth birthday during his junior year of high school and served in the Guard for nine years. In addition to being passionate about building a stronger America, he loves playing music, is an obsessive reader, and religiously follows his favorite team, the Minnesota Twins.

Chuck and his wife live with their two daughters in their hometown of Brainerd, Minnesota.

Acknowledgments

I would like to thank Jason DeGray of Toole Design, both for his leadership in the field of engineering as well as for his passion in helping me edit this book. A native of Springfield, he challenged me on a number of things that I had written in early drafts and provided a lot of local information as well as missing details. Any mistakes are mine, but the rest would not have happened without Jason.

I also want to thank Steven Shultis, Elizabeth Lawton, and Luna Lucia for inviting me into their home and being so generous over many years. Your actions have always spoken louder than your words (and that is really saying something, especially for Steve).

I want to thank Wiley, particularly Brian Neill, for working with me during all of the tumult of 2020. You always put me and my writing process first, even when you were going through more difficulty than I was. That makes you the most valued of partners.

This book would not have happened without the team at Strong Towns helping me think through ideas, providing timely edits, and generally picking up the slack. Many thanks to Rachel Quednau, Michelle Erfurt, Daniel Herriges, John Pattison, Alexa Mendieta, Lauren Fisher, Linda Twillman, Christa Theilen, and Shina Shayesteh.

I am also blessed with the support and friendship of Andrew Burleson, Ian Rasmussen, and John Reuter, who have served as my bosses on the Strong Towns Board of Directors since 2014. Your leadership has always been the clarifying force for my otherwise random thoughts.

Thank you to Chloe and Stella for being patient with me when my mind was not fully there with you. And, of course, everything I do is possible only because of my wife, Kirsti. So long as she is proud of what I have written, nothing else really matters.

About Strong Towns

Strong Towns is a movement of thousands of people across North America working to make their communities financially strong and resilient.

Everyone deserves the opportunity to live a good life in a prosperous place. Future generations deserve that same opportunity, too. But there's a problem. For decades, North American communities have been growing—or at least, they've been building:

- Endless roads paved
- Countless buildings raised
- Trillions of dollars of infrastructure put into the ground

Yet we've given little thought to whether future generations can afford to maintain the world we're passing on to them—or how many of the things we build are making our communities worse places to live in today. We're wasting time and squandering resources that should be used to make our communities more prosperous.

The good news: people like you are changing all that. And we're here to help.

The Strong Towns approach is a radically new way of thinking about how we build our world. We believe that in order to truly thrive, our cities and towns must:

- Stop valuing efficiency and start valuing resilience.
- Stop betting our futures on huge, irreversible projects, and start taking small, incremental steps and iterating based on what we learn.
- Stop fearing change and start embracing a process of continuous adaptation.
- Stop building our world based on abstract theories and start building it based on how our places actually work and what our neighbors actually need today.

- Stop obsessing about future growth and start obsessing about our current finances.

The Strong Towns organization is working to make the Strong Towns approach real in every city and town in North America. We do this in four key ways:

1. Strong Towns Media: Articles and podcasts annually reach an audience of more than 2 million people.
2. Strong Towns Academy: A growing library of online courses covers a range of topics—transportation, housing, urban design, and more.
3. Strong Towns Action Lab: This new platform gives you the tools, resources, and connections you need to take action in your community.
4. Strong Towns Events: Our in-person and online live events reach more than 10,000 people each year.

Most importantly, we believe that Strong Citizens from all walks of life—from citizens to leaders, professionals to neighbors, and everyone in between—can and must participate in the Strong Towns approach. And that means we need you.

Are you ready to build *your* strong town? **To get started, or to learn more, visit StrongTowns.org.**

Index

Page numbers followed by *f* and *t* refer to figures and tables, respectively.